The
Scottis
Bus Hand

British Bus Publishing

Body codes used in the Bus Handbook series:

Type:
A	Articulated vehicle
B	Bus, either single-deck or double-deck
BC	Interurban - high-back seated buses and high-capacity school transport 3+2 seated vehicles.
C	Coach
M	Minibus with design capacity of sixteen seats or less
N	Low-floor bus (*Niederflur*), either single-deck or double-deck
O	Open-top bus (CO = convertible; PO = partial open-top)

Seating capacity is then shown. For double-decks the upper deck capacity is followed by the lower deck.

Door position:
C	Centre entrance/exit
D	Dual doorway.
F	Front entrance/exit
R	Rear entrance/exit (no distinction between doored and open)
T	Three or more access points

Equipment:
L	Lift for wheelchair	TV	Training vehicle.
M	Mail compartment	RV	Used as tow bus or engineer's vehicle.
T	Toilet	w	Vehicle is withdrawn and awaiting disposal.

e.g. - B32/28F is a double-deck bus with thirty-two seats upstairs, twenty-eight down and a front entrance/exit.
   N43D is a low-floor bus with two or more doorways.

Re-registrations:
Where a vehicle has gained new index marks, the details are listed at the end of each fleet showing the current mark, followed in sequence by those previously carried starting with the original mark. Marks carried more than once are not always repeated.

Regional books in the series:
The Scottish Bus Handbook
The Ireland & Islands Bus Handbook
The North East Bus Handbook
The Yorkshire Bus Handbook
The North West Bus Handbook
The East Midlands Bus Handbook
The West Midlands Bus Handbook
The Welsh Bus Handbook
The Eastern Bus Handbook
The London Bus Handbook
The South East Bus Handbook
The South West Bus Handbook

Annual books are produced for the major groups:
The Stagecoach Bus Handbook
The Go-Ahead Bus Handbook
The First Bus Handbook
The Arriva Bus Handbook
The National Express Handbook (bi-annual)
Most editions for earlier years are available direct from the publisher.

Associated series:
The Hong Kong Bus Handbook
The Malta Bus Handbook
The Leyland Lynx Handbook
The Model Bus Handbook
The Postbus Handbook
The Overall Advertisement Bus Handbook - Volume 1
The Toy & Model Bus Handbook - Volume 1 - Early Diecasts
The Fire Brigade Handbook (fleet list of each local authority fire brigade)
The Police Range Rover Handbook

Some earlier editions of these books are still available. Please contact the publisher on 01952 255669.

Contents

The Scottish Bus Handbook

This fifth edition of the Scottish Bus Handbook is part of a series that details the fleets of bus and express coach operators from across Britain. A list of current editions is shown on page 2. The operators included in this edition are some of those who provide tendered and commercial services in Scotland. The publishers have also included a number of operators who provide significant coaching activities.

Quality photographs for inclusion in the series are welcome, for which a fee is payable. The publishers unfortunately cannot accept responsibility for any loss and they require that you show your name on each picture or slide. High-resolution digital images of six megapixels or higher are also welcome on CD or DVD discs.

To keep the fleet information up-to-date, the publishers recommend the Ian Allan magazine *Buses* published monthly, or for more detailed information, the PSV Circle monthly news sheets.

The writer and publisher would be glad to hear from readers should any information be available which corrects or enhances that given in this publication.

Series Editor: Bill Potter
Principal Editors for *The Scottish Bus Handbook:* Stuart Martin, David Donati, and Bill Potter.

Acknowledgments:
We are grateful to the operating companies, John Burnett, Murdoch Currie, Bob Downham, and Tom Johnson for their assistance in the compilation of this book.

The cover photograph and frontispiece are by Richard Walters and Bob Downham

Earlier editions of the Scottish Bus Handbook:
1st Edition - 1994 - 1-897990-09-X
2nd Edition - 1996 - 1-897990-20-2
3rd Edition - 2000 - 1-897990-65-5
4th Edition - 2002 - 1-897990-33-2

ISBN 1 904875 01 7 (5th Edition) - May 2006
Published by British Bus Publishing Ltd, 16 St Margaret's Drive, Telford, TF1 3PH
Telephone: 01952 255669 - Facsimile 01952 222397 - www.britishbuspublishing.co.uk

AAA Coaches

AAA Coaches Ltd, 7 Camps Industrial Estate, Kirknewton, EH27 8DF

Reg	Chassis	Body	Seating	Year	Previous operator
R200STL	Volvo B10M-62	Caetano Enigma	C49FT	1998	Edinburgh Coach Lines, 2005
V431EAL	Volvo B10M-62	Jonckheere Mistral 50	C51FT	2000	Lochs & Glens, Aberfoyle, 2003
SN51AAA	Volvo B10M-62	Jonckheere Mistral 50	C33FT	2001	
SO51AAA	Volvo B12M	Jonckheere Mistral 50	C33FT	2002	
SN02AAA	Mercedes-Benz Vario 0814	Onyx	C24F	2002	
RR52AAA	Mercedes-Benz Vario 0814	Mellor	C33F	2002	
AR03AAA	Bova Futura FHD12.340	Bova	C53F	2003	
SC53VOM	Ford Transit	Ford	M16	2004	
SC53VPP	Ford Transit	Ford	M16	2004	
AR04AAA	Volvo B12m	Sunsundegri Sideral 330	C49FT	2004	
NR04AAA	Volvo B12m	Sunsundegri Sideral 330	C49FT	2004	
PF04SVJ	MAN 18.310 12m	Marcopolo Viaggio II 330	BC70F	2004	
PO54VZT	MAN 12.220 9.9m	Marcopolo Viaggio II 330	B35F	2004	Holmeswood Coaches, 2005
PN05BJY	MAN 18.310 12m	Marcopolo Viaggio II 330	BC70F	2005	
YX05DKK	Mercedes-Benz Vario 0814	Autibus Nouvelle 2	C33F	2005	
SN55FEF	MAN 18.310 12m	Marcopolo Viaggio II 330	BC70F	2005	

Previous registrations:
AR03AAA   WA03EYP   R200STL   R200STL, PSU612

AAA Coaches operates from Edinburgh using a modern fleet that includes Sunsundegri NR04AAA, seen in Linlithgow while heading for Larbert. *Mark Doggett*

ALLANDER TRAVEL

Allander Coaches Ltd, 19 Cloberfield, Milngavie, Glasgow, G62 7LN

AT33	T104GSE	Bova Futura FHD10.340	Bova	C38FT	1999	
AT44	OFS690Y	Leyland Olympian ONTL11/2R	Eastern Coach Works	B50/31D	1983	Lothian Buses, 2000
AT45	OFS691Y	Leyland Olympian ONTL11/2R	Eastern Coach Works	B50/31D	1983	Lothian Buses, 2000
AT48	Y633TYS	Volvo B10MT	Van Hool T9 Alizée	C49FT	2001	
AT49	Y58THS	Bova Futura FHD12.370	Bova	C49FT	2001	
AT50	4143AT	Toyota Coaster HZB50R	Caetano Optimo III	C18F	1996	Carter, North Acton, 2001
AT54	E607KSP	Volvo B10M-61	Plaxton Paramount 3200 III	C53F	1987	Docherty's Midland Cs, 2001
AT63	9237AT	Volvo B7R	TransBus Prima	C55F	2003	
AT69	A236GHN	Leyland Olympian ONTL11/2R	Eastern Coach Works	B45/32F	1984	Irvine, Law, 2003
AT71	K579PHU	Dennis Javelin 12m	Wadham Stringer Vanguard II	BC70F	1992	MoD, 2003
AT72	K578PHU	Dennis Javelin 12m	Wadham Stringer Vanguard II	BC70F	1992	MoD, 2003
AT73	K538PHU	Dennis Javelin 12m	Wadham Stringer Vanguard II	BC70F	1992	MoD, 2003
AT74	9446AT	Volvo B7R	Jonckheere Mistral 45	C55F	2003	
AT77	7921AT	Volvo B12M	Jonckheere Mistral 50	C51FT	2004	
AT78	4670AT	Volvo B12M	Jonckheere Mistral 50	C51FT	2004	
AT79	GIL1685	Volvo B10M-62	Jonckheere Mistral 50	C49FT	2001	Park's of Hamilton, 2004
AT80	XAT11X	Volvo B10M-62	Jonckheere Mistral 50	C49FT	2001	Park's of Hamilton, 2004
AT81	Y573RSE	Mercedes-Benz Vario 0815	Sitcar Beluga	C29F	2001	Maynes of Buckie, 2004
AT82	8578AT	Bova Futura FCL12.270	Bova	C53F	1995	City of Nottingham, 2004
AT83	SF05KWB	Volvo B12M	Jonckheere Mistral 50	C51FT	2005	
AT84	SF05KWA	Volvo B12M	Jonckheere Mistral 50	C51FT	2005	
AT85	R319NRU	Volvo B10M-62	Berkhof Excellence	C49FT	1997	Stephenson, Tolthorpe, 2005
AT86	3788AT	Bova Futura FHD12.270	Bova	C53F	1993	Hellyers, Fareham, 2005
AT87	2367AT	Bova Futura FCL12.270	Bova	C53F	1994	Galleon, Hunsdon, 2005
AT88	SF05NRY	VDL Bova Futura FHD12.340	VDL Bova	C49FT	2005	
AT89	N113NYS	Mercedes-Benz 711D	LCB	B24FL	1996	Glasgow BC, 2005
AT90	AT2472	Bova Futura FLD12.270	Bova	C49FT	1996	Burton, Kendal, 2005

Previous registrations:

2367AT	M272SBT, LSK607	AT2472	P157XNW
3786AT	L962OEY	E607KSP	248D334, JD3164
4143AT	P162ANR	GIL1685	Y178KCS
4670AT	SF04SXY	R319NRU	KNP1X
7726AT	-	SF03ACJ	SF03ACJ, 3786AT
7921AT	SF04SXX	T104GSE	GLZ1270, 2367AT
8578AT	M784RUY, 77RTO	XAT11X	Y176KCS
9237AT	SF03ACU	Y58THS	Y58YHS, 7726AT
9446AT	SF03MGO	Y573RSE	Y555GSM, AT2472

Web: www.allandercoaches.co.uk

ANDERSON COACHES

IF Anderson Coaches Ltd, Seaview, Tayvallich, Lochgilphead, PA31 8PJ

M373MUV	Dennis Dart	East Lancs	BC31F	1994	Metropolitan Police, 2002
N753OYR	Dennis Dart	East Lancs	BC31F	1995	Metropolitan Police, 2002
N23KYS	Mercedes-Benz 709D	Wadham Stringer	B29F	1995	

Depots: Tayvallich, Lochgilphead; Achnabreck, Lochgilphead and Dalvore Farm, Kilmartin

Allander Travel's livery comprises a striking combination of black, red and gold for their coaches. Seen in bus colours is former MoD single-deck AT72, K578PHU. This Dennis Javelin has a Wadham Stringer Vanguard body now fitted with seventy seats in a 3+2 combination, and is primarily used on school services. *Billy Nicol*

Based in the town of Lochgilphead, in Argyll and Bute is the small operation of Andersons. One minibus bought new is Wadham Stringer-bodied Mercedes-Benz minibus N23KYS, seen in its home town. *Murdoch Currie*

AVONDALE COACHES

Avondale Coaches Ltd, 189 Dumbarton Road, Clydebank, G81 1UF

E511YSU	Mercedes-Benz 709D	Alexander AM	B25F	1988	Kelvin Central, 1995
F311DET	Mercedes-Benz 709D	Reeve Burgess Beaver	B25F	1988	Slaemuir, Port Glasgow, 2003
G169FJC	Mercedes-Benz 709D	Reeve Burgess Beaver	BC25F	1989	Arriva Cymru, 2000
G175FJC	Mercedes-Benz 709D	Reeve Burgess Beaver	BC25F	1989	Arriva Cymru, 2000
G293TSL	Mercedes-Benz 709D	Alexander Sprint	B23F	1989	Pugh, St Helens, 2004
J10WBT	Dennis Dart 8.5m	Northern Counties Paladin	B31F	1991	Warrington Borough Transport, 2004
K221VTB	Dennis Dart 9m	Northern Counties Paladin	B35F	1992	Warrington Borough Transport, 2004
K222VTB	Dennis Dart 9m	Northern Counties Paladin	B35F	1992	Warrington Borough Transport, 2004
K223VTB	Dennis Dart 9m	Northern Counties Paladin	B35F	1992	Warrington Borough Transport, 2004
K224VTB	Dennis Dart 9m	Northern Counties Paladin	B35F	1992	Warrington Borough Transport, 2004
K225VTB	Dennis Dart 9m	Northern Counties Paladin	B35F	1992	Warrington Borough Transport, 2004
K151LGO	Dennis Dart 8.5m	Plaxton Pointer	B26F	1992	London General, 2004
K153LGO	Dennis Dart 8.5m	Plaxton Pointer	B26F	1992	London General, 2004
K581MGT	Dennis Dart 9m	Plaxton Pointer	B32F	1993	London General, 2004
K583MGT	Dennis Dart 9m	Plaxton Pointer	B32F	1993	London General, 2004
K593MGT	Dennis Dart 9m	Plaxton Pointer	B32F	1993	London General, 2004
K244SUS	Mercedes-Benz 709D	Alexander Sprint	B23F	1993	Dublin Bus, 2001
L374BGA	Mercedes-Benz 709D	Eurocoach	B23F	1994	Dublin Bus, 2001
L375BGA	Mercedes-Benz 709D	Eurocoach	B23F	1994	Dublin Bus, 2001
L376BGA	Mercedes-Benz 709D	Eurocoach	B23F	1994	Dublin Bus, 2001
L395BGA	Mercedes-Benz 709D	Eurocoach	B23F	1993	Dublin Bus, 2001
L416BGA	Mercedes-Benz 709D	Eurocoach	B23F	1994	Dublin Bus, 2001
L464BGA	Mercedes-Benz 709D	Eurocoach	B23F	1994	Dublin Bus, 2001
L465BGA	Mercedes-Benz 709D	Eurocoach	B23F	1994	Dublin Bus, 2001
L481BGA	Mercedes-Benz 709D	Eurocoach	B23F	1994	Dublin Bus, 2001
L482BGA	Mercedes-Benz 709D	Eurocoach	B23F	1994	Dublin Bus, 2001
L493BGA	Mercedes-Benz 709D	Eurocoach	B23F	1994	Dublin Bus, 2001

Avondale Clydebank operates services in that town as well as services into central Glasgow. K581MGT is one of several buses in the fleet formerly run by London General. This Plaxton Pointer-bodied Dennis Dart was acquired during 2004. *Billy Nicol*

Recent deliveries for Avondale carry the colours of SPT, the Passenger Transport Authority and Executive for Strathclyde. A trio of Darts arrived in 2003 and despite the Dennis and Plaxton badges the buses were built by TransBus after they intended those names to disappear. Following the collapse of TransBus, some assets, including the Falkirk assembly plant, have been bought by a new company now named Alexander Dennis Limited. *Bob Downham*

L851WDS	Mercedes-Benz 709D	Wadham Stringer Wessex II	B28FL	1994	Marbill, Beith, 1998
L139XDS	Mercedes-Benz 709D	Wadham Stringer Wessex II	B29F	1994	
L140XDS	Mercedes-Benz 709D	Wadham Stringer Wessex II	B29F	1994	
L300RHU	Mercedes-Benz 711D	Talbot	B24FL	1994	Wilson's of Rhu, 1998
M211EGF	Dennis Dart 9m	Plaxton Pointer	B35F	1995	London General, 2004
VU02TSO	Optare Solo M920	Optare	N33F	2002	Brylaine Travel, Boston, 2005
VU02TTO	Optare Solo M920	Optare	N33F	2002	Brylaine Travel, Boston, 2005
SN03LFV	TransBus Dart 8.8m	TransBus Mini Pointer	N29F	2003	
SN03LFW	TransBus Dart 8.8m	TransBus Mini Pointer	N29F	2003	
SN03LFX	TransBus Dart 8.8m	TransBus Mini Pointer	N29F	2003	
YJ05XNP	Optare Solo M850	Optare	N29F	2005	
YJ05XNR	Optare Solo M850	Optare	N29F	2005	
YJ05XNS	Optare Solo M850	Optare	N29F	2005	
YJ05XNT	Optare Solo M850	Optare	N29F	2005	

Previous registrations:

K244SUS	93D8011		L464BGA	94D2014
L374BGA	94D2020		L465BGA	94D2015
L375BGA	94D2018		L481BGA	94D2013
L376BGA	94D2019		L482BGA	93D2015
L395BGA	93D10010		L493BGA	93D8012
L416BGA	93D10004			

AYRWAYS COACH TRAVEL

Ayrways Coach Travel Ltd, 1 Dallowie Road, Patna, Ayr, KA6 7ND

Reg	Chassis	Body	Seating	Year	History
EBM439T	Leyland Leopard PSU5C/4R	Duple Dominant II	C57F	1979	McIntosh, Dalmellington, 2002
TWH686T	Leyland Leopard PSU3E/4R	Plaxton Supreme IV	C51F	1979	McIntosh, Dalmellington, 2002
GHG348W	Leyland Atlantean AN68A/2R	East Lancs	B50/36F	1981	Metro, Blackpool, 2003
EJR104W	Leyland Atlantean AN68A/2R	Alexander AL	B49/37F	1981	Moffat & Williamson, 2003
A227LFX	Volvo B10M-61	Duple Caribbean	C51F	1984	Rayner, Esh Winning, 2003
D36ONY	Bedford Venturer YNV	Duple 320	C57F	1987	Shirran-Lumsden, 2005
HIL8645	Volvo B10M-60	Van Hool Alizée	C49F	1987	Gannan, Loanhead, 2006
F427DUG	Volvo B10M-60	Plaxton Paramount 3200 III	C57F	1988	Durham City Travel, 2004
F481WFX	Volvo B10M-60	Duple 340	C51F	1988	Milligan, Mauchline, 2003
G807LAG	Scania N113DRB	East Lancs	B51/37F	1990	Coliseum, Southampton, 2005
H223LOM	Scania N113DRB	Alexander RH	B45/31F	1990	Coliseum, Southampton, 2005
H224LOM	Scania N113DRB	Alexander RH	B45/31F	1990	Coliseum, Southampton, 2005
J500CCH	Volvo B10M-60	Berkhof Excellence 2000	C50FT	1992	Milligan, Mauchline, 2003
M631KVU	Volvo B10M-60	Van Hool Alizée HE	C49FT	1995	Dodsworth, Boroughbridge, 2003
P646MSE	Mercedes-Benz 814D	Plaxton Beaver	BC33F	1996	White, Cumnock, 2006

Previous registrations:

JUI4680	TNH882X, 226DMW,JFO108X, 325CCE, ONL810X, MIL2979		
A227LFX	A227LFX, 723CTH, GIL6240	F481WFX	F481WFX, MIL5830
ABZ9122	F257OFP	J500CCH	J500CCH, MIL8028
F427DUG	F427DUG, WSV573	HIL8645	D539MVR

Ayrways Coach Travel operates principally school services around Ayrshire. Their newest coach is M631KVU, a Van Hool Alizée-bodied Volvo that was new to Shearings. It is seen at Preston rail station while working a rail replacement service from Carlisle. *Bob Downham*

BILLY DAVIES

WAA Davies, Transport House, Plean Industrial Estate, Plean, Stirling, FK7 8BS

B821RSH	Leyland Tiger TRCTL11/3RH	Alexander TC	C57F	1985	Hunter, Sauchie, 1999
MRJ40W	MCW Metrobus DR102/21	MCW	B43/30F	1981	Burnley & Pendle, 2002
MRJ55W	MCW Metrobus DR102/21	MCW	B43/30F	1981	Burnley & Pendle, 2002
ULS618X	MCW Metrobus DR102/23	Alexander	B45/33F	1981	First, 2004
ANA173Y	MCW Metrobus DR102/21	MCW	B43/30F	1983	Burnley & Pendle, 2002
ANA184Y	MCW Metrobus DR102/21	MCW	B43/30F	1983	First, 2005
L8BUS	Plaxton 425	Lorraine	C53F	1993	Mitchell, Plean, 2002
RIB6563	Volvo B10M-62	Plaxton Paramount 3500 II	C51FT	1986	Mitchell, Plean, 2003
R189LBC	Volvo B10M-62	Caetano Algarve 2	C49FT	1997	Smith, Ashington, 2004
CNZ2978	Volvo B10M-62	Plaxton Première 350	C49FT	1998	White Lion, Tredegar, 2005
P100BUS	Mercedes-Benz Vario 0814	Onyx	C24F	2002	Myles, Plean, 2005

Previous registrations:

B821RSH	B530LSG, GSU377		R189LBC	R189LBC, VFW721
CNZ2978	R554JDF		RIB6563	C175LWB
P100BUS	MIL02ONH			

Web: www.daviescoaches.co.uk

Almost half of Billy Davies' vehicles are MCW Metrobuses which are required for school contracts. Pictured in a line-up at Plean are SND120X, ANA173Y and MRJ48W. All these were latterly with Greater Manchester Buses.
Bob Downham

BOWMANS

Bowman Coaches (Mull) Ltd, Scallastle, Craignure, Isle of Mull, PA65 6BA

A121XNH	DAF SB2300	Jonckheere Jubilee P50	C53FT	1984	Nationwide, Lanark, 1989
D126ACX	DAF MB230	Plaxton Paramount 3500 III	C53F	1987	Mackie, Alloa, 1997
H837AHS	Volvo B10M-60	Plaxton Paramount 3500 III	C49FT	1991	Goode, West Bromwich, 2000
J782KHD	DAF MB230	Van Hool Alizée H	C51FT	1992	Pullman, Crofty, 2003
J235NNC	Volvo B10M-60	Van Hool Alizée H	C49FT	1992	National Holidays, 2001
M481CSD	Volvo B10M-62	Van Hool Alizée H	C55F	1995	Crawford, Neilston, 2003
M627RCP	DAF SB3000	Van Hool Alizée HE	C51FT	1995	TLC Travel, West Bromwich, 2003
N982FWT	DAF SB3000	Van Hool Alizée HE	C49FT	1996	Trueman, Ash Vale, 2005
P696BRS	Volvo B10M-62	Van Hool Alizée HE	C53F	1996	Peace, Skene, 2002
T608DGD	Volvo B10M-62	Van Hool T9 Alizée	C46FT	2000	Allander, Milngavie, 2004

Previous registrations:

M481CSD	GJI627
N982FWT	J17TRU, 1287RU, N982FWT

Providing almost all the transport on the Isle of Mull is Bowman's. The full-size coaches are a mix of Volvo and DAF products with T608DGD being one of the former. The coachwork is the T9 version of the Van Hool Alizée and was pictured while meeting the Oban ferry at Craignure on Mull. *Murdoch Currie*

The Scottish Bus Handbook

BRYANS of DENNY

W Bryans, 39 Sutherland Drive, Denny, FK6 5ER

E308KES	Dennis Javelin 12m	Duple 320	C57F	1987	Travel Tayside, 2004
K818NKH	Dennis Dart 9m	Plaxton Pointer	B34F	1992	Metroline, Harrow, 2002
R983FYS	Toyota Coaster BB50R	Caetano Optimo IV	C21F	1997	
T222GSM	Dennis Javelin 12m	Berkhof Excellence	C49FT	1999	Maynes of Buckie, 2004
Y264KNB	Optare Solo M850	Optare	N29F	2001	
SL52CPE	Mercedes-Benz Sprinter 413cdi	KVC	M16	2003	Wood, Tillicoultry, 2005
SN05FLR	ADL Dart 8.8m	ADL Mini Pointer	N29F	2005	

Previous registration:
E308KES   E308KES, PSU340

Depot: Myothill Road, Head of Muir, Denny

The fleet of Bryans of Denny is represented by Optare Solo Y264KNB, seen here in an all-over white livery. It was photographed on Larbert local service E3 in June 2004. *Bob Downham*

BUS NA COMHAIRLE

Nan Eilean Siar Comhairle, Marybank Depot, Stornoway, Isle of Lewis, HS2 0DB

J495DJS	Dennis Javelin 11m	Plaxton Derwent II	BC57F	1991	
M6SEL	Dennis Javelin 12m	Plaxton Expressliner 2	C46FT	1994	Selwyn, Runcorn, 2004
M7SEL	Dennis Javelin 12m	Plaxton Expressliner 2	C46FT	1994	Selwyn, Runcorn, 2004
M365AMA	Dennis Javelin 12m	Plaxton Expressliner 2	C46FT	1995	Selwyn, Runcorn, 2004
M366AMA	Dennis Javelin 12m	Plaxton Première 350	C48FT	1995	Selwyn, Runcorn, 2004
M602BCA	Dennis Javelin 12m	Plaxton Première 350	C49FT	1995	
R777GSM	Dennis Javelin 12m	Plaxton Première 350	C49FT	1997	
SG04FKK	Ford Transit	Ford	M16	2004	
YN04HJD	Mercedes-Benz Vario 0814	TransBus Beaver 2	BC29F	2004	
YN04HJE	Mercedes-Benz Vario 0814	TransBus Beaver 2	BC29F	2004	
YN04HJF	Mercedes-Benz Vario 0814	TransBus Beaver 2	BC29F	2004	
YN04HJK	Mercedes-Benz Vario 0814	TransBus Beaver 2	BC29F	2004	
YU04XJT	Mercedes-Benz Vario 0814	TransBus Beaver 2	BC29F	2004	
YN54XYK	Mercedes-Benz Vario 0814	TransBus Beaver 2	BC29F	2005	

Previous registrations:

M365AMA	M365AMA, 352STG	R777GSM	R777GSM, ODY395

One of the most remote British operators is Bus na Comhairle which is based on the Isle of Lewis in the Outer Hebrides. The current fleet comprises Dennis Javelin coaches and Mercedes-Benz Vario minibuses. Originally used on English National Express services, M6SEL and M7SEL are now based at Stornoway. *Richard Walter*

The Scottish Bus Handbook

CALEDONIA BUSES

Caledonia Buses - Linn Park Buses

Caledonian Coach Co Ltd, 6 Portree Avenue, Greenfield Gardens, Kilmarnock, KA3 2GB

HUI4553	Dennis Dorchester	Plaxton Paramount 3500	C44FT	1983	Faydon Travel, Hayes, 2005
RIL9404	Dennis Dart 8.5m	Carlyle Dartline	B28F	1990	Bayview, Helensburgh, 2004
RIL9410	Dennis Dart 8.5m	Carlyle Dartline	B28F	1990	Bayview, Helensburgh, 2004
H141MOB	Dennis Dart 8.5m	Carlyle Dartline	B28F	1991	Beta Buses, Glasgow, 2004
J967JNL	Optare MetroRider MR	Optare	B25F	1991	Wilson, Greenock, 2005
J968JNL	Optare MetroRider MR	Optare	B25F	1991	Wilson, Greenock, 2005
JDZ2405	Dennis Dart 9m	Wright HandyBus	B36F	1991	Pete's Travel, West Bromwich, 2003
JDZ2409	Dennis Dart 9m	Wright HandyBus	B36F	1991	Pete's Travel, West Bromwich, 2003
JDZ2413	Dennis Dart 9m	Wright HandyBus	B36F	1991	Pete's Travel, West Bromwich, 2003
JDZ2414	Dennis Dart 9m	Wright HandyBus	B36F	1991	Pete's Travel, West Bromwich, 2003
K416MGN	Dennis Dart 8.5m	Plaxton Pointer	B35F	1992	Metroline, Harrow, 2003
K163FYG	Optare MetroRider MR03	Optare	B29F	1992	Stagecoach North East, 2002
K186YDW	Optare MetroRider MR01	Optare	B31F	1992	Stagecoach West, 2002
K359SCN	Optare MetroRider MR03	Optare	B26F	1993	A2B, Southampton, 2005
L807TFY	Optare MetroRider MR11	Optare	B22F	1993	Stagecoach North West, 2002
L377TFT	Optare MetroRider MR13	Optare	B22F	1993	Go-Ahead Northern, 2004
L383TFT	Optare MetroRider MR13	Optare	B22F	1993	Go-Ahead Northern, 2004
L385TFT	Optare MetroRider MR13	Optare	B22F	1993	Go-Ahead Northern, 2004
L386TFT	Optare MetroRider MR13	Optare	B22F	1993	Go-Ahead Northern, 2004
L387TFT	Optare MetroRider MR13	Optare	B22F	1993	Go-Ahead Northern, 2004
L389AVK	Optare MetroRider MR13	Optare	B22F	1993	Go-Ahead Northern, 2004

Caledonia Buses has built up a considerable collection of Optare MetroRiders for its services to the west of Glasgow. New to Cardiff Bus in 1992, K186YDW is seen in Glasgow city centre while preparing to head to Castlemilk. The MetroRider was originally built by Laird Group subsidiary MCW, but when production at Washwood Heath ceased, the design was sold to Optare who commenced production of an improved version at Leeds. *Mark Doggett*

Five former Metroline MAN 11.220s with Marshall Capital bodywork now operate for Caledonian Buses. Representing the type, N128XEG, is seen here in Glasgow while operating route 66 to East Kilbride.
Mark Doggett

L472YVK	Optare MetroRider MR13	Optare	B22F	1993	Go-Ahead Northern, 2004
L103GBO	Optare MetroRider MR	Optare	B31F	1994	Cardiff Bus, 2005
L106GBO	Optare MetroRider MR	Optare	B31F	1994	Cardiff Bus, 2005
M110KBO	Optare MetroRider MR15	Optare	B31F	1995	Cardiff Bus, 2005
M116KBO	Optare MetroRider MR15	Optare	B31F	1995	Cardiff Bus, 2005
M123KBO	Optare MetroRider MR15	Optare	B31F	1995	Cardiff Bus, 2005
M124KBO	Optare MetroRider MR15	Optare	B31F	1995	Cardiff Bus, 2005
M125KBO	Optare MetroRider MR15	Optare	B31F	1995	Cardiff Bus, 2005
M127KBO	Optare MetroRider MR15	Optare	B31F	1995	Cardiff Bus, 2005
M129KBO	Optare MetroRider MR15	Optare	B31F	1995	Cardiff Bus, 2005
M665JFP	Mercedes-Benz 709D	Alexander Sprint	B29F	1995	City of Nottingham, 2001
M238UTM	Mercedes-Benz 709D	Marshall C19	B21D	1995	Stagecoach, 2005
N139PTG	Optare MetroRider MR15	Optare	B31F	1996	Cardiff Bus, 2005
N128XEG	MAN 11.220	Marshall Capital	N38F	1996	Metroline, Harrow, 2003
P470JEG	MAN 11.220	Marshall Capital	N38F	1996	Metroline, Harrow, 2003
P474JEG	MAN 11.220	Marshall Capital	N38F	1996	Metroline, Harrow, 2003
P476JEG	MAN 11.220	Marshall Capital	N38F	1996	Metroline, Harrow, 2003
P478JEG	MAN 11.220	Marshall Capital	N38F	1996	Metroline, Harrow, 2003
T415LGP	Dennis Dart SLF 10.7m	Caetano Compass	N41F	1999	Connex, London, 2005
T416LGP	Dennis Dart SLF 10.7m	Caetano Compass	N41F	1999	Connex, London, 2005
T417LGP	Dennis Dart SLF 10.7m	Caetano Compass	N41F	1999	Connex, London, 2005

Previous registration:
HUI4553   HNF262Y, BUT23Y

Depot: Drakemire Drive, Linn Park Ind Est, Glasgow

CITY SPRINTER

A Arnott, 24 Parkinch, Erskine, PA8 7HZ

D502NWG	Mercedes-Benz L608D	Alexander AM	B20F	1986	Dunn, Port Glasgow, 1999
D541RCK	Mercedes-Benz L608D	Reeve Burgess	B20F	1986	Dart Buses, Paisley, 1997
F736FDV	Mercedes-Benz 709D	Reeve Burgess Beaver	BC25F	1988	Stagecoach Devon, 2000
F758FDV	Mercedes-Benz 709D	Reeve Burgess Beaver	BC25F	1988	Stagecoach Devon, 2000
F410KDD	Mercedes-Benz 709D	Reeve Burgess Beaver	BC25F	1989	Stagecoach Devon, 2000
G201RKK	Mercedes-Benz 709D	Reeve Burgess Beaver	B25F	1989	Arriva Cymru, 2000
G202RKK	Mercedes-Benz 709D	Reeve Burgess Beaver	B25F	1989	Arriva Cymru, 2000
G203RKK	Mercedes-Benz 709D	Reeve Burgess Beaver	B25F	1989	Arriva Cymru, 2000
G681AAD	Mercedes-Benz 709D	PMT Ami	B25F	1989	Stagecoach Cheltenham, 2000
G160YRE	Mercedes-Benz 709D	LHE Commuter	B29F	1989	Arriva Cymru, 2001
G161YRE	Mercedes-Benz 709D	LHE Commuter	B29F	1989	Arriva Cymru, 2001
G162YRE	Mercedes-Benz 709D	LHE Commuter	B29F	1989	Arriva Cymru, 2001
G948TDV	Mercedes-Benz 709D	Carlyle	B29F	1989	McPherson, Port Glasgow, 1999
G951TDV	Mercedes-Benz 709D	Carlyle	B29F	1989	McPherson, Port Glasgow, 1999
K132XRE	Mercedes-Benz 709D	Dormobile Routemaker	B29F	1992	Arriva Scotland West, 2000
K242SFJ	Mercedes-Benz 709D	Plaxton Beaver	B25F	1992	Slaemuir, Port Glasgow, 2003
M208EGF	Dennis Dart	Plaxton Pointer	B35F	1994	Go-Ahead London, 2004
M209EGF	Dennis Dart	Plaxton Pointer	B35F	1994	Go-Ahead London, 2004
M103BLE	Dennis Dart 9.5m	Plaxton Pointer	B40F	1994	Metroline, Harrow, 2004
M506ALP	Dennis Dart 9.5m	Plaxton Pointer	B40F	1994	Metroline, Harrow, 2004
N249PGD	Mercedes-Benz 709D	UVG	B25F	1995	Slaemuir, Port Glasgow, 2003
N250PGD	Mercedes-Benz 709D	UVG	B25F	1995	Slaemuir, Port Glasgow, 2003
P294MLD	Dennis Dart	Plaxton Pointer	B39F	1996	Metroline, Harrow, 2004

Depot: Braehead Ind Est, Old Govan Road, Renfrew

City Sprinter of Erskine competes with First on their service linking the south side of Glasgow with the city. Carrying a permanent destination indicator is Dennis Dart M208EGF which latterly operated with Go-Ahead London. *Mark Doggett*

CLYDE COAST

Clyde Coast Coaches Ltd, 55ᴀ Montgomerie Street, Ardrossan, KA22 8HR

RRS320X	Leyland Olympian ONLXB/1R	Eastern Coach Works	B45/32F	1982	Fife Scottish, 1999
TSO24X	Leyland Olympian ONLXB/1R	Eastern Coach Works	B45/32F	1982	Fife Scottish, 1999
OFS674Y	Leyland Olympian ONLXB/2R	Eastern Coach Works	B50/31D	1983	Lothian Buses, 2000
OFS675Y	Leyland Olympian ONLXB/2R	Eastern Coach Works	B50/31D	1983	Lothian Buses, 2000
OFS678Y	Leyland Olympian ONLXB/2R	Eastern Coach Works	B50/31D	1983	Lothian Buses, 2000
OFS689Y	Leyland Olympian ONLXB/2R	Eastern Coach Works	B50/31D	1983	Lothian Buses, 2000
WDC218Y	Leyland Olympian ONLXB/1R	Eastern Coach Works	B43/32F	1983	UK North, Manchester, 2004
TJI4024	Volvo B10M-61	Van Hool Alizée	C49DT	1984	Bruce, Shotts, 2003
GIL5407	Volvo B10M-61	Van Hool Alizée	C57F	1987	McGowan, Neilston, 2000
GIL2754	Volvo B10M-61	Van Hool Alizée	C57F	1987	, 2002
D522DSX	Leyland Tiger TRBTL11/2RH	Alexander TB	B57F	1987	Dart, Paisley, 2002
XJF448	Volvo B10M-61	Van Hool Alizée	C49FT	1989	Steele, Stevenston, 2002
TJI6264	Volvo B10M-60	Van Hool Alizée	C49FT	1992	Shearings, 1999
WSC571	Volvo B10M-62	Van Hool T9 Alizée	C49FT	1997	IBT Travel, Prestwick, 2002
GNZ9360	Volvo B10M-62	Van Hool T9 Alizée	C53F	1998	Logan, Ballymoney, 2005
FN04JZK	Volvo B12M	Sunsundegui Sideral 330	C49FT	2004	
FN04JZM	Volvo B12M	Sunsundegui Sideral 330	C49FT	2004	
SN05FPG	Volvo B12B	Van Hool T9 Alicron	C49FT	2005	Whytes, Newmachar, 2006

Previous registrations:

GIL2754	?	TJI4024	A612UGD
GIL5407	D555MVR	TJI6264	J241NNC
GNZ9360	R784WSB	WSC571	R132JGA
RRS320X	TSO19X, 9492SC	XJF448	F764ENE, LSK505, F253MGB

Web: www.clydecoast.com

Clyde Coast of Ardrossan is one of several operators to take mid-life Olympians from Lothian Buses primarily for use on school contracts. OFS674Y is one of five from the 1983 intake now in blue livery, complete with the original second door. *Billy Nicol*

COAKLEY

Coakley Bus Company Ltd, 19 Newhut Road, Braidhurst Ind Est, Motherwell, ML1 3ST

WIB9256	Mercedes-Benz 811D	Reeve Burgess Beaver	B31F	1990	Bryce, Coatbridge, 2004
H177JVT	Mercedes-Benz 811D	Wright NimBus	B29F	1990	Ferguson, Cleland, 2004
H916XYT	Volvo Citybus B10M-55	East Lancs EL2000 (1992)	B41F	1990	Arriva North East & Scotland, 2005
H921XYT	Volvo Citybus B10M-55	East Lancs EL2000 (1992)	B41F	1990	Arriva Yorkshire, 2005
H922XYT	Volvo Citybus B10M-55	East Lancs EL2000 (1992)	B41F	1990	Arriva Yorkshire, 2005
KDZ5801	Dennis Dart 9m	Wright HandyBus	B34F	1991	Haywood, Bedworth, 2005
J316XVX	Dennis Dart 9m	Wright HandyBus	B35F	1991	Arriva Southern Counties, 2005
J612XHL	Dennis Dart 9m	Plaxton Pointer	B34F	1991	Mackie, Alloa, 2004
K470SKO	Dennis Dart 9.8m	Plaxton Pointer (1995)	B40F	1992	Arriva Southern Counties, 2005
K433OKH	Dennis Dart 9m	Plaxton Pointer	B34F	1993	Arriva Scotland, 2001
L52LSG	Mercedes-Benz 709D	Plaxton Beaver	B25F	1993	Arriva Scotland, 2001
L53LSG	Mercedes-Benz 709D	Plaxton Beaver	B25F	1993	Arriva Scotland, 2001
L54LSG	Mercedes-Benz 709D	Plaxton Beaver	B25F	1993	Arriva Scotland, 2003
NDZ7927	Mercedes-Benz 811D	Wright NimBus	B26F	1993	Wiilson, Carnwath, 2002
NDZ7928	Mercedes-Benz 811D	Wright NimBus	B26F	1993	Wiilson, Carnwath, 2002
NDZ7930	Mercedes-Benz 811D	Wright NimBus	B26F	1993	Wiilson, Carnwath, 2002
L737PUA	Optare MetroRider MR15	Optare	B31F	1993	Arriva Yorkshire, 2004
L866LFS	Mercedes-Benz 711D	Plaxton Beaver	B25F	1994	Arriva Scotland, 2003
L870LFS	Mercedes-Benz 711D	Plaxton Beaver	B25F	1994	Arriva Scotland, 2003
L868LFS	Mercedes-Benz 711D	Plaxton Beaver	B25F	1994	Arriva Scotland, 2003
L413BGA	Mercedes-Benz 709D	Eurocoach	B23F	1994	Avondale, Greenock, 2002
L906ANS	Mercedes-Benz 811D	Dormobile Routemaker	B33F	1994	Clyde Coast, Ardrossan, 1997
L705AGA	Mercedes-Benz 709D	Wadham Stringer Wessex II	B29F	1994	Arriva Scotland, 2003
M880DDS	Mercedes-Benz 709D	Wadham Stringer Wessex II	B29F	1994	Arriva Scotland, 2003
M742UUA	Optare MetroRider MR15	Optare	B31F	1994	Arriva Yorkshire, 2004
M743UUA	Optare MetroRider MR15	Optare	B31F	1994	Arriva Yorkshire, 2004
M744UUA	Optare MetroRider MR15	Optare	B31F	1994	Arriva Yorkshire, 2004
M745UUA	Optare MetroRider MR15	Optare	B31F	1994	Arriva Yorkshire, 2004
M115KBD	Optare MetroRider MR15	Optare	B31F	1994	Cardiff Bus, 2005
M121KBD	Optare MetroRider MR15	Optare	B31F	1995	Cardiff Bus, 2005
M132KBD	Optare MetroRider MR15	Optare	B31F	1995	Cardiff Bus, 2005
M791EUS	Mercedes-Benz 709D	TBP	B27F	1995	Arriva Scotland, 2003
M201EGF	Dennis Dart 9m	Plaxton Pointer	B35F	1995	London General, 2004
M202EGF	Dennis Dart 9m	Plaxton Pointer	B35F	1995	London General, 2004
M206EGF	Dennis Dart 9m	Plaxton Pointer	B35F	1995	London General, 2004
M207EGF	Dennis Dart 9m	Plaxton Pointer	B35F	1995	London General, 2004
M215EGF	Dennis Dart 9m	Plaxton Pointer	B35F	1995	London General, 2004
M216EGF	Dennis Dart 9m	Plaxton Pointer	B35F	1995	London General, 2004
N142PTG	Optare MetroRider MR15	Optare	B31F	1996	Cardiff Bus, 2005
P291MLD	Dennis Dart 9.8m	Plaxton Pointer	B39F	1996	Metroline, Harrow, 2004

Many former Arriva buses are entering service with smaller operators. One of several MetroRiders working in Scotland is Coakley's M742UUA. It is seen in June 2005 while operating route 109 between Bellshill and Hamilton.
Bob Downham

After almost ten years in London, M206EGF was one of several 9-metre Darts purchased by Coakley from London General. It is seen in Motherwell while working route 61 from Birkenshaw. *Bob Downham*

P294MLD	Dennis Dart 9.8m	Plaxton Pointer	B39F	1996	Metroline, Harrow, 2004
P295MLD	Dennis Dart 9.8m	Plaxton Pointer	B39F	1996	Metroline, Harrow, 2004
P301MLD	Dennis Dart 9.8m	Plaxton Pointer	B39F	1996	Metroline, Harrow, 2004
P318MLD	Dennis Dart 9.8m	Plaxton Pointer	B39F	1996	Metroline, Harrow, 2004
P203OLX	Dennis Dart SLF 10m	Plaxton Pointer	N36F	1997	Metroline, Harrow, 2005
P204OLX	Dennis Dart SLF 10m	Plaxton Pointer	N36F	1997	Metroline, Harrow, 2005
P205OLX	Dennis Dart SLF 10m	Plaxton Pointer	N36F	1997	Metroline, Harrow, 2005
P207OLX	Dennis Dart SLF 10m	Plaxton Pointer	N36F	1997	Metroline, Harrow, 2005
P208OLX	Dennis Dart SLF 10m	Plaxton Pointer	N36F	1997	Metroline, Harrow, 2005
P210OLX	Dennis Dart SLF 10m	Plaxton Pointer	N36F	1997	Metroline, Harrow, 2005
P736FMS	Dennis Dart SLF 10.7m	UVG UrbanStar	N43F	1997	Mackie, Alloa, 2004
P737FMS	Dennis Dart SLF 10.7m	UVG UrbanStar	N43F	1997	Mackie, Alloa, 2004
P738FMS	Dennis Dart SLF 10.7m	UVG UrbanStar	N43F	1997	Mackie, Alloa, 2004
P40BLU	Dennis Dart SLF 10.1m	Wright Crusader	N32F	1997	Tanner, St Helens, 2005
P50BLU	Dennis Dart SLF 10.1m	Wright Crusader	N32F	1997	Tanner, St Helens, 2005
P484GNB	Dennis Dart SLF 10.1m	Wright Crusader	N32F	1997	Tanner, St Helens, 2005
R113RLY	Dennis Dart SLF 10m	Plaxton Pointer	N36F	1997	Metroline, Harrow, 2005
R115RLY	Dennis Dart SLF 10m	Plaxton Pointer	N36F	1997	Metroline, Harrow, 2005
R118RLY	Dennis Dart SLF 10m	Plaxton Pointer	N36F	1997	Metroline, Harrow, 2005
R119RLY	Dennis Dart SLF 10m	Plaxton Pointer	N36F	1997	Metroline, Harrow, 2005
R120RLY	Dennis Dart SLF 10m	Plaxton Pointer	N36F	1997	Metroline, Harrow, 2005
R121RLY	Dennis Dart SLF 10m	Plaxton Pointer	N36F	1997	Metroline, Harrow, 2005
R178VLA	Dennis Dart SLF 10.1m	Plaxton Pointer 2	N35F	1998	Metroline, Harrow, 2005
R179VLA	Dennis Dart SLF 10.1m	Plaxton Pointer 2	N35F	1998	Metroline, Harrow, 2005
R183VLA	Dennis Dart SLF 10.1m	Plaxton Pointer 2	N35F	1998	Metroline, Harrow, 2005
SN05LFT	ADL Dart 9m	ADL Pointer	N34F	2005	
SN05LFU	ADL Dart 9m	ADL Pointer	N34F	2005	
SN05LFV	ADL Dart 9m	ADL Pointer	N34F	2005	
SN05LFW	ADL Dart 9m	ADL Pointer	N34F	2005	
SF55GXJ	ADL Dart 8.8m	ADL Mini Pointer	N29F	2005	
SF55GXL	ADL Dart 8.8m	ADL Mini Pointer	N29F	2005	
SF55HBC	ADL Dart 10.1m	ADL Pointer	N34F	2005	
SF55HBD	ADL Dart 10.1m	ADL Pointer	N34F	2005	

Depots: Braidhurst Ind Est, Motherwell; Blairlinn Ind Est, Cumbernauld and Marshall Street, Wishaw.

The Scottish Bus Handbook

HENRY CRAWFORD

H Crawford Coaches Ltd, Shilford Mill, Neilston, Glasgow, G78 3BA

JNM742Y	Leyland Tiger TRCTL11/2R	Plaxton Paramount 3200	C57F	1983	Miller, Calderbank, 2005
RNY307Y	Leyland Tiger TRCTL11/2R	Plaxton Paramount 3200	C53F	1983	Miller, Calderbank, 2005
935BRU	Volvo B10M-61	Duple 320	C55F	1988	Riddler, Arbroath, 2000
973BUS	Volvo B10M-61	Duple 320	C57F	1989	Galloway, Harthill, 2001
L98WSW	Mercedes-Benz 609D	Onyx	C24F	1994	
NSK919	Volvo B10M-62	Van Hool Alizée HE	C57F	1994	Holmeswood Coaches, 2004
NSK920	Volvo B10M-62	Van Hool Alizée HE	C57F	1994	Holmeswood Coaches, 2004
NSK921	Volvo B10M-62	Van Hool Alizée HE	C57F	1994	
NNF922	Volvo B10M-62	Van Hool Alizée HE	C57F	1996	
XLM923	Volvo B10M-62	Van Hool Alizée HE	C57F	1996	Chalfont, Southall, 2004
HCC60	Mercedes-Benz 614D	Crystals	C24F	1998	
HCC882	Volvo B10M-62	Van Hool T9 Alizée	C57F	1998	
HCC551	Volvo B10M-62	Van Hool T9 Alizée	C53F	1998	
HCC296	Volvo B10MT	Van Hool T9 Alizée	C49FT	1999	
HCC440	Volvo B10MT	Van Hool T9 Alizée	C49FT	2000	
S20HCC	Mercedes-Benz Vario 0814	Plaxton Cheetah	C25F	2000	
S26HCC	Volvo B10M-62	Van Hool T9 Alizée	C50FT	2000	
S27HCC	Volvo B10M-62	Van Hool T9 Alizée	C49FT	2001	
HCC49	Mercedes-Benz Sprinter 413	Ferqui	M16	2001	
S28HCC	Volvo B12M	Van Hool T9 Alizée	C49FT	2002	
S29HCC	Volvo B12M	Van Hool T9 Alizée	C49FT	2002	
S30HCC	Volvo B12B	Van Hool T9 Alicron	C49FT	2003	
HCC974	Volvo B12M	Van Hool T9 Alizée	C57F	2004	
OO05HCC	Mercedes-Benz Vario 0814	Indcar Maxim	C25F	2005	
OO04HCC	Mercedes-Benz Vario 0814	Indcar	C24F	2006	
OO06HCC	Bova Futura FHD.340	Bova	C38FT	2006	
HCC296	Volvo B12B	Van Hool T9 Alicron	C49FT	2006	

Previous registrations:

935BRU	E100LBC	NSK919	L708PHE, HCC440
973BUS	F256OFP	NSK920	L709PHE, HCC974
L98WSW	L906LFS, HCC246, HCC49	NSK921	M269POS
HCC49	FX51BNN, S19HCC	NNF922	N277HSD
HCC60	R126LKS	S20HCC	W637MKY
HCC296	T284UCS, S24HCC	S26HCC	Y286TSU
HCC440	W285WCS, S25HCC	S27HCC	Y287TSU
HCC551	S283JGA, S23HCC	S28HCC	SC02LVD
HCC882	S282JGA, S22HCC	S29HCC	SC02LVE
HCC974	SJ04LLE, S21HCC	S30HCC	SJ03HMY
		XLM923	N197DYB, HCC882

Many of the coaches in Henry Crawford's fleet use his batch of Select 'HCC' index marks as shown on the last Volvo B10M purchased new. S27HCC carries a Van Hool T9 Alizée body and is seen in Glasgow while picking up passengers for a David Urquhart Tour. *Bob Downham*

D B TRAVEL

D P Bishop, Auld Street, Dalmuir, G81 4HB

E72MVV	Mercedes-Benz 709D	Robin Hood	B25F	1988	Coakley Bus, Motherwell, 2001
E73MVV	Mercedes-Benz 709D	Robin Hood	B25F	1988	Coakley Bus, Motherwell, 2001
F624XMS	Mercedes-Benz 811D	Alexander Sprint	B28F	1988	John Morrow, Glasgow, 2004
F49CWY	Mercedes-Benz 811D	Optare StarRider	B26F	1989	Arvonia, Llanrug, 2004
F214DCC	Mercedes-Benz 709D	Robin Hood	BC25F	1988	Arriva Cymru, 2001
F218DCC	Mercedes-Benz 709D	Robin Hood	BC25F	1988	Arriva Cymru, 2001
F219DCC	Mercedes-Benz 709D	Robin Hood	B27F	1988	Wilson, Carnwath, 2001
F427EJC	Mercedes-Benz 709D	Robin Hood	BC25F	1989	Arriva Cymru, 2001
F428GAT	Mercedes-Benz 811D	Robin Hood	B31F	1989	Slaemuir, Port Glasgow, 2004
L202ONU	Optare MetroRider MR15	Optare	B30F	1993	Harte, Greenock, 2005
L203ONU	Optare MetroRider MR15	Optare	B30F	1993	Harte, Greenock, 2005
L733MWV	Optare MetroRider MR15	Optare	B30F	1993	Puma, Glasgow, 2005
L738PUA	Optare MetroRider MR15	Optare	B31F	1994	Colchri, Glasgow, 2005
N796PDS	Mercedes-Benz 814D	Mellor	BC33F	1996	Rubensaat, Tamworth, 2006

DAVIDSON BUSES

Davidson Buses Ltd, PO Box 12542, Bathgate, EH48 2YD

K243SFJ	Mercedes-Benz 709D	Plaxton Beaver	B25F	1992	Citybus, Plymouth, 2003
K245SFJ	Mercedes-Benz 709D	Plaxton Beaver	B25F	1992	Citybus, Plymouth, 2003
K247SFJ	Mercedes-Benz 709D	Plaxton Beaver	B25F	1992	Citybus, Plymouth, 2003
K113XHG	Mercedes-Benz 709D	Alexander Sprint	B25F	1993	Stagecoach, 2005
L255YOD	Mercedes-Benz 709D	Plaxton Beaver	B25F	1993	Citybus, Plymouth, 2005
P692RWU	Dennis Dart SLF 10m	Plaxton Pointer	N35F	1997	Armchair, Brentford, 2003
P698RWU	Dennis Dart SLF 10m	Plaxton Pointer	N35F	1997	LocalLink, Bishop's Stortford, 2003
SJ53AXB	TransBus Dart SLF 8.8m	TransBus Pointer MPD	N29F	2004	
SN05HDC	ADL Dart 8.8m	ADL Mini Pointer	N29F	2005	
SN05HDD	ADL Dart 8.8m	ADL Mini Pointer	N29F	2005	
SN05HDE	ADL Dart 8.8m	ADL Mini Pointer	N29F	2005	
SN05HDF	ADL Dart 8.8m	ADL Mini Pointer	N29F	2005	

Depot: Westwood Works, West Calder

Latterly used by Armchair, Dart P692RWU is one of a pair that emigrated from Brentford in 2003 and is seen here awaiting time in Livingston for its next journey to Loganlea. The pair has recently been joined by four Alexander-Dennis Mini Pointers. *Bob Downham*

DICKSON'S

S Dickson, 27 Broomlands Gardens, Erskine, PA8 7BL

F424EJC	Mercedes-Benz 709D	Robin Hood	BC25F	1989	Arriva Cymru, 2000
F319EJO	Mercedes-Benz 709D	Reeve Burgess Beaver	BC25F	1989	Stagecoach Cambus, 1999
G238FJC	Mercedes-Benz 709D	Robin Hood	B25F	1989	Arriva Cymru, 2001
G288TSL	Mercedes-Benz 709D	Alexander Sprint	B23F	1990	Stagecoach Western Buses, 2002
J384GKH	Dennis Dart 8.5m	Plaxton Pointer	B24F	1990	Metrobus, 2003
J397GKH	Dennis Dart 8.5m	Plaxton Pointer	B24F	1990	Metrobus, 2003
K866ODY	Mercedes-Benz 709D	Alexander Sprint	B25F	1993	Stagecoach South, 2003
L748LWA	Mercedes-Benz 709D	Alexander Sprint	B25F	1994	Hendersons, Hamilton, 2005
L703AGA	Mercedes-Benz 709D	Wadham Stringer Wessex	B29F	1994	Davidson Buses, Bathgate, 1998
L245CCK	Volvo B6	Alexander Dash	BC40F	1994	Stagecoach, 2004
N102EMB	Mercedes-Benz 814D	Crystals	BC31F	1996	Lofty's, Bridge Trafford, 1997
N746YVR	Mercedes-Benz 711D	Marshall	B27F	1996	Stagecoach, 2004
N207GCS	Mercedes-Benz 709D	Wadham Stringer Wessex II	B28F	1996	Puma, Glasgow, 2003
N950MGG	Mercedes-Benz 709D	Wadham Stringer Wessex II	B29F	1996	Dart Buses, Paisley, 2002
N798FSD	Mercedes-Benz 709D	Wadham Stringer Wessex II	B16FL	1995	Marbill, Beith, 2004
N275FNS	Mercedes-Benz 811D	Wadham Stringer Wessex II	B33F	1996	Tyrer, Burnley, 2004
N744LUS	Mercedes-Benz 811D	Wadham Stringer Wessex II	B33F	1996	City of Nottingham, 2004
P675RWU	Dennis Dart SLF 10m	Plaxton Pointer	N35F	1997	Armchair, Brentford, 2003
SF04RHX	Mercedes-Benz Vario 814	Mellor	BC33F	2004	

Depot: Scotts Road, Paisley

In 2004 Dickson's purchased two Volvo B6s with Alexander Dash bodywork that were formerly operated by Stagecoach in north west England, although one has already left the fleet. The survivor, L245CCK, is seen in its home town of Paisley. *Billy Nicol*

DOCHERTY'S MIDLAND COACHES

J & E Docherty, Priory Park, Crown Wynd, Auchterarder, PH3 1AE

JDS77J	Mercedes-Benz Vario 0814	Plaxton Beaver	BC33F	1993	
P77JDS	Volvo B10M-62	Van Hool Alizée HE	C53F	1997	
W7JDS	Volvo B10M-62	Van Hool T9 Alizée	C53F	2000	
W77JDS	Volvo B10M-62	Van Hool T9 Alizée	C49FT	2000	
N77JDS	Volvo B10M-62	Van Hool T9 Alizée	C49FT	2000	Brown, Edinburgh, 2004
X77JDS	Volvo B10M-62	Van Hool T9 Alizée	C49FT	2000	
Y77JDS	Volvo B12M	Van Hool T9 Alizée	C49FT	2002	
SK02VNX	Mercedes-Benz Sprinter 413	KVC	M16	2002	
SK52HYP	Scania L94UB	Wrightbus Solar	N43F	2002	
YR52VEX	Scania L94UB	Wrightbus Solar	N43F	2002	
YN03WYD	Mercedes-Benz Vario 0814	Plaxton Cheetah	C33F	2003	
YN04XZC	Optare Solo M850	Optare	N33F	2004	
SF04LKG	Volvo B12M	Van Hool T9 Alizée	C49FT	2004	
SN05FHM	Volvo B12M	Van Hool T9 Alizée	C49FT	2005	
SN05FHL	Mercedes-Benz Vario 0815	Sitcar Beluga	C29F	2005	
SP06DGE	Mercedes-Benz Vario 0815	Sitcar Beluga	C29F	2006	
SP06DFZ	Volvo B12M	Van Hool T9 Alizée	C49FT	2006	
SP06DGF	Scania K114IB4	Irizar Century	C49FT	2006	

Special event vehicle:

JA5515	Leyland TS7	Windover (1950)	C32F	1936	WHM, Little Waltham, 1999

Previous registrations:

4488WD	Y77JDS		
7067ED	M407XSL		
		JDS77J	C318HYP
		N77JDS	V64GSX

Web: www.dochertysmidlandcoaches.co.uk

Docherty's special event coach is JA5515, a Leyland TS7 with Windover bodywork dating from 1936. It is seen at a Lathalmond gathering, but is frequently found in use with wedding parties. A more modern Docherty's bus is on the rear cover. *Phillip Stephenson*

DODDS COACHES

Dodds of Troon Ltd, 4 East Road, Ayr, KA8 9BA

WFS147W	Leyland Leopard PSU3F/4R	Alexander AYS	BC53F	1980	Stagecoach Western Buses, 1999 -
XMS423Y	Leyland Leopard PSU3G/4R	Alexander AYS	B53F	1982	Stagecoach Western Buses, 1999
TJI5393	Volvo B10M-61	Plaxton Paramount 3200 II	C53F	1986	Shearings, 1993
TJI5394	Volvo B10M-61	Plaxton Paramount 3200 II	C53F	1986	Shearings, 1993
TJI5392	Volvo B10M-61	Van Hool Alizée	C53F	1988	Excelsior, Bournemouth, 1989
YXI7906	Volvo B10M-61	Van Hool Alizée	C53F	1989	Skills, Nottingham, 2001
D5DOT	Volvo B10M-62	Van Hool Alizée HE	C53F	1994	Reay, Fletchertown, 2000
D11DOT	Volvo B10M-62	Van Hool Alizée HE	C46FT	1995	Shearings, 2002
D20DOT	Volvo B10M-62	Van Hool Alizée HE	C46FT	1995	Shearings, 2002
M70TCC	Toyota Coaster HZB50R	Caetano Optimo III	C18F	1995	Stort Valley, Stansted, 1998
N830DKU	Scania K113TRB	Irizar Century 12.37	C49FT	1996	Capital, West Drayton, 2000
N7DOT	Dennis Javelin 10m	Plaxton Première 320	C43F	1996	Cavalier, Hounslow, 2001
YXD507	Volvo B10M-62	Jonckheere Mistral 50	C51FT	2001	Park's of Hamilton, 2004
YWE840	Volvo B10M-62	Jonckheere Mistral 50	C51FT	2001	Park's of Hamilton, 2004
T3DOT	Toyota Coaster BB50R	Caetano Optimo IV	C22F	2004	
V9DOT	Toyota Coaster BB50R	Caetano Optimo IV	C22F	2004	
AA05DOT	Volvo B12M	Jonckheere Mistral 50	C51FT	2005	
BB05DOT	Volvo B12M	Jonckheere Mistral 50	C51FT	2005	
-06	Volvo B12M	Jonckheere Mistral 50	C51FT	2006	
-06	Volvo B12M	Jonckheere Mistral 50	C51FT	2006	

Special event vehicles:

OKM317	AEC Regent III	Saunders-Roe	B30/26R	1951	
GSD779	Guy Arab IV	Roe	B37/28RD	1955	
SJW515	Guy Warrior WUF	Burlingham Seagull	C41F	1957	Stagecoach Bluebird Buses, 1999
BAO867T	AEC Reliance 6U3ZR	Plaxton Supreme IV Express	C53F	1979	Marshall, Troon, 1992

Previous registrations:

D5DOT	L645AYS, HSK650 , RIL1558	TJI5393	C519DND
D11DOT	M641KVU	TJI5394	C520DND
D20DOT	M642KVU	YWE840	LSK501, Y524UOS
N7DOT	P431JDT, A20HAV	YXD507	LSK502, Y177KCS
T3DOT	BX04BZV	YXI7906	P744ENE
TJI5392	E314OPR		

Web: www.doddsoftroon.com

Dodds of Troon has been providing coach and bus services since 1910. The company is still a family business and retains an impressive collection of vintage vehicles. A fleet of modern coaches is operated in a green and cream livery, an older one being Van Hool Alizée TJI5392.
Mark Doggett

DOIG'S of GLASGOW

Doig's Ltd, Transport House, 7 Summer Street, Glasgow, G40 3TB

Reg	Chassis	Body	Seating	Year
V664FPO	Dennis Dart SLF	Caetano Compass	N43F	2000
W724WAK	Mercedes-Benz Sprinter 413CDi	Excel	M16	2000
SF51RCY	Mercedes-Benz O1223L	Optare/Ferqui Solera	C35F	2001
SJ51LPA	Scania L94UA	Wrightbus Solar Fusion	ANC58D	2001
SG02ONA	Scania K114EB4	Irizar Century 12.35	C49FT	2002
SA02RMZ	Scania K124IB4	Irizar Century 12.35	C49FT	2002
SA02RNE	Scania K114IB4	Irizar Century 12.35	C49FT	2002
BL03NRE	LDV Convoy	Concept	M16	2003
SF03OMP	Scania K114IB4	Irizar Century 12.35	C40FT	2003
SF04LKY	MAN 18.310	Marcopolo Viaggio II 330	C55F	2004
YN05HFY	Scania OmniDekka N94UD	East Lancs	NC47/33F	2005
YN05HFZ	Scania K94IB4	Irizar S-Kool	BC70F	2005
SN05FCF	Mercedes-Benz Sprinter 413CDi	KVC	M16	2005
FJ05ANX	Volvo B12B	Sunsundegui Sideral 330	C49FT	2005
YN55PVX	Scania K124IB4	Irizar PB	C49FT	2005

Web: www.doigs.com

Among the many modern coaches, two interesting vehicles are operated. In 2001 Doig's purchased an articulated Scania L94UA with Wrightbus Solar Fusion bodywork, unusual in that it is fitted with high-back seating for the private hire and contract work undertaken by the company. YN05HFY is also a Scania, and the only semi-integral OmniDekka currently in Scotland. It, too, is fitted with high-back seating which is visible in this view taken in Renfrew Street, Glasgow. *Murdoch Currie*

DUNN'S COACHES

C & M Dunn, 35 South Street, Port Glasgow, PA14 5TA

JSV331	Volvo B10M-61	Van Hool Alizée	C49FT	1982	Gilchrist, East Kilbride, 1996
8212RU	Volvo B10M-61	Jonckheere Jubilee P599	C49FT	1983	Webber, Bodmin, 2002
K322BTM	Volvo B10M-61	Plaxton Première 320	C53F	1993	Stevenson, Mexborough, 2003
XAM826A	DAF MB3200	Jonckheere Jubilee P50	C49FT	1983	Lowe, Cuminestown, 2004
PIL3752	Mercedes-Benz 709D	Alexander AM	B25F	1988	McPherson, Port Glasgow, 2000
E564YBU	Mercedes-Benz 709D	Reeve Burgess Beaver	B25F	1988	Arriva Midlands North, 2000
E205YGC	Mercedes-Benz 709D	Reeve Burgess Beaver	BC25F	1988	Dickson Direct, Renfrew, 2001
PIL3750	Mercedes-Benz 811D	Alexander AM	BC33F	1988	Hughes, Gourock, 1999
E564YBU	Mercedes-Benz 709D	Reeve Burgess Beaver	B25F	1988	Arriva Midlands North, 2000
F281GNB	Mercedes-Benz 609D	Made-to-Measure	B24F	1988	Scottish Travel, Port Glasgow, 2001
F207DGT	Mercedes-Benz 709D	Reeve Burgess Beaver	BC25F	1988	Dickson Direct, Renfrew, 2001
F189PRE	Mercedes-Benz 709D	Reeve Burgess Beaver	B25F	1988	Arriva Midlands North, 2000
F69LNU	Mercedes-Benz 709D	Robin Hood	B29F	1989	Beeline, Warminster, 1998
G233FJC	Mercedes-Benz 709D	Robin Hood	B27F	1990	Clarke, Glasgow, 2003
GBZ7212	Mercedes-Benz 811D	Wright Wishaw	B29F	1991	Pride of the Clyde, 2005
J55BUS	Mercedes-Benz 709D	Plaxton Beaver	B30F	1992	Slaemuir, Port Glasgow, 2004
K893BEG	Mercedes-Benz 709D	Marshall C19	B27F	1992	Watermill, Fraserburgh, 2005
K226BJA	Mercedes-Benz 709D	Plaxton Beaver	B27F	1993	Slaemuir, Port Glasgow, 2004
L642DNA	Mercedes-Benz 709D	Plaxton Beaver	B27F	1993	Arriva Cymru, 2001
L638DNA	Mercedes-Benz 709D	Alexander Sprint	B25F	1994	Arriva Cymru, 2001
L715WCC	Mercedes-Benz 709D	Marshall C19	B27F	1994	Arriva Cymru, 2001
L716WCC	Mercedes-Benz 709D	Marshall C19	B27F	1994	Arriva Cymru, 2001

Previous registrations:

8212RU	MRP845Y, 9485RU	K322BTM	K322BTM, PSK320
E205YGC	E205YGC, GIB6135	PIL3750	F365TSX
JSV331	KGG727Y	PIL3752	E506YSU
K226BJA	BUSIN	XAM826A	OTC711Y, XAM826A

Depot: Ingleston Street, Greenock.

Whilst the majority of vehicles in Dunn's fleet are minibuses, the operation also includes coaches. Seen near Cumbernauld is E555UHS, a recently withdrawn Plaxton Paramount.
Mark Doggett

E & M HORSBURGH

E & M Horsburgh, 180 Uphall Station Road, Pumpherston, Livingston, EH53 0PD

GCS57V	Leyland Leopard PSU3E/4R	Alexander AY	B53F	1980	Stagecoach Western Buses, 1999
KSX105X	Leyland National 2 NL116AL11/2R		B42D	1982	Lothian Buses, 2004
KPJ281W	Leyland Atlantean AN68B/1R	Roe	B43/30F	1981	, 1999
A346ASF	Mercedes-Benz L508D	Mercedes-Benz	B16FL	1983	Braid House, Livingston, 1998
A725YFS	Leyland Olympian ONTL11/2R	Eastern Coach Works	B51/32D	1983	Lothian Buses, 2001
A726YFS	Leyland Olympian ONTL11/2R	Eastern Coach Works	B51/32D	1983	Lothian Buses, 2001
A734YFS	Leyland Olympian ONTL11/2R	Eastern Coach Works	B51/32D	1983	Lothian Buses, 2001
A736YFS	Leyland Olympian ONTL11/2R	Eastern Coach Works	B51/32D	1983	Lothian Buses, 2001
B141KSF	Leyland National 2 NL116TL11/2R		B42D	1985	Lothian Buses, 2004
B142KSF	Leyland National 2 NL116TL11/2R		B42D	1985	Lothian Buses, 2004
B143KSF	Leyland National 2 NL116TL11/2R		B42D	1985	Lothian Buses, 2004
B144KSF	Leyland National 2 NL116TL11/2R		B42D	1985	Lothian Buses, 2004
B145KSF	Leyland National 2 NL116TL11/2R		B42D	1985	Lothian Buses, 2004
B146KSF	Leyland National 2 NL116TL11/2R		B42D	1985	Lothian Buses, 2004
B147KSF	Leyland National 2 NL116TL11/2R		B42D	1985	Lothian Buses, 2004
C63PSG	Leyland Tiger TRCTL11/3RH	Duple Laser 2	C53F	1985	Lothian Buses, 2001
C64PSG	Leyland Tiger TRCTL11/3RH	Duple Laser 2	C53F	1985	Lothian Buses, 2001
C776SFS	Leyland Olympian ONTL11/2R	Eastern Coach Works	B51/32D	1985	Lothian Buses, 2004
C780SFS	Leyland Olympian ONTL11/2R	Eastern Coach Works	B51/32D	1985	Lothian Buses, 2004
C781SFS	Leyland Olympian ONTL11/2R	Eastern Coach Works	B51/32D	1985	Lothian Buses, 2004
C782SFS	Leyland Olympian ONTL11/2R	Eastern Coach Works	B51/32D	1985	Lothian Buses, 2004
C786SFS	Leyland Olympian ONTL11/2R	Eastern Coach Works	B51/32D	1985	Lothian Buses, 2004
E993YNS	Mercedes-Benz 609D	Scott	B16FL	1988	Scottish Spastics, 1996
J292NNB	Mercedes-Benz 709D	Carlyle C19	B29F	1991	Arriva Scotland, 2000
J293NNB	Mercedes-Benz 709D	Carlyle C19	B29F	1991	Arriva Scotland, 2000
K930HSO	Ford Transit VE6	Ford	M8L	1993	van conversion, 1999
L749JSX	Ford Transit VE6	Ford	M14L	1994	van conversion, 1999
M37FGG	Ford Transit VE6	Ford	M14L	1995	van conversion, 2001
M480FGG	Mercedes-Benz 609D	Devon Conversions	B18FL	1995	Glasgow City Council, 2001
M481FGG	Mercedes-Benz 609D	Devon Conversions	B18FL	1995	Glasgow City Council, 2001
M490FGG	Mercedes-Benz 410D	Aitken	M16L	1995	Glasgow City Council, 2001
M491FGG	Mercedes-Benz 410D	Aitken	M16L	1995	Glasgow City Council, 2001
M664UCT	Mercedes-Benz 711D	Autobus Classique	C24F	1995	
N602FWA	Ford Transit VE6	Ford	M14	1995	private owner, 2001
N120NYS	Mercedes-Benz 711D	Leicester Carriage	B24FL	1996	Glasgow City Council, 2001
N250MNS	Mercedes-Benz 609D	Stewart	B13FL	1995	private owner, 2003
N104WRC	Mercedes-Benz 711D	Plaxton Beaver	B30F	1995	City of Nottingham, 2002
N105WRC	Mercedes-Benz 711D	Plaxton Beaver	B30F	1995	City of Nottingham, 2002
N107WRC	Mercedes-Benz 711D	Plaxton Beaver	B30F	1995	City of Nottingham, 2002

The low-floor Optare Solo has been popular with many operators in Scotland. E&M Horsburgh currently operates eleven, including YN03NDY seen on route 274 in Linlithgow.
Mark Doggett

E & M Horsburgh operates nine Leyland Olympians that were previously with Lothian Buses. These have Eastern Coach Works dual-door bodies. Representing the type is A725YFS which is seen crossing Waverley Bridge in Edinburgh. *Billy Nicol*

P671MSC	Mercedes-Benz 611D	Heggie	B15L	1996	private owner, 2003
P613RGB	Mercedes-Benz 609D	Anderson	BC24F	1997	
R785GGU	Ford Transit VE6	Fisher	M14L	1997	van conversion, 2001
R584SKW	Ford Transit VE6	Fisher	M14L	1997	van conversion, 2001
R459VSD	Mercedes-Benz Vario 0614	Anderson	BC24F	1998	
S456LGN	Dennis Dart SLF 8.8m	Plaxton Pointer MPD	N29F	1998	Epsom Buses, 2004
S457LGN	Dennis Dart SLF 8.8m	Plaxton Pointer MPD	N29F	1998	Epsom Buses, 2004
S458LGN	Dennis Dart SLF 8.8m	Plaxton Pointer MPD	N29F	1998	Epsom Buses, 2004
S463LGN	Dennis Dart SLF 8.8m	Plaxton Pointer MPD	N29F	1998	Epsom Buses, 2004
T75JBA	Dennis Dart SLF 8.8m	Plaxton Pointer MPD	N29F	1999	Epsom Buses, 2004
W594PFS	Mercedes-Benz Vario 0814	Plaxton Beaver 2	BC31F	2000	
W595PFS	Mercedes-Benz Vario 0814	Plaxton Beaver 2	BC31F	2000	
W596PFS	Mercedes-Benz Vario 0814	Plaxton Beaver 2	BC31F	2000	
W597PFS	Mercedes-Benz Vario 0814	Plaxton Beaver 2	BC31F	2000	
W189WNS	LDV Convoy		M16L	2000	private owner, 2003
X415CSC	LDV Convoy	Aitken	M16L	2000	
X416CSC	LDV Convoy	Aitken	M16L	2000	
X417CSC	LDV Convoy	Aitken	M16L	2000	
YJ51XSH	Optare Solo M920	Optare	N31F	2001	
YJ51XSK	Optare Solo M920	Optare	N31F	2001	
YJ51XSL	Optare Solo M920	Optare	N31F	2001	
YJ51XSM	Optare Solo M920	Optare	N31F	2001	
YJ51XSN	Optare Solo M920	Optare	N31F	2001	
YJ51XSO	Optare Solo M920	Optare	N31F	2001	
SP02HMV	Ford Transit	Fisher	M14L	2002	
YN02TOV	Optare Solo M920	Optare	N31F	2002	
YN03NDY	Optare Solo M850	Optare	N29F	2003	
YN03NDZ	Optare Solo M850	Optare	N29F	2003	
MX55MCW	Optare Solo M850	Optare	N29F	2005	

Web: www.horsburghcoaches.com
Depot: Uphall Station Road, Pumpherston and Houston Ind Est, Livingston

EVE

Eve Coaches Ltd, Spott Road, Dunbar, EH42 1RR

ESU512	Volvo Citybus B10M-50	Northern Counties	B47/39F	1989	London General, 2001
GSU370	Volvo Citybus B10M-50	Northern Counties	B47/39F	1989	London General, 2001
K10EVE	Volvo B10M-60	Jonckheere Deauville P50	C53F	1993	Brown, Edinburgh, 1998
L98PTW	Toyota Coaster HZB50R	Caetano Optimo III	C21F	1994	Frank Harris, Grays, 1998
N1EVE	Toyota Coaster BB50R	Caetano Optimo IV	C21F	1995	Sunfun Holidays, Earith, 1999
P798KSF	Mercedes-Benz Vario 0814	Plaxton Beaver 2	BC33F	1996	Glen Coaches, Port Glasgow, 1998
P390OFS	Mercedes-Benz Vario 0814	Plaxton Beaver 2	BC33F	1996	Glen Coaches, Port Glasgow, 1998
S400EVE	Scania K124IB4	Van Hool T9 Alizée	C44FT	1998	Dunn-Line, Nottingham, 2005
S27DTS	Scania K124IB4	Van Hool T9 Alizée	C44FT	1998	Dunn-Line, Nottingham, 2005
T3EVE	Volvo B10M-62	Van Hool T9 Alizée	C49FT	1999	Park's of Hamilton, 2003
Y10EVE	Scania K124IB4	Van Hool T9 Alizée	C49FT	2001	Allan, Gorebridge, 2003
MX51VCT	Mercedes-Benz Sprinter 413cdi	Olympus	M16	2001	
YG52DFX	Optare Solo M920	Optare	N31F	2002	
OO05GXZ	Scania K94IB4	Irizar S-kool	BC70F	2005	Wheal Britain, 2006
OO05EVE	Scania K94IB4	Irizar S-kool	BC70F	2005	

Previous registrations:

ESU512	G107NGN	S400EVE	S26DTS
GSU370	G109NGN	T3EVE	12HM, KSK980, T609OGD
K10EVE	K918RGE	Y10EVE	B18DWA, Y604JSH
N1EVE	R903FYS		

EVE Cars and Coaches' G107NGN is one of a trio of Northern Counties-bodied Volvo Citybuses that were acquired from London General in 2001. The Citybus is a version of the B10M coach with underfloor engine strengthened to take a double-deck body. *Billy Nicol*

ESSBEE

Essbee Coaches Ltd, Highland & Islands Coaches Ltd
7 Hollandhurst Road, Coatbridge, ML5 2EG

10	HHA122L	Leyland National 1151/1R [Volvo]		B51F	1973	Arriva North East (T), 1998
9	NTC640M	Leyland National 1151/1R [Volvo]		B52F	1974	Arriva Teesside, 1998
20	MIL6676	Leyland National 11351/1R [DAF]		B50F	1974	Arriva North West, 1999
	MIL7620	Leyland National 11351/1R [DAF]		B50F	1974	Arriva North West, 1999
	MIL7622	Leyland National 11351/1R [DAF]		B50F	1974	Arriva North West, 1999
	UHG741R	Leyland National 11351A/1R [Volvo]		B49F	1976	McKindless, Wishaw, 2003
19	OOX801R	Leyland National 11351/1R [DAF]		B50F	1977	Arriva North West, 1999
7	TVP863S	Leyland National 11351A/1R [Volvo]		B50F	1978	Arriva Teesside, 1998
5	SKF5T	Leyland National 11351A/1R		B49F	1979	Merseyside, 1995
8	XOV748T	Leyland National 11351A/1R [Volvo]		B49F	1979	Arriva North East, 1998
	KKG109W	Leyland National 2 NL116AL11/1R		B52F	1981	Arriva Scotland West, 2000
	NIB6535	Volvo B10M-61	Jonckheere Jubilee	C51FT	1983	Landles, Calderbank, 1998
	PAZ6344	DAF MB230DKFL615	Duple 340	C53FT	1986	McNairn, Coatbridge, 1994
	NIB2796	Volvo B10M-61	Plaxton Paramount 3500 II	C53F	1986	Skills, Nottingham, 1997
	408UFC	Volvo B10M-61	Plaxton Paramount 3500 II	C49FT	1986	Rapsons, Inverness, 1997
	VIB3264	Volvo B10M-61	Duple 340	C49FT	1987	Express Travel, Speke, 1996
	NIL7707	Volvo B10M-61	Duple 340	C49FT	1988	Landles, Calderbank, 1998
	A8AAA	Volvo B10M-61	Duple 320	C53F	1988	Arriva East Herts & Essex, 1999
	XCS961	Volvo B10M-61	Duple 320	C57F	1989	Galloway, Harthill, 1996
	OJI9456	Mercedes-Benz 709D	PMT	BC25F	1990	van, 1993

Essbee still operates a number of Leyland Nationals on school contract work. New to Merseyside PTE, SKF5T is seen in Glasgow. *Billy Nicol*

The number of Duple-bodied coaches in operation continues to decline. Essbee currently uses three of the higher 340 model and a pair of the lower 320. One of the latter, A8AAA, is seen in Albion Street, Glasgow. The last Duple coaches were built at the end of 1989 after which work transferred to Plaxton's. *Murdoch Currie*

	T796BGD	Mercedes-Benz Vario 0814	Crystals	C29F	1999	
	W585PFS	Mercedes-Benz Vario 0814	Plaxton Cheetah	C33F	2000	Wilsons of Rhu, 2003
	X441JHS	Mercedes-Benz Vario 0814	Plaxton Cheetah	C30F	2001	Hilton, Newton-le-Willows, 2004
	X442JHS	Mercedes-Benz Vario 0814	Plaxton Cheetah	C33F	2001	Armstrong, Inverkeithing, 2002
11	SA02BOU	Mercedes-Benz Vario 0814	Essbee	BC24F	2002	
18	SF04LKV	Mercedes-Benz Vario 0814	Essbee	BC24F	2004	
19	SF04YEK	Mercedes-Benz 1223L	Essbee	BC24F	2004	
20	SF04ZPV	Mercedes-Benz 1223L	Essbee	BC24F	2004	
	SF04LKX	Mercedes-Benz Sprinter 413cdi	Essbee	M16	2004	
	SF05KWR	Mercedes-Benz Sprinter 413cdi	Essbee	M16	2005	
22	SF05HNM	Mercedes-Benz Vario 0814	Essbee	BC24F	2005	
21	SF05KWE	Mercedes-Benz Vario 0814	Essbee	BC24F	2005	
	SF55HGO	Mercedes-Benz Sprinter 413cdi	Essbee	M16	2005	

Previous registrations:

408UFC	C115DWR, ESK934	NIL7707	E980LRN
A8AAA	E892KYW, 185CLT, E949JJN	OJI9456	F834SGM
MIL6676	TOE490N	PAZ6344	C775MVH, ESK934, C379MDS
MIL7620	TOE512N	VIB3264	D614FSL, D448FSP, NXI9007, D753CFV
MIL7622	ROK469M	XCS961	F480WFX, VIB3264
NIB2796	C106DWR		
NIB6535	A230RNS		

Depots: Drumgellough Street, Airdrie; Elgin Place, Coatbridge; Hollandshurst Road, Coatbridge; Lochburie Lane, Glenmavis; Range Street. Motherwell and Livingston Drive, Plains.

FAIRLINE

Fairline Coaches Ltd, 331 Charles Street, Glasgow, G21 2QA

Reg	Chassis	Body	Seating	Year	Notes
TSJ61S	Volvo B10M-62	Jonckheere Deauville 45	C49FT	1994	Edinburgh Castle Coaches, 2001
EGB60T	Volvo B10M-62	Jonckheere Deauville 45	C49FT	1996	Allander, Milngavie, 2001
OOB32X	Volvo B10M-62	Jonckheere Deauville 45	C49FT	1996	Barratt's, Nantwich, 2002
OBX51	Bova Futura FHD12.340	Bova	C49FT	1998	Meney, Saltcoats, 2002
GSO84V	Bova Futura FHD12.340	Bova	C49FT	1999	Long's, Salsburgh, 2004
EPK1V	Bova Futura FHD12.370	Bova	C51FT	2000	Bailey, Biddisham, 2004
S445OGB	Ford Transit	Ford	M14	1998	Currie, Carluke, 2001
R823RDS	Mercedes-Benz Vario 0614	Crest	BC24F	1998	Haggis Back Packers, Edinburgh, '01
W592PFS	Mercedes-Benz Vario 0614	Onyx	BC24F	2000	Going Forth, Edinburgh, 2001
X233USC	Mercedes-Benz Vario 0614	Onyx	BC24F	2000	
X274SRM	Mercedes-Benz Vario 0814	Autobus Nouvelle 2	C33F	2000	Stainton, Kendal, 2004
SA52OCX	Bova Futura FHD12.340	Bova	C49FT	2002	
SN03NLJ	Mercedes-Benz Vario 0814	Onyx	BC24F	2003	
SN03NLK	Mercedes-Benz Vario 0814	TransBus Cheetah	C33F	2003	
SN03NLL	Mercedes-Benz Vario 0814	TransBus Beaver 2	B27F	2003	
RX03HNN	Volkswagen Transporter	Volkswagen	C33F	2003	
SF05BEJ	Mercedes-Benz Sprinter 611D	Mercedes-Benz	M14	2005	Keenan, Coalhall, 2005
YJ55BJZ	Optare Solo M850	Optare	N27F	2006	
YN06CYV	Mercedes-Benz Vario 0814	Plaxton Cheetah	C33F	2006	
YJ06FZE	Optare Solo M850	Optare	N27F	2006	
YJ06FZF	Optare Solo M850	Optare	N27F	2006	

Previous registrations:

EGB60T	N813AHS, 4143AT, N813AHS	TSJ61S	L749YGE
OBX51	R300RMS	XIW1184	M303KRY
OOB32X	N815NHS, N7BCL		

Web: www.fairlinecoaches.co.uk

Airport Express is the name used by Fairline Mini Coaches for its service linking Glasgow airport with the city centre. Pictured in a livery of maroon on a silver base is newly delivered YJ55BJZ. This bus features additional luggage accommodation. *Murdoch Currie*

FIRST STOP

First Stop Travel (LLC) Ltd, Clyde Street, Renfrew, PA4 8SL

G901UPP	Mercedes-Benz 709D	Reeve Burgess Beaver	B23F	1989	Sovereign, 1999
G909UPP	Mercedes-Benz 709D	Reeve Burgess Beaver	B23F	1989	Grayson, Widnes, 2000
H201TWE	Mercedes-Benz 811D	Reeve Burgess Beaver	B33F	1990	RoadCar, Lincoln, 2005
H213TWE	Mercedes-Benz 811D	Reeve Burgess Beaver	B31F	1990	RoadCar, Lincoln, 2005
J392AWB	Mercedes-Benz 811D	Reeve Burgess Beaver	B33F	1990	RoadCar, Lincoln, 2005
K229SFJ	Mercedes-Benz 709D	Plaxton Beaver	B25F	1992	Plymouth Citybus, 2000
K236SFJ	Mercedes-Benz 709D	Plaxton Beaver	B25F	1992	Plymouth Citybus, 2000
K238SFJ	Mercedes-Benz 709D	Plaxton Beaver	B25F	1992	Plymouth Citybus, 2000
K392SLB	Mercedes-Benz 709D	Plaxton Beaver	B25F	1993	Sovereign, 1999
K393SLB	Mercedes-Benz 709D	Plaxton Beaver	B25F	1993	Sovereign, 1999
L248YOD	Mercedes-Benz 709D	Plaxton Beaver	B25F	1993	Citybus, Plymouth, 2003
L260YOD	Mercedes-Benz 709D	Plaxton Beaver	B25F	1993	Citybus, Plymouth, 2003
L735PUA	Optare MetroRider MR31	Optare	B25F	1994	McGill's, Barrhead, 2005

One of the many Mercedes-Benz 709Ds with Plaxton Beaver bodywork operated by First Stop Travel is K235SFJ pictured on service in Paisley. *Phillip Stephenson*

Recent changes to the First Stop Travel fleet have seen a large reduction in the fleet strength. During 2003 several Dennis Darts were acquired from McKinless of Wishaw and these have all now been withdrawn. All bar three were the 8.5-metre Dartlines built by Carlyle delivered new to London Buses. H134MOB is seen here in the fleet livery. *Mark Doggett*

L947HTM	Mercedes-Benz 709D	Plaxton Beaver	B31F	1994	Gibson Direct, Renfrew, 2002
L948HTM	Mercedes-Benz 709D	Plaxton Beaver	B31F	1994	Gibson Direct, Renfrew, 2002
L299BGA	Mercedes-Benz 709D	Eurocoach	B23F	1994	Avondale Coaches, Greenock, 2001
M753WWR	Optare MetroRider MR31	Optare	B25F	1995	A&P, Erskine, 2005
T966JAO	Mercedes-Benz 614D	Excel	B21F	1999	
T967JAO	Mercedes-Benz 614D	Excel	B21F	1999	

Previous registration:
L299BGA   94D2012

GALSON MOTORS

Galson - Stornoway Motor Services Ltd, 1 Lower Barvas, Isle of Lewis, HS2 0QZ

GS41	B294KPF	Leyland Tiger TRCTL11/3RH	Plaxton Paramount 3200 II E	C51F	1985	Andy James, Tetbury, 1996
GS42	M599GMR	Mercedes-Benz 811D	Autobus Classique II	B31F	1995	Andy James, Tetbury, 1996
GS51	TJI3142	Volvo B10M-60	Plaxton Paramount 3500 III	C50F	1989	Galloway, Harthill, 1999
GS52	JIL3713	Volvo B10M-61	Plaxton Paramount 3200 III	C53F	1988	Amport & District, 1999
GS53	F252DLS	Volvo B10M-61	Plaxton Paramount 3200 III	C57F	1988	Kirkpatrick, Aberdeen, 1999
GS54	W235AGA	Ford Transit	Ford	M16L	2000	
GS55	TIL7490	Volvo B10M-60	Plaxton Paramount 3200 III	C53F	1990	McColl, Balloch, 2002
GS56	JSV486	Volvo B10M-60	Plaxton Paramount 3200 III	C53F	1989	Wallace Arnold, 2002
GS57	SK02NYU	Mercedes-Benz Vario 0814	Plaxton Beaver 2	BC33F	2002	
GS59	SF53NZU	LDV Convoy	LDV	M16	2003	
GS60	L345ERU	Volvo B10M-62	Plaxton Première 320	C49FT	1993	Slaemuir, Port Glasgow, 2003
GS61	N224THO	Volvo B10M-60	Plaxton Première 320	C49FT	1995	Blackburn Buses, 2003
GS	K17CJT	Volvo B10M-60	Plaxton Première 320	C57F	1992	MacKay, Tarbert, 2004
GS	K300SOU	Volvo B10M-60	Plaxton Première 320	C57F	1992	MacKay, Tarbert, 2004
GS	M658ROS	Volvo B10M-62	Van Hool Alizée HE	C55F	1995	Hutchinson, Overtown, 2004
GS	PCZ2674	Ford Transit	Ford	M15	2003	
GS	T383GTH	Ford Transit	Ford	M16	1999	Day's, Shantea, 2004

Previous registrations:

F252DLS	F103HSO, LSK572	M599GMR	M33ARJ
K17CJT	K301MFB, 3138DP	M658ROS	PSV223
JIL3713	E314OMG	N224THO	A13EXC, YJV316
JSV486	G837VAY	TIL7490	H69CFJ, MUD490
L345ERU	213ONU, XEL31	TJI3142	F430DUG

Plaxton-bodied Volvo coaches form the backbone of Galson's operations on the Isle of Lewis. Seen heading for Ness is GS60, L345ERU, a Première 320. *Richard Walter*

GARELOCHHEAD COACHES

Garelochhead Minibuses & Coaches Ltd, Woodlea Garage, Main Road, Garelochhead, G84 0EG

WSF989Y	Volvo B10M-61	Van Hool Alizée	C53F	1983	Ayrways, Ayr, 2004
L742NHE	Ford Transit VE6	AVB	M14	1994	
M634FJF	Mercedes-Benz 811D	Marshall	B31F	1995	Stagecoach Manchester, 2003
N200BUS	Volvo B10M-62	Van Hool Alizée HE	C53F	1996	Park's of Hamilton, 1999
P227YGG	Volvo B10M-62	Van Hool Alizée HE	C53F	1997	Flights, Birmingham, 2001
X443JHS	Mercedes-Benz Vario 0814	Plaxton Beaver 2	BC33F	2000	
PK02WVV	Ford Transit	Jaycas	M14	2002	
SC02HLD	Mercedes-Benz Vario 0814	Plaxton Cheetah	C33F	2002	
SA02LHC	Volvo B12M	Van Hool T9 Alizée	C51F	2002	
VX54CKL	Mercedes-Benz Vario 0814	Plaxton Cheetah	C33F	2004	Stonehouse Coaches, 2005
MX05ENC	Optare Solo M850	Optare	N28F	2005	
MX55BYH	Optare Solo M850	Optare	N28F	2005	
GN55XTD	Ford Transit	Ford	M16	2006	

Previous registrations:

N200BUS	KSK986, N416PYS		P227YGG	KSK950, LSK497

Seen in Garelochhead Coach's current grey and red livery is Plaxton-bodied Mercedes-Benz 814D. *Billy Nicol*

GIBSON

Gibson Direct Ltd, 16 Braehead Works, Old Govan Way, Renfrew, PA4 8XN

P694RWU	Dennis Dart SLF	Plaxton Pointer	N35F	1997	Davidson, Bathgate, 2004
S374PGB	Mercedes-Benz Vario 0814	Marshall Master	B31F	1998	Scotways, Glasgow, 2002
S581PGB	Dennis Dart SLF 8.8m	Plaxton Pointer MPD	N29F	1998	Canovan, Kilsyth, 2006
V100CBC	Dennis Dart SLF 10.7m	Plaxton Pointer 2	N37F	1999	Coakley Bus, Motherwell, 2001
V400CBC	Dennis Dart SLF 10.7m	Plaxton Pointer 2	N37F	1999	Coakley Bus, Motherwell, 2001
V700CBC	Dennis Dart SLF 10.7m	Plaxton Pointer 2	N37F	1999	Coakley Bus, Motherwell, 2001
W386WGE	Dennis Dart SLF 10.7m	Plaxton Pointer 2	N39F	2000	McHugh, Old Swan, 2001
Y214BGB	Dennis Dart SLF 10.7m	Plaxton Pointer 2	N37F	2000	
Y216BGB	Dennis Dart SLF 10.7m	Plaxton Pointer 2	NC33F	2000	
Y483TSU	Dennis Dart SLF	SCC Compass	N44F	2000	Johnston, Motherwell, 2002
Y484TSU	Dennis Dart SLF	SCC Compass	N44F	2000	Johnston, Motherwell, 2002
Y485TSU	Dennis Dart SLF	SCC Compass	N44F	2000	Johnston, Motherwell, 2002
SJ51GCV	Mercedes-Benz Vario 0814	Plaxton Beaver 2	B25F	2001	
SF03SCZ	Mercedes-Benz Vario 0814	Mellor	BC33F	2003	
SF04ZXC	TransBus Dart 8.8m	TransBus Mini Pointer	N29F	2004	
SF54HWG	Optare Solo M850	Optare	N20F	2005	
SF54HWH	Optare Solo M850	Optare	N20F	2005	
SF54ORA	Optare Solo M850	Optare	N20F	2005	
SF54ORC	Optare Solo M850	Optare	N20F	2005	
SF54ORJ	Optare Solo M850	Optare	N20F	2005	
SF54ORK	Optare Solo M850	Optare	N20F	2005	
SF54ORL	Optare Solo M850	Optare	N20F	2005	
SF54ORM	Optare Solo M850	Optare	N20F	2005	
SF54ORN	Optare Solo M850	Optare	N20F	2005	
SF54ORP	Optare Solo M850	Optare	N20F	2005	
SF05FMV	Mercedes-Benz Vario 0814	Plaxton Beaver 2	BC33F	2005	
YJ55BGY	Optare Solo M1020	Optare	N37F	2006	
YJ55BGZ	Optare Solo M1020	Optare	N37F	2006	
YJ55BHA	Optare Solo M1020	Optare	N37F	2006	
YJ55BHD	Optare Solo M1020	Optare	N37F	2006	
YJ55BHE	Optare Solo M1020	Optare	N37F	2006	
YJ55BHK	Optare Solo M1020	Optare	N37F	2006	

Apart from the four Mercedes-Benz Vario buses, the whole of the Gibson fleet is now low-floor, dominated by the Optare Solo and the Dart. One of the latter that was built by Dennis is S200CBC, pictured in Paisley.
Phillip Stephenson

GIBSON of MOFFAT

J & M Gibson, 16 Church Street, Moffat, DG10 9HD

	HIL7590	Volvo B10M-61	Van Hool Alizée HE	C53F	1982
	HIL7589	Volvo B10M-61	Duple	C51F	1984	Tedd, Thruxton, 1984, 1988
	OAZ9372	Volvo B10M-60	Van Hool Alizée	C50F	1993	McGeehan, Fintown, 1997
	WDZ4724	Volvo B10M-60	Van Hool Alizée	C50F	1993	Wallace Arnold, 1997
w	OIL2939	Volvo B10M-62	Van Hool Alizée HE	C53F	1995	Robertson, Cuminestone, 2006
	P301VWR	Volvo B10M-62	Van Hool Alizée HE	C46FT	1997	Wallace Arnold, 2002
	R50TPB	Bova Futura FHD12.340	Bova	C49FT	1998	Patterson, Kilbirnie, 2003
	R60TPB	Bova Futura FHD12.340	Bova	C49FT	1998	Patterson, Kilbirnie, 2003
	W749GSE	Volvo B10MT	Van Hool T9 Alizée	C48FT	2000	Whytes, Newmachar, 2005
	W365OSM	Bova Futura FHD12.370	Bova	C49FT	2000
	SA02VKH	Bova Futura FHD12.340	Bova	C49FT	2002

Previous registrations:

HIL7589	A228LFX		OIL2939	M804HGB
HIL7590	CSM915X		WDZ9724	K872HUM
OAZ9372	K823HUM			

Depots: St Ann's, Lockerbie and Eastherd, Moffat

Gibson of Moffat operates a coach fleet comprising Bova and Volvo products. Typical of the fleet is Van Hool Alizée-bodied OIL2939 which is seen on one of the regular excursions to Blackpool. *Bob Downham*

GOLDEN EAGLE

Golden Eagle Coaches Ltd, Muirhall Garage, 197 Main Street, Salsburgh, Shotts, ML7 4LS

GOG208W	MCW Metrobus DR101	MCW	B43/34F	1981	Metroline, London, 2005
A246SVW	Leyland Tiger TRCTL11/3RP	Duple Caribbean	C57F	1984	Arriva Southend, 2000
C318BUV	MCW Metrobus DR102	MCW	B47/28D	1985	Arriva London, 2004
C402BUV	MCW Metrobus DR102	MCW	B47/28D	1985	Arriva London, 2004
JIL8561	Volvo B10M-61	Van Hool Alizée	C53F	1986	
JIL8562	Volvo B10M-61	Van Hool Alizée	C53FT	1988	
JIL8559	Volvo B10M-60	Van Hool Alizée	C53FT	1989	Eales, Ecclesfield, 2001
F171JKH	Volvo B10M-61	Plaxton Paramount 3500 III	C53F	1989	East Yorkshire, 2005
JIL8553	Volvo B10M-60	Van Hool Alizée	C49FT	1990	Whytes, Newmachar, 1995
JIL8560	Volvo B10M-60	Van Hool Alizée	C53F	1992	
YIL6691	Dennis Javelin 12m	Wadham Stringer Vanguard II	BC70F	1993	MoD, 2005
YIL1206	Volvo B10M-62	Van Hool Alizée HE	C53F	1996	
YIL1207	Volvo B10M-62	Van Hool Alizée HE	C55F	1997	MacPhail, Newarthill, 2000
YIL1208	Bova Futura FHD12.370	Bova	C49FT	2000	Maynes of Buckie, 2002
Y998TGG	Volvo B10M-62	Jonckheere Mistral 50	C53F	2001	
SG03ZER	Volvo B12M	Jonckheere Mistral 50	C53F	2003	Park's of Hamilton, 2006

Previous registrations:

F171JKH	F300JNC, HIL7746, A9EYC	SG03ZER	2WR
JIL8553	G804OSS, HSK176, G341VSE	Y798TGG	J15JEC
JIL8559	D65CUT, LIL2186, 25PMX, D101TMF	YIL1206	N985ODS
JIL8560	J39HSU	YIL1207	P763VDS
JIL8561	D864PGB	YIL1208	W444GSM
JIL8562	E129BSU	YIL6691	75KK24

Web: www.goldeneaglecoaches.com

Operating on a David Urquhart Travel tour is Golden Eagle's JIL8560, seen here at Salsburgh. *Bob Downham*

GULLIVERS TRAVEL

Gullivers Travel Ltd, Janefield West, Main Road, Longbank, Paisley, PA14 6XP

K725UTT	Iveco TurboDaily 59.12	Mellor Duet	B29F	1993	Stagecoach Devon, 2003
K816WFJ	Iveco TurboDaily 59.12	Mellor Duet	B29F	1993	Stagecoach Devon, 2003
K173CAV	Iveco TurboDaily 59.12	Marshall C31	B25F	1993	Stagecoach Devon, 2003
M628HDV	Iveco TurboDaily 59.12	WS Wessex II	B21D	1994	Stagecoach, 2004
M636HDV	Iveco TurboDaily 59.12	WS Wessex II	B21D	1994	Stagecoach, 2004
M637HDV	Iveco TurboDaily 59.12	WS Wessex II	B21D	1994	Stagecoach, 2004
M640HDV	Iveco TurboDaily 59.12	WS Wessex II	B21D	1994	Stagecoach, 2004
M191HTT	Iveco TurboDaily 59.12	WS Wessex II	B21D	1994	Stagecoach, 2004
M193HTT	Iveco TurboDaily 59.12	WS Wessex II	B21D	1994	Stagecoach, 2004
N182CMJ	Iveco TurboDaily 59.12	Alexander Sprint	B29F	1996	Stagecoach, 2005
N183CMJ	Iveco TurboDaily 59.12	Alexander Sprint	B29F	1996	Stagecoach, 2005

HARRIS COACHES

N & M Mackay, Scott Road, Tarbert, Isle of Harris, HS3 3DL

H38	W15HCT	Mercedes-Benz Vario 0814	Plaxton Cheetah	C33F	2000	
H39	M534NCG	Volvo B10M-62	Plaxton Première 320	C53F	1994	Shaw of Maxey, 2001
H40	V58KWO	Volvo B10M-62	Plaxton Première 320	C53F	2000	Bebb, Llantwit Fardre, 2000
H41	M893WLG	Mercedes-Benz Sprinter 308		M16L	1997	Mainwaring, 2000

Gullivers Travel's M193HTT is seen in Paisley while operating route 1 to Barrhead. The fleet comprises entirely the Iveco TurboDaily 59.12 model. All formerly operated for Stagecoach and originated with the acquisition of the Transit Group. In this view the letters LBC, for Local Bus Company, are displayed. *Bob Downham*

HEBRIDEAN COACHES

D & A MacDonald, 2 Howmore, Isle of Uist, HS8 5SH

N406SPC	Dennis Javelin 12m	Plaxton Première 320	C53F	1994	Epsom Coaches, 2004
N407SPC	Dennis Javelin 12m	Plaxton Première 320	C53F	1994	Epsom Coaches, 2004
N409SPC	Dennis Javelin 12m	Plaxton Première 320	C49FT	1994	Epsom Coaches, 2004
N479VPA	Dennis Javelin 12m	Plaxton Première 320	C46FT	1994	Epsom Coaches, 2004
P707DPA	Dennis Javelin 12m	Plaxton Première 320	C57F	1995	Epsom Coaches, 2004
V828GGA	Mercedes-Benz Vario O814	Plaxton Beaver 2	B33F	1999	Myles, Plean, 2003
SV52AXV	Mercedes-Benz Vario O814	Essbee	BC24F	2002	Essbee, Coatbridge, 2004
V958HEB	Mercedes-Benz Sprinter 412	Mercedes-Benz	M16	1999	
MX54VWJ	Mercedes-Benz Sprinter 413	Mercedes-Benz	M16	2004	

Depot: Parkend Ind Est, Sandwick.

Retaining the colours of Epsom Coaches, its previous owners, N479VPA, is now to be found with Hebridean Coaches, and is pictured on Stornoway service W10. *Richard Walter*

The Scottish Bus Handbook

HENDERSON TRAVEL

Henderson Travel - Value Bus

JC & DC Henderson, 4 Whistleberry Industrial Park, Hamilton, ML3 0ED

E766MSC	Mercedes-Benz 609D	Alexander AM	B25F	1988	
L483BGA	Mercedes-Benz 709D	Alexander Sprint	B23F	1993	Avondale Cs, Greenock, 2002
L91NSF	Mercedes-Benz 709D	Alexander Sprint	B25F	1994	
M609WFS	Mercedes-Benz 709D	Alexander Sprint	B29F	1995	Bell, South Hylton, 2001
M366KVR	Mercedes-Benz 709D	Alexander Sprint	B27F	1995	Colchri, Barrhead, 2004
M367KVR	Mercedes-Benz 709D	Alexander Sprint	B27F	1995	Colchri, Barrhead, 2004
P683HND	Mercedes-Benz 709D	Alexander Sprint	B27F	1996	Cross Gates Coaches, 2001
P414MFS	Mercedes-Benz 711D	Alexander Sprint	B29F	1996	
P454MFS	Mercedes-Benz 711D	Alexander Sprint	B29F	1997	
P455MFS	Mercedes-Benz 711D	Alexander Sprint	B29F	1997	
P240OSF	Mercedes-Benz 711D	Alexander Sprint	B29F	1997	
S905DUB	Mercedes-Benz 0405	Optare Sigma	B49F	1998	Black Prince, Morley, 2005
T92JBA	Mercedes-Benz Vario 0814	Plaxton Beaver 2	B31F	1999	

Henderson Travel operates a network of minibus services from its base in Hamilton. Illustrating the blue and white colour scheme is Mercedes-Benz 711 P414MFS. Bodywork is the Alexander Sprint. *Mark Doggett*

Henderson has been progressively replacing its Mercedes-Benz minibuses with Optare Solo buses, mostly of the standard 8.5-metre version. Pictured in Hamilton is MX03YDB, one of the longer 9.2-metre examples.
Bob Downham

W425CWX	Optare MetroRider MR17	Optare	B29F	2000
W426CWX	Optare MetroRider MR17	Optare	B29F	2000
YN03ZXE	Optare Solo M850	Optare	N29F	2003
MX03YCM	Optare Solo M850	Optare	N29F	2003
MX03YCV	Optare Solo M850	Optare	N29F	2003
MX03YCW	Optare Solo M850	Optare	N29F	2003
MX03YDB	Optare Solo M920	Optare	N29F	2003
MV04GXF	Optare Solo M920	Optare	N33F	2004
YN04LWZ	Optare Solo M920	Optare	N33F	2004
YN04LXE	Optare Solo M850	Optare	N29F	2004
YN04LXS	Optare Solo M920	Optare	N33F	2004
SF04LHU	Optare Solo M850	Optare	N29F	2004
MX54KXZ	Optare Solo M880	Optare	N28F	2005
YJ54UXB	Optare Solo M880	Optare	N20FL	2005
YJ54UXC	Optare Solo M880	Optare	N20FL	2005
YJ54UXD	Optare Solo M880	Optare	N20FL	2005
YJ54UXE	Optare Solo M880	Optare	N20F	2005
YJ54UWN	Optare Solo M920	Optare	N33F	2005
YJ54UWO	Optare Solo M920	Optare	N33F	2005
YJ05XOS	Optare Solo M850	Optare	N29F	2005
YJ05XOT	Optare Solo M850	Optare	N29F	2005
YJ05XOU	Optare Solo M850	Optare	N29F	2005
YN55YHC	Optare Solo M880	Optare	N29F	2006
Y-06	Optare Solo M880	Optare	N29F	2006
Y-06	Optare Tempo X1060	Optare	N--F	2006

Previous registrations:

L483BGA	93D8010		
		P683HND	P682HND

HIGHLAND HERITAGE

Highland Heritage Ltd, Dalmally Hotel, Dalmally, PA33 1AY

11	SN05DVW	Volvo B12T	Van Hool T9 Alizée	C59F	2005
12	SN05DVX	Volvo B12T	Van Hool T9 Alizée	C59F	2005
13	SN05DVY	Volvo B12T	Van Hool T9 Alizée	C59F	2005
14	SN05DVZ	Volvo B12T	Van Hool T9 Alizée	C59F	2005
15	SN05DWA	Volvo B12T	Van Hool T9 Alizée	C59F	2005
16	SN05DWC	Volvo B12T	Van Hool T9 Alizée	C59F	2005
17	SN05DWD	Volvo B12T	Van Hool T9 Alizée	C59F	2005
18	SN05DWE	Volvo B12T	Van Hool T9 Alizée	C59F	2005
19	SN05DWF	Volvo B12T	Van Hool T9 Alizée	C59F	2005
20	SN05DWG	Volvo B12T	Van Hool T9 Alizée	C59F	2005
21	SN05DWJ	Volvo B12T	Van Hool T9 Alizée	C59F	2005
22	SN05DWK	Volvo B12T	Van Hool T9 Alizée	C59F	2005
23	SN05DWL	Volvo B12T	Van Hool T9 Alizée	C59F	2005
24	SN54LRL	Volvo B12T	Van Hool T9 Alizée	C59F	2005
25	SN54LRO	Volvo B12T	Van Hool T9 Alizée	C59F	2005
26	SN06ACO	Volvo B12T	Van Hool T9 Alizée	C59F	2006
27	SN06ACU	Volvo B12T	Van Hool T9 Alizée	C59F	2006

Named vehicles: 11 Clan Campbell; 12 Clan Cameron; 13 Clan MacGregor; 14 Clan MacDonald; 15 Clan MacDougall, 16 Clan Stewart;17 Clan MacIntyre; 18 Clan MacNab; 19 Clan MacBean; 20 Clan MacLaven; 21 Clan McFarlane; 22 Clan Murray; 23 Clan Lamont; 24 Clan Bruce; 25 Clan Graham; 26 Clan MacQuarrie and 27 Clan MacMillan.

2005 saw a major investment by Highland Heritage, when the whole fleet was replaced with Van Hool-bodied Volvo B12Ts, the tri-axle rear-engined coach chassis from Volvo. Illustrating the new livery is 18, SN05DWE, which is seen while on tour in Dunoon. *Murdoch Currie*

HUTCHISON

Hutchison - Scottish Pullman

Hutchison's Coaches (Overtown) Ltd, 5 Castlehill Road, Overtown, ML2 0QS

J17BUS	Volvo B10M-55	Duple 300	B53F	1992	
L684UYS	Volvo B10B	Northern Counties Paladin	B51F	1993	
M679CSU	MAN 11.190	Optare Vecta	B42F	1994	
M868FSU	MAN 11.190	Optare Vecta	B42F	1995	
N608OGE	MAN 11.190	Optare Vecta	B42F	1996	
P995RHS	MAN 11.190	Optare Vecta	B42F	1996	
KSK930	Volvo B10M-62	Van Hool Alizée HE	C48DT	1996	
KSK933	Volvo B10M-62	Van Hool Alizée HE	C53F	1996	
KSK934	Volvo B10M-62	Van Hool Alizée HE	C53F	1996	
P502VUS	Volvo B10M-62	Van Hool Alizée HE	C51F	1996	
P507VUS	Volvo B10M-62	Plaxton Première 320	C57F	1997	
P508VUS	Volvo B10M-62	Plaxton Première 320	C57F	1997	
HCO514	Optare Excel L1070	Optare	N40F	1997	
R27VSM	DAF SB3000	Van Hool Alizée HE	C51FT	1998	MacEwan, Amisfield Town, 2000
R28VSM	DAF SB3000	Van Hool Alizée HE	C51FT	1998	MacEwan, Amisfield Town, 2000
R91HUS	Volvo B10M-62	Plaxton Première 320	C53F	1998	
R92HUS	Volvo B10M-62	Plaxton Première 320	C53F	1998	
R93HUS	Optare Excel L1070	Optare	N39F	1998	
R94HUS	Optare Excel L1070	Optare	N39F	1998	
R95HUS	Optare Excel L1070	Optare	N39F	1998	
S556OGB	Optare Excel L1070	Optare	N39F	1999	
T732JGB	Volvo B10M-62	Berkhof Axial 50	C51FT	1999	
PSV223	Volvo B10MT	Van Hool T9 Alizée	C49FT	1999	
XUF456	Volvo B10MT	Van Hool T9 Alizée	C49FT	1999	

Hutchinson currently operates four Volvo B10BLEs, two with Wrightbus Renown bodywork and two with Alexander ALX300 bodies. Illustrating one of the Renowns is Y182BGB. In 2001 the Wright coachbuilder made internal changes within the firm resulting in the coachbuilder being re-branded Wrightbus. *Billy Nicol*

While Volvo buses have been the norm for Hutchinson, 2002-03 saw the arrival of four Scania L94s with Wrightbus Solar bodywork. Pictured in Wishaw is the first to arrive, SK02ZYG, which illustrates the Solar bodywork. Interestingly, Hutchinson returned to Volvo for the 2004 delivery. *Billy Nicol*

T735JGB	Optare Excel L1070	Optare	N39F	1999
T736JGB	Optare Excel L1070	Optare	N39F	1999
W49WDS	Optare Excel L1070	Optare	N39F	2000
W52WDS	Optare Excel L1070	Optare	N39F	2000
X303JGE	Volvo B10BLE	Alexander ALX300	N44F	2000
X304JGE	Volvo B10BLE	Alexander ALX300	N44F	2000
Y181BGB	Volvo B10BLE	Wrightbus Renown	N44F	2001
Y182BGB	Volvo B10BLE	Wrightbus Renown	N44F	2001
SK02ZYG	Scania L94UB	Wrightbus Solar	N43F	2002
SK02ZYH	Scania L94UB	Wrightbus Solar	N43F	2002
SK02ZYJ	Scania K114IB4	Irizar Century 12.35	C49FT	2002
SK02ZYL	Scania K114IB4	Irizar Century 12.35	C49FT	2002
SN03CLZ	Scania K114IB4	Irizar Century 12.35	C49FT	2003
SN03CME	Scania K114IB4	Irizar Century 12.35	C49FT	2003
SN03CLX	Scania L94UB	Wrightbus Solar	N43F	2003
SN03CLY	Scania L94UB	Wrightbus Solar	N43F	2003
SF04SPZ	Volvo B12B	Van Hool T9 Alicron	C49FT	2004
SF04SRU	Volvo B12B	Van Hool T9 Alicron	C49FT	2004
SF04HXW	Volvo B7RLE	Wrightbus Eclipse Urban	N38F	2004
SF04HXX	Volvo B7RLE	Wrightbus Eclipse Urban	N38F	2004
SF04ZPE	Volvo B7RLE	Wrightbus Eclipse Urban	N38F	2004
SF04ZPG	Volvo B7RLE	Wrightbus Eclipse Urban	N38F	2004

Previous registrations:

PSV223	T733JGB	XUF456	T734JGB

Web: www.hutchinsoncoaches.co.uk

The Scottish Bus Handbook

IRVINE'S

P Irvine, MMR Walker, Lawmuir Road Garage, Law, Carluke, ML8 5JB

CHL772	Daimler CVD6SD	Willowbrook	B35F	1950	Go-Goodwins, Eccles, 2005
B301KVO	Volvo Citybus B10M-50	East Lancs	B51/35D	1985	City of Nottingham, 2000
B302KVO	Volvo Citybus B10M-50	East Lancs	B51/35D	1985	City of Nottingham, 2000
B303KVO	Volvo Citybus B10M-50	East Lancs	B51/35D	1985	Rowe & Tudhope, Muirkirk, 2002
B304KVO	Volvo Citybus B10M-50	East Lancs	B51/35D	1985	Rowe & Tudhope, Muirkirk, 2002
B305KVO	Volvo Citybus B10M-50	East Lancs	B51/35D	1985	Rowe & Tudhope, Muirkirk, 2002
B307KVO	Volvo Citybus B10M-50	East Lancs	B51/35D	1985	Rowe & Tudhope, Muirkirk, 2002
E327BVO	Volvo Citybus B10M-50	East Lancs	B47/38D	1987	City of Nottingham, 2005
E329BVO	Volvo Citybus B10M-50	East Lancs	B47/38D	1987	Redline, Penwortham, 2005
F113TML	Volvo Citybus B10M-50	Alexander RV	B46/29D	1989	Redline, Penwortham, 2004
F122PHM	Volvo Citybus B10M-50	Alexander RV	B46/29D	1989	2Travel, Swansea, 2005
F134PHM	Volvo Citybus B10M-50	Alexander RV	B46/29D	1989	Blue Triangle, Rainham, 2004
F135PHM	Volvo Citybus B10M-50	Alexander RV	B46/29D	1989	Redline, Penwortham, 2004
NSU552	Volvo B10M-53	Van Hool Alizée	C49FT	1990	Steven's, Birmingham, 2003
HSK857	Volvo B10M-60	Van Hool Alizée	C52FT	1992	Holmeswood Coaches, 2002
JIL8813	Volvo B10M-60	Plaxton Première 350	C51F	1992	Eastbond, Tamworth, 2004
SIL1895	Volvo B10M-60	Plaxton Première 350	C49FT	1992	Dunn-Line, Nottingham, 2002
J812HMC	Scania N113DRB	Alexander RH	B47/31F	1992	Metroline, Harrow, 2003
J814HMC	Scania N113DRB	Alexander RH	B47/31F	1992	Metroline, Harrow, 2003
J818HMC	Scania N113DRB	Alexander RH	B47/31F	1992	Metroline, Harrow, 2003
J387GKH	Dennis Dart 8.5m	Plaxton Pointer	B28F	1992	Metroline, Harrow, 2003
J388GKH	Dennis Dart 8.5m	Plaxton Pointer	B28F	1992	Metroline, Harrow, 2003
J389GKH	Dennis Dart 8.5m	Plaxton Pointer	B28F	1992	Metroline, Harrow, 2003
J392GKH	Dennis Dart 8.5m	Plaxton Pointer	B28F	1992	Metroline, Harrow, 2003
PSV114	Volvo B10M-62	Caetano Algarve 2	C49FT	1995	Reliant, Heather, 2005
XXI3248	DAF SB3000	Plaxton Première 350	C53F	1996	North Kent Express, 2003

Pictured while operating route 200 to Monklands Hospital, Dart J387GKH is seen in Law. It was latterly with Metroline as its DR87. *Bob Downham*

Irvine's Coaches operates five Optare Solo buses, including a pair in the longer 9.2-metre length. Illustrating the standard 8.5-metre model is YN53YHJ which joined the fleet in 2003. It is seen in Law bus station while preparing to operate the afternoon journey to Biggar. *Bob Downham*

P11RVN	Scania L94IB4	Irizar Century 12.35	C49FT	1997	Pointon, Nuneaton, 2002
S332SET	Scania L94IB4	Irizar Century 12.35	C49FT	1998	Atherstone, Bulkington, 2002
S461LGN	Dennis Dart SLF 8.8m	Plaxton Pointer MPD	N29F	1998	Epsom Coaches, 2005
T9RVN	Scania K113CRB	Van Hool T9 Alizée	C49FT	1999	Redline, Penwortham, 2002
W322YSB	Scania L94IB4	Irizar Century 12.35	C49FT	2000	Bus Eireann, 2004
Y500MRT	Optare Solo M850	Optare	N29F	2001	Boyd's, Rochdale, 2003
Y173CGC	Volvo B7R	Plaxton Prima	C53F	2001	Hardings, Betchworth, 2004
SJ51BZA	Dennis Dart SLF 8.8m	Plaxton Pointer MPD	N29F	2001	HAD, Shotts, 2004
SJ51UDW	Dennis Dart SLF 8.8m	Plaxton Pointer MPD	N29F	2001	HAD, Shotts, 2004
123TRL	Volvo B10M-62	Plaxton Paragon	C49FT	2001	Bus Eireann, 2004
GXI153	Volvo B10M-62	Plaxton Paragon	C49FT	2001	Bus Eireann, 2004
VU02TSV	Optare Solo M920	Optare	N33F	2002	
VU02TSV	Optare Solo M920	Optare	N33F	2002	
BP02FMX	Scania K114CRB	Van Hool T9 Alizée	C49FT	2002	Wharton, Crossdoney, 2004
EU03EUD	TransBus Dart 8.8m	TransBus Pointer	N29F	2003	LocalLink, Bishop's Stortford, 2004
YN53YHJ	Optare Solo M850	Optare	N29F	2003	
SF54KHV	ADL Dart 8.8m	Caetano Nimbus	N28F	2005	
FJ05HXX	ADL Dart 8.8m	Caetano Nimbus	N28F	2005	
SN55DUU	ADL Dart 8.8m	ADL Mini Pointer	N28F	2005	
-06	VDL Bova FHD12.340	Bova Futura	C49FT	2006	

Previous registrations:

123TRL	X436BTT, 01D8068		PSV114	M40CLA, REL575
BP02FMX	01KK2221		S332SET	99D4099
GXI153	X437BTT, 01D8083		SIL1895	J261NNC
HSK857	J989JNS, RJI8712, J293TFP		T9RVN	T147HHG, T9RED
JIL8813	J750CWT		W322YSB	00KK41909
NSU552	G958JJC, PAN58R, G760CRW		XXI3248	P167RWR
P11RVN	P97GHE		Y173CGC	Y4HCT

JAY COACHES

Jays Coach Travel Ltd, 249 Greengairs Road, Greengairs, Airdrie, ML6 7SZ

MIL6679	Leyland National 11351/1R		B50F	1976	Hunter, Sauchie, 2003
UNA863S	Leyland Atlantean AN68A/1R	Park Royal	B43/32F	1977	Western Buses, 1999
ECS65V	Ailsa B55-10	Alexander AV	B44/35F	1979	Clyde Coast, 2003
OSC54V	Ailsa B55-10	Alexander AV	B44/35F	1979	Stagecoach Fife, 2000
LHS747V	Ailsa B55-10	Alexander AV	B44/35F	1979	Allander Travel, Milngavie, 2002
PNW59W	Leyland National NL116L11/1R		B52F	1980	Hunter, Sauchie, 2002
ORA450W	Leyland Atlantean AN68C/1R	East Lancs	B47/31D	1980	Tait, Irvine, 2002
NFS172Y	Leyland Leopard PSU3G/4R	Alexander AT	BC49F	1982	Marshall, Baillieston, 2003
NFS179Y	Leyland Leopard PSU3G/4R	Alexander AT	BC49F	1982	Stagecoach Fife, 1999
RSC192Y	Leyland Leopard PSU3G/4R	Alexander AT	BC49F	1982	Stagecoach Fife, 1999
AEF223Y	Leyland Olympian ONLXB/1R	Eastern Coach Works	B45/37F	1983	Allander Travel, Milngavie, 2005
YSO40Y	Leyland Olympian ONLXB/1R	Alexander RL	B45/37F	1983	Allander Travel, Milngavie, 2005
PIL2167	Volvo B10M-61	Plaxton Paramount 3500	C28FT	1984	Classic, Annfield Plain, 2003
C783SFS	Leyland Olympian ONTL11/2R	Eastern Coach Works	B51/32D	1986	Lothian Buses, 2004
C784SFS	Leyland Olympian ONTL11/2R	Eastern Coach Works	B51/32D	1986	Lothian Buses, 2004
F852YJX	DAF SB2305	Plaxton Paramount 3200 III	C57F	1989	Maynes of Buckie, 2003
J420JBV	Volvo B10M-55	East Lancs	B51F	1991	Blackburn Transport, 2005
J422JBV	Volvo B10M-55	East Lancs	B51F	1991	Blackburn Transport, 2005
TJI1983	Volvo B10M-62	Van Hool Alizée	C49FT	1994	Long's, Salsburgh, 2004
6308YG	Volvo B10M-62	Van Hool Alizée	C53F	1994	Long's, Salsburgh, 2004
M601RFS	Mercedes-Benz 609D	Aitken	BC24F	1995	Milne, New Byth, 1998
B16AFC	Volvo B10M-62	Van Hool Alizée H	C40FT	1996	Ellison, St Helens, 1997
P279VUS	Volvo B10M-61	Van Hool Alizée	C53F	1997	Long's, Salsburgh, 2004
R83RBY	Scania K113CRB	Berkhof Axial 50	C30FT	1998	Peter Carol, Bristol, 2005
ESK675	Iveco EuroRider 391.12.35	Beulas Stergo ε	C49FT	1999	Redwing, Herne Hill, 2002
Y8AMS	Bova Futura FHD12.370	Bova	C49F	2001	Aberfeldy Motor Services, 2004
KU52YJX	TransBus Dart 8.8m	TransBus Mini Pointer	N29F	2002	HAD, Shotts, 2004
KU52YJY	TransBus Dart 8.8m	TransBus Mini Pointer	N29F	2002	HAD, Shotts, 2004
KU52YJZ	TransBus Dart 8.8m	TransBus Mini Pointer	N29F	2002	HAD, Shotts, 2004
B1AFC	Bova Futura FHD12.370	Bova	C49FT	2004	
GSK675	Bova Futura FHD12.340	Bova	C49FT	2005	
W1JAY	Bova Futura FHD13.340	Bova	C57F	2005	
W2JAY	Bova Futura FHD13.340	Bova	C57F	2005	

Previous registrations:

6308YG	P278VUS	GSK675	-
B16AFC	N651EWJ, FDJ7S, N706UEC	TJI1983	M268POS

While most of the Mercedes-Benz minibuses with John Morrow Coaches are bodied by Plaxtons, R716TRV is a exception in having a UVG body. The Citystar model is seen in Clydebank. *Phillip Stephenson*

JOHN MORROW COACHES

J J Morrow, 18 Albion Industrial Estate, Halley Street, Glasgow, G13 4DJ

YPJ207Y	Leyland Tiger TRCTL11/3R	East Lancashire (1992)	B59F	1982	Arriva Midlands, 2003
K719DAO	Volvo B10M-55	Alexander PS	B49F	1992	Stagecoach, 2005
K732DAO	Volvo B10M-55	Alexander PS	B53F	1993	Stagecoach, 2005
K773DAO	Volvo B10M-55	Alexander PS	B53F	1993	Stagecoach, 2005
R716TRV	Mercedes-Benz Vario 0814	UVG CityStar	B31F	1997	Glyn Williams, Pontllanfraith, 1999
R878FGE	Mercedes-Benz Vario 0810	Plaxton Beaver 2	B29F	1997	
R185OCW	Mercedes-Benz Vario 0814	Plaxton Beaver 2	B27F	1997	Alpine, Hull, 2003
R585HDS	Mercedes-Benz Vario 0810	Plaxton Beaver 2	B29F	1998	
S975CSG	Mercedes-Benz Vario 0814	Plaxton Beaver 2	B27F	1999	
T87JBA	Mercedes-Benz Vario 0814	Plaxton Beaver 2	B31F	1999	Henderson, Harwood, 2003
T341LGB	Mercedes-Benz Vario 0814	Plaxton Beaver 2	B27F	1999	Gibson Direct, Renfrew, 2003
SJ54GDA	Optare Solo M880	Optare	N29F	2004	
SJ54GDE	Optare Solo M880	Optare	N29F	2004	

John Morrow operates commercial and tendered services in Glasgow and Clydebank. Two Optare Solo buses arrived in 2004 and SJ54GDA is seen in Clydebank shortly after delivery. *Billy Nicol*

KEENAN OF AYR

John Keenan & Sons (Darwin Garage) Ltd, Coalhall, Ayr, KA6 6ND

TSJ71S	Leyland Leopard PSU3D/4R	Alexander AY	B53F	1977	Stagecoach, 2005
BSJ931T	Leyland Leopard PSU3E/4R	Alexander AY	B53F	1978	Rowe, Kilmarnock, 2004
HGD214T	Leyland Atlantean AN68A/1R	Alexander AL	B45/33F	1979	Graham's, Paisley, 1990
AVK155V	Leyland Atlantean AN68A/2R	Alexander AL	B49/37F	1980	Go-Ahead Northern, 2000
AVK165V	Leyland Atlantean AN68A/2R	Alexander AL	B49/37F	1980	Go-Ahead Northern, 2000
WDS343V	Leyland Leopard PSU3E/4R	Alexander AY	B53F	1980	Stagecoach Western Buses, 2000
GCS48V	Leyland Leopard PSU3E/4R	Alexander AY	B53F	1980	Stagecoach Western Buses, 1999
ORJ393W	Leyland Atlantean AN68A/1R	Northern Counties	B43/32F	1981	, 2005
AEF91A	DAF MB200	Duple Caribbean	C57F	1985	Southend, 1993
YIJ3053	DAF MB200	Duple Laser 2	C57F	1985	Southend, 1993
TJI1328	Volvo B10M-61	Plaxton Paramount 3500 II	C53F	1985	Clynnog & Trefor, 1995
A1VOL	Volvo B10M-61	Plaxton Paramount 3500 II	C53F	1986	Stonehouse Coaches, 1995
YIJ3053	Leyland Tiger TRCTL11/3RZ	Plaxton Derwent 2	BC70F	1986	Crown, Bristol, 2003
246AJF	Volvo B10M-61	Van Hool Alizée	C53F	1986	Epsom Coaches, 1996
B10VOL	Volvo B10M-61	Van Hool Alizée	C57F	1988	Marbill, Beith, 2000
OJD11R	Mercedes-Benz 609D	Whittaker Europa	C21F	1989	Whittaker demonstrator, 1989
LIL9814	Volvo B10M-60	Van Hool Alizée	C53F	1990	Compass Royston, Stockton, 2004
TIW9829	Volvo B10M-60	Van Hool Alizée	C53F	1991	Beaton, Blantyre, 2005
GCS38V	Mercedes-Benz 709D	Alexander Sprint	B25F	1992	Stagecoach, 2004
B3VOL	Volvo B10M-62	Van Hool Alizée HE	C53F	1994	Allander Travel, Milngavie, 2000
B4VOL	Volvo B10M-62	Van Hool Alizée HE	C46FT	1994	Shearings, 2003
B5VOL	Volvo B10M-62	Van Hool Alizée HE	C46FT	1994	Shearings, 2003
SF04ETK	Mercedes-Benz Vario 0814	Plaxton Cheetah	C33F	2004	

Previous registrations:

246AJF	C331DND	GCS38V	K488FFS
A1VOL	C176LWB, C411SSB, UBM880, C799SSB, SJI1977	LIL9814	G340HSC
AEF91A	B252CVX	ORJ393W	ORJ393W, NIL9313, NIL9312
B3VOL	LSK844, L635AYS, XAT11X, L502AYS	TIW9829	H192DVM
B4VOL	M652KVU	TJI1328	C486HAK, C484HAK, XSU653
B5VOL	M648KVU	WDS343V	GLS38V
B10VOL	E641UNE, LSK871, E959GCA, GJI926, E582CNS	YIJ3053	65KG96, D511FTS, E818NOU

Livery: White, yellow, orange and red

HGD214T is one of three Leyland Atlanteans used by Keenan of Ayr on school duties. All three have Alexander AL bodies, and this example features the rounded dome option of the AL.
Bob Downham

KEY COACHES

S Forbes, 102 Dundonald Avenue, Johnstone, PA5 0LT

M81	RIL7381	Mercedes-Benz 709D	Alexander Sprint	BC25F	1988	JP Travel, Middleton, 2000
M49	RIL3749	Mercedes-Benz 709D	Reeve Burgess Beaver	BC25F	1989	McPherson, Port Glasgow, 1999
M50	RIL4450	Mercedes-Benz 609D	Reeve Burgess Beaver	B20F	1989	Blue Bus, Bucknall, 1999
M26	G926WGS	Mercedes-Benz 709D	Reeve Burgess Beaver	B23F	1990	Hardie's Cs, Port Glasgow, 2001
M38	J938WHJ	Mercedes-Benz 709D	Reeve Burgess Beaver	B23F	1990	Hardie's Cs, Port Glasgow, 2001
M11	J211KTT	Mercedes-Benz 709D	Reeve Burgess Beaver	B25F	1992	Slaemuir, Port Glasgow, 2000
M25	K31WND	Mercedes-Benz 609D	Made-to-Measure	B24F	1993	Arriva The Shires, 2000
M32	K32WND	Mercedes-Benz 609D	Made-to-Measure	B24F	1993	Arriva The Shires, 2000
M96	K96RGA	Mercedes-Benz 709D	Dormobile Routemaker	B29F	1993	Miller, Foxton, 2004
M64	L649DNA	Mercedes-Benz 709D	Marshall C19	B27F	1994	Arriva North West, 2001
M33	R733EGD	Mercedes-Benz Vario 0810	Plaxton Beaver 2	B27F	1998	Dickinson of Erskine, 2004

Previous registrations:

RIL3749	F313EJO		
RIL4450	F377UCP, JIL5227, F57GUJ	RIL7881	E324OSC

Depot: Braehead Ind Est, Renfrew

Many of the minibuses operated by Key Coaches are conversions of the Mercedes-Benz 709 van series. Two examples with Made-to-Measure bodywork are operated, these being new to Birmingham Omnibus of Tividale in the West Midlands. The example here, K32WND, was photographed in Paisley. *Phillip Stephenson*

KINEIL

Kineil Coaches Ltd, 7 Pitblae Place, Fraserburgh, AB43 7BG

RIL9964	Volvo B58-61	Plaxton Panorama Elite	C53F	1974	Cheyne, Turriff, 2002
VIA488	Volvo B58-61	Caetano	C49FT	1980	Whytes, Newmachar, 1992
PDL252X	Bedford YNT	Plaxton Supreme	C53F	1981	Maynes of Buckie, 1995
TYS259W	Dennis Dominator DD135B	Alexander AL	B45/34F	1981	Scott, Oldham, 1998
OSN870Y	Volvo Citybus B55	East Lancs	B48/36F	1983	Travel Tayside, 1998
OSN875Y	Volvo Citybus B55	East Lancs	B48/36F	1983	Travel Tayside, 1998
PDX782	DAF MB200	Van Hool Alizée	C50F	1983	Cowie, Peterhead, 1995
A39XHE	Leyland Tiger TRCTL11/2RH	Alexander TE	BC65F	1983	APT Travel, Rayleigh, 2002
A44XHE	Leyland Tiger TRCTL11/2RH	Alexander TE	BC65F	1984	APT Travel, Rayleigh, 2004
A717ASJ	Volvo B10M-61	Van Hool Alizée	C50FT	1984	Campbell, Clydebank, 2002
TIW7700	Volvo B10M-61	Van Hool Alizée	C50FT	1984	Millington, Streetly, 1996
KIW4388	Volvo B10M-61	Jonckheere Jubilee	C53FT	1985	Cedric's, Wivenhoe, 1995
953HBU	Volvo B10M-61	Van Hool Alizée	C51FT	1987	Clan, Kyle of Lochalsh, 2002
671YWC	Volvo B10M-61	Van Hool Alizée	C49DT	1987	Clan, Kyle of Lochalsh, 2002
RIB7742	Volvo B10M-60	Van Hool Alizée	C53F	1989	Wilson, Carnwath, 1995
JSU384	Volvo B10M-60	Van Hool Alizée	C50F	1989	Clan, Kyle of Lochalsh, 2002
K5SKY	Volvo B10M-60	Van Hool Alizée	C49FT	1993	Clan, Kyle of Lochalsh, 2002
L502YGD	DAF 400	Onyx	M14	1993	Milne, New Byth, 2002
L314KSS	Mercedes-Benz 814D	Plaxton Beaver	BC33F	1993	Reid, Rhynie, 2002
L930UGA	Mercedes-Benz 609D	Made-to-Measure	BC26F	1993	Maynes of Buckie, 1995
L4LCC	Volvo B10M-60	Van Hool Alizée	C55F	1994	Longs, Salsburgh, 2000
DSU755	Volvo B10M-62	Van Hool Alizée	C53F	1995	McQueen, Garelochhead, 2002
VIA963	Volvo B10M-62	Van Hool Alizée	C57F	1996	Maynes of Buckie, 2001
R611OFS	Mercedes-Benz Vario 0614	Onyx	BC24F	1997	
R321HDS	Mercedes-Benz Vario 0614	Plaxton Cheetah	C33F	1998	Peace, Skene, 2003
T9TAP	Mercedes-Benz Vario 0614	Onyx	BC24F	1999	Bruce, Maud, 2002
V326XDO	Mercedes-Benz Sprinter 412	ACL	M16	2000	Allen, Coventry, 2003
X974NRS	Mercedes-Benz Vario 0614	Onyx	BC24F	2000	Dawson, Stuartfield, 2002
SV03JZK	Mercedes-Benz Vario 0815	Sitcar Beluga	C33F	2003	
SN53DYA	Mercedes-Benz Vario 0614	Onyx	BC24F	2003	
SN04GFE	Mercedes-Benz Vario 0814	Plaxton Cheetah	C33F	2004	
YN54WWZ	Mercedes-Benz Vario 0814	Plaxton Cheetah	C33F	2004	

Previous registrations:

671YWC	A608UGD, GIL7364, GIL3573, A842ASJ	PDX782	From ne
953HBU	D800EST, D846FST, 12EWO, D583SBS	RIB7742	F812XSG
A717ASJ	NVY148	RIL9964	PTO14M, 3380SR
DSU755	HSK647, N525PYS	TIW7700	WAC828, A221XTL, 5670SC, A733YOX
JSU384	F782UJS	VIA488	WCO734V, 7173WW, KRS558V
KIW4388	B493GBD, KIW4392	VIA963	P500GSM

Depot: Westshore Ind Est, Fraserburgh

Lippen have acquired a series of L-PPN index marks, with the first almost presenting the fleet name. This is now attached to a Marshall-bodied Mercedes-Benz Vario. It is seen leaving Paisley for Linwood.
Bob Downham

LIPPEN

Lippen - Graham's of Paisley

C Graham, 53 Scotts Road, Paisley, PA2 7AN

G146LRM	Mercedes-Benz 609D	Reeve Burgess Beaver	B18F	1989	GM North, 1995
GBZ9059	Mercedes-Benz 709D	Wright NimBus	B29F	1991	
K579MGT	Dennis Dart 9m	Plaxton Beaver	B32F	1992	Go-Ahead London, 2003
K580MGT	Dennis Dart 9m	Plaxton Beaver	B32F	1992	Go-Ahead London, 2003
L776AUS	Mercedes-Benz 609D	North West	B17F	1993	A1A, Birkenhead, 1998
P408RGG	Mercedes-Benz 609D	Anderson	C24F	1996	Coakley Bus, Motherwell, 1999
L11PPN	Mercedes-Benz 412D	Mercedes-Benz	M16	1996	
R776MGB	Ford Transit VE6	Mayflower	M16	1998	
L4PPN	Mercedes-Benz Vario O814	Plaxton Beaver 2	B31F	1998	Evans, Oxton, 2002
GBZ8812	Mercedes-Benz Vario O814	Plaxton Beaver 2	BC31F	1999	
L1PPN	Mercedes-Benz Vario O814	Marshall Master	B31F	1999	
L2PPN	Mercedes-Benz Vario O814	Plaxton Beaver 2	B31F	2000	
L3PPN	Mercedes-Benz Vario O814	Plaxton Beaver 2	B33F	2000	
L8PPN	LDV Convoy	LDV	M16	2001	
L9PPN	Mercedes-Benz Sprinter 313cdi	Concept	M16	2003	
L5PPN	Optare Solo M920	Optare	N30F	2004	
L7PPN	Mercedes-Benz Sprinter 313cdi	Concept	M16	2005	

Previous registrations:

GBZ8812	R23JSG		L8PPN	X319RSD
L1PPN	V720GGE		L11PPN	P530UGA
L4PPN	S312DLG		L776AUS	L2BUS

Depots: Meadowside Street, Renfrew and Scotts Road, Paisley

Lippen's first and so far only Dennis Darts are a pair of Plaxton Pointers sold by Go-Ahead London where they operated under the London General name. K579MGT is one of the 9-metre models which were built to single door format. It is seen in Paisley. *Billy Nicol*

LOCHS & GLENS HOLIDAYS

Lochs & Glens Transport Ltd, The Old Schoolhouse, Gartocharn, Alexandria, G83 8RW

FN52HRU	Volvo B12M	Jonckheere Mistral 50	C51FT	2003
FJ04ETD	Volvo B12B	VDL Jonckheere Mistral 50	C51FT	2004
FJ04ETE	Volvo B12B	VDL Jonckheere Mistral 50	C51FT	2004
FJ04ETF	Volvo B12B	VDL Jonckheere Mistral 50	C51FT	2004
FJ04ETK	Volvo B12B	VDL Jonckheere Mistral 50	C51FT	2004
FJ04ETL	Volvo B12B	VDL Jonckheere Mistral 50	C51FT	2004
FJ05AOM	Volvo B12B 13.5m	VDL Jonckheere Mistral 70	C57FT	2005
FJ05AON	Volvo B12B 13.5m	VDL Jonckheere Mistral 70	C57FT	2005
FJ05AOO	Volvo B12B 13.5m	VDL Jonckheere Mistral 70	C57FT	2005
FJ05AOP	Volvo B12B 13.5m	VDL Jonckheere Mistral 70	C57FT	2005
FJ05AOR	Volvo B12B 13.5m	VDL Jonckheere Mistral 70	C57FT	2005
FJ06BSO	Volvo B12B 13.5m	VDL Jonckheere Mistral 70	C57FT	2006
FJ06BSU	Volvo B12B 13.5m	VDL Jonckheere Mistral 70	C57FT	2006
FJ06BSV	Volvo B12B 13.5m	VDL Jonckheere Mistral 70	C57FT	2006
FJ06BSX	Volvo B12B 13.5m	VDL Jonckheere Mistral 70	C57FT	2006
FJ06BSY	Volvo B12B 13.5m	VDL Jonckheere Mistral 70	C57FT	2006

Depot: Inversnaid Hotel, Aberfoyle

FJ06BSV is one of five 13.5-metre tri-axle Volvo B12B coaches added to the fleet in 2006. All of Lochs & Glens Holidays fleet comprises coaches bodied by Jonckheere using the Mistral design. The Belgium coachbuilder Jonckheere, which assembles buses at its factory in Roeselare, became part of VDL Groep in 2001 and adopted the VDL name in 2003. VDL is an international industrial company with its head office in Eindhoven in the Netherlands, and includes the former DAF Bus, Bova and Berkhof identities in its portfolio. *Volvo Bus*

LOTHIAN BUSES

Lothian Buses plc, Annandale Street, Edinburgh, EH7 4AZ

1	TR	JSJ749	AEC Routemaster R2RH	Park Royal	O43/32R	1959	MacTours, 2002
2	TR	VLT163	AEC Routemaster R2RH	Park Royal	O43/32R	1959	MacTours, 2002
3	TR	VLT235	AEC Routemaster R2RH	Park Royal	O43/25R	1960	MacTours, 2002
4	TR	JSJ746	AEC Routemaster R2RH	Park Royal	O43/25R	1959	MacTours, 2002
5	TR	JSJ747	AEC Routemaster R2RH	Park Royal	O43/25R	1959	MacTours, 2002
6	TR	JSJ748	AEC Routemaster R2RH	Park Royal	O43/25R	1959	MacTours, 2002
7	TR	VLT143	AEC Routemaster R2RH	Park Royal	O43/25R	1959	MacTours, 2002
8	TR	VLT237	AEC Routemaster R2RH	Park Royal	O43/25R	1960	MacTours, 2002
9	TR	VLT242	AEC Routemaster R2RH	Park Royal	O43/25R	1960	MacTours, 2002
10	TR	VLT281	AEC Routemaster R2RH	Park Royal	O43/25R	1960	MacTours, 2002
11	TR	CUV241C	AEC Routemaster R2RH	Park Royal	B36/29R	1965	London Bus Exports, 2002
12	TR	CUV248C	AEC Routemaster R2RH	Park Royal	B36/29R	1965	MacTours, 2002
13	TR	CUV210C	AEC Routemaster R2RH	Park Royal	B32/25R	1965	MacTours, 2002
14	TR	803DYE	AEC Routemaster R2RH	Park Royal	O32/25R	1965	MacTours, 2002
15	TR	858DYE	AEC Routemaster R2RH	Park Royal	O32/25R	1961	MacTours, 2002
16	TR	WLT371	AEC Routemaster R2RH	Park Royal	O32/25R	1960	MacTours, 2002
17	TR	485CLT	AEC Routemaster R2RH	Park Royal	B32/25R	1960	Stagecoach, 2005
18	TR	CUV203C	AEC Routemaster R2RH	Park Royal	B36/25R	1965	MacTours, 2002
19	T	NMY646E	AEC Routemaster R2RH/2	Park Royal	B32/24F	1967	MacTours, 2002
20	T	NMY634E	AEC Routemaster R2RH/2	Park Royal	B32/24F	1967	Stagecoach, Bluebird, 2002
21	TR	LST873	Leyland Titan PD2/40	Park Royal	O27/26R	1958	MacTours, 2002
22	TR	YSL334	Leyland Tiger PS1	Guernseybus	O35F	1951	MacTours, 2002
23	TR	OAS624	Leyland Tiger PS1	Guernseybus	CO35F	1951	MacTours, 2002
24	TR	OSJ636R	Leyland Leopard PSU3C/3R	Alexander AY	O49F	1977	Western Buses, 1999
27	T	XIL1483	Mercedes-Benz 709D	Alexander Sprint	B23F	1990	Stagecoach, 2005
31	E	W631PSX	Dennis Trident	Plaxton President	ON51/26F	2000	
32	E	W632PSX	Dennis Trident	Plaxton President	ON51/26F	2000	
33	E	W633PSX	Dennis Trident	Plaxton President	ON51/26F	2000	
34	ER	W634PSX	Dennis Trident	Plaxton President	ON51/26F	2000	
45	ER	A158FPG	Leyland Olympian ONTL11/1R	Roe	O43/29F	1984	Guide Friday, 2002
46	ER	A159FPG	Leyland Olympian ONTL11/1R	Roe	O43/29F	1984	Guide Friday, 2002
47	ER	A145DPE	Leyland Olympian ONTL11/1R	Roe	O43/29F	1983	Guide Friday, 2002

Notable members of Lothian's fleet of Plaxton Presidents are three open-top Tridents that joined the fleet in 2000. Pictured in City Sightseeing livery is 31, W631PSX.
Billy Nicol

In a boost to the single-deck fleet, and as replacements for Leyland Lynx, thirty Volvo B7RLEs with Wrightbus Eclipse Urban bodywork joined the Lothian fleet in 2004, with a further five the following year. These carry the harlequin livery as shown by 125, SN04NHV. *Richard Walter*

51-100   Dennis Dart SLF 11.3m   Plaxton Pointer SPD   N42F   2002-03

51	C	SK52OHU	64	C	SK52OJH	77	L	SK52OJX	89	L	SN53AVC
52	C	SK52OHV	65	C	SK52OJJ	78	L	SK52OJY	90	L	SN53AVD
53	C	SK52OHW	66	C	SK52OJL	79	L	SK52OJZ	91	L	SN53AVE
54	C	SK52OHX	67	C	SK52OJM	80	L	SK52OKA	92	L	SN53AVF
55	C	SK52OHY	68	C	SK52OJN	81	L	SK52OKB	93	L	SN53AVG
56	C	SK52OHZ	69	C	SK52OJO	82	L	SK52OKC	94	L	SN53AVK
57	C	SK52OJA	70	C	SK52OJP	83	L	SK52OKD	95	L	SN53AVL
58	C	SK52OJB	71	C	SK52OJR	84	L	SK52OKE	96	L	SN53AVM
59	C	SK52OJC	72	L	SK52OJS	85	L	SK52OKF	97	L	SN53AVO
60	C	SK52OJD	73	L	SK52OJT	86	L	SN53AUW	98	L	SN53AVP
61	C	SK52OJE	74	L	SK52OJU	87	L	SN53AUX	99	L	SN53AVR
62	C	SK52OJF	75	L	SN53JNO	88	L	SN53AUY	100	L	SN53AVT
63	C	SK52OJG	76	L	SK52OJW						

101-130   Volvo B7RLE   Wrightbus Eclipse Urban   N42F   2004

101	C	SN04NFZ	109	C	SN04NGZ	117	C	SN04NHH	124	C	SN04NHU
102	C	SN04NGE	110	C	SN04NHA	118	C	SN04NHJ	125	C	SN04NHV
103	C	SN04NGF	111	C	SN04NHB	119	C	SN04NHK	126	C	SN04NHX
104	C	SN04NGG	112	C	SN04NHC	120	C	SN04NHL	127	C	SN04NHY
105	C	SN04NGJ	113	C	SN04NHD	121	C	SN04NHM	128	C	SN04NHZ
106	C	SN04NGU	114	C	SN04NHE	122	C	SN04NHP	129	C	SN04NJE
107	C	SN04NGX	115	C	SN04NHF	123	C	SN04NHT	130	C	SN04NJF
108	C	SN04NGY	116	C	SN04NHG						

131-135   Volvo B7RLE   Wrightbus Eclipse Urban   N40F   2005

131	C	SN55BJJ	133	C	SN55BJO	134	C	SN55BJU	135	C	SN55BJV
132	C	SN55BJK									

151-175   Dennis Dart SLF   Plaxton Pointer SPD   N42F   2000

151	L	V151EFS	158	L	V158EFS	164	M	V164EFS	170	M	V170EFS
152	L	V152EFS	159	L	V159EFS	165	M	V165EFS	171	M	V171EFS
153	L	V153EFS	160	L	V160EFS	166	M	V166EFS	172	M	V172EFS
154	L	V154EFS	161	M	V161EFS	167	M	V167EFS	173	M	V173EFS
155	L	V155EFS	162	M	V162EFS	168	M	V168EFS	174	M	V174EFS
156	L	V156EFS	163	M	V163EFS	169	M	V169EFS	175	M	V175EFS
157	L	V157EFS									

The Scottish Bus Handbook

Four of the remaining Alexander Dash-bodied Dennis Darts carry MacTours livery. Representing the type is 200, K123CSG, which is seen outside Holyrood House. *Phillip Stephenson*

176-192   Dennis Dart SLF   Plaxton Pointer SPD   N42F   2001

176	M	Y176CFS	181	M	Y181CFS	185	M	Y185CFS	189	M	Y189CFS
177	M	Y177CFS	182	M	Y182CFS	186	M	Y186CFS	191	M	Y191CFS
178	M	Y178CFS	183	M	Y183CFS	187	M	Y187CFS	192	M	SN51FZB
179	M	Y179CFS	184	M	Y184CFS	188	M	Y188CFS			

194-200   Dennis Dart 9m   Alexander Dash   B35F   1992

194	T	K117CSG	196	T	K119CSG	198	L	K121CSG	200	T	K123CSG
195	L	K118CSG	197	L	K120CSG	199	T	K122CSG			

201-234   Volvo Olympian YN2RC16Z4   Alexander RH   B51/30D   1995

201	C	M201VSX	210	C	M210VSX	218	C	M218VSX	227	C	M227VSX
202	C	M202VSX	211	C	M211VSX	219	C	M219VSX	228	C	M228VSX
203	C	M203VSX	212	C	M212VSX	220	C	M220VSX	229	C	M229VSX
204	C	M204VSX	213	C	M213VSX	221	C	M221VSX	230	C	M230VSX
205	C	M205VSX	214	C	M214VSX	223	C	M223VSX	231	C	M231VSX
206	C	M206VSX	215	C	M215VSX	224	C	M224VSX	232	C	M232VSX
207	C	M207VSX	216	C	M216VSX	225	C	M225VSX	233	C	M233VSX
208	C	M208VSX	217	C	M217VSX	226	C	M226VSX	234	C	M234VSX
209	C	M209VSX									

251-285   Volvo Olympian YN2RC16Z4   Alexander Royale   B51/30D   1997

251	M	P251PSX	260	L	P260PSX	269	L	P269PSX	277	L	P277PSX
252	M	P252PSX	261	L	P261PSX	270	L	P270PSX	278	L	P278PSX
253	M	P253PSX	262	L	P262PSX	271	L	P271PSX	279	L	P279PSX
254	L	P254PSX	263	L	P263PSX	272	L	P272PSX	281	L	P281PSX
255	L	P255PSX	264	L	P264PSX	273	L	P273PSX	282	L	P282PSX
256	L	P256PSX	265	L	P265PSX	274	L	P274PSX	283	L	P283PSX
257	L	P257PSX	266	L	P266PSX	275	L	P275PSX	284	L	P284PSX
258	L	P258PSX	267	L	P267PSX	276	L	P276PSX	285	L	P285PSX
259	L	P259PSX	268	L	P268PSX						

The model of bus most associated with Lothian in recent years is the Alexander RH-bodied Olympian. Many of these have now left the fleet, while others are used on peripheral or special services. One that has been converted to partial open-top and to single-door is 314, E314MSG, which is shown here in the colours of The Edinburgh Tour. *Richard Walter*

291-297 — Volvo B7LE — Plaxton President — N45/30F — 2000

| 291 | M | W291PFS | 293 | M | W293PFS | 295 | M | W295PFS | 296 | M | W296PFS |
| 292 | M | W292PFS | 294 | M | W294PFS | 297 | M | WDF297 | | | |

300-335 — Leyland Olympian ONCL10/2RZ Alexander RH — B51/30D* — 1988 — *seating varies, many single door

300	E	E300MSG	307	E	E307MSG	314	E	E314MSG	320	L	E320MSG
301	E	E301MSG	308	E	E308MSG	315	L	E315MSG	321	L	E321MSG
302	ER	E302MSG	309	E	E309MSG	316	L	E316MSG	322	L	E322MSG
303	ER	E303MSG	310	E	E310MSG	317	L	E317MSG	333	TR	E333MSG
304	ER	E304MSG	311	E	E311MSG	318	L	E318MSG	334	TR	E334MSG
305	ER	E305MSG	312	E	E312MSG	319	L	E319MSG	335	TR	E335MSG
306	ER	E306MSG	313	E	E313MSG						

336-365 — Leyland Olympian ONCL10/2RZ Alexander RH — B51/30D* — 1988 — *seating varies, many single door

336	TR	G336CSG	341	L	G341CSG	354	R	F354WSC	361	R	F361WSC
337	TR	G337CSG	342	L	G342CSG	356	E	F356WSC	362	L	F362WSC
338	TR	G338CSG	343	C	G343CSG	357	TR	F357WSC	363	L	F363WSC
339	L	G339CSG	344	C	G344CSG	358	TR	F358WSC	364	C	F364WSC
340	L	G340CSG	345	C	G345CSG	360	R	F360WSC	365	C	F365WSC

366-371 — Leyland Olympian ONCL10/2RZ Alexander RH — BC47/31F — 1989

| 366 | M | F366WSC | 368 | M | F368WSC | 370 | M | F370WSC | 371 | M | F371WSC |
| 367 | M | F367WSC | 369 | M | F369WSC | | | | | | |

401-430 — Volvo Olympian YN2RC16Z4 Alexander Royale B51/30D* 1996 421-30 are B51/29D

401	M	N401GSX	409	M	P409KSX	417	M	P417KSX	424	M	P424KSX
402	M	N402GSX	410	M	P410KSX	418	M	P418KSX	425	M	P425KSX
403	M	N403GSX	411	M	P411KSX	419	M	P419KSX	426	M	P426KSX
404	M	N404GSX	412	M	P412KSX	420	M	P420KSX	427	M	P427KSX
405	M	N405GSX	413	M	P413KSX	421	M	P421KSX	428	M	P428KSX
406	M	N406GSX	414	M	P414KSX	422	M	P422KSX	429	M	P429KSX
407	M	N407GSX	415	M	P415KSX	423	M	P423KSX	430	M	P430KSX
408	M	P408KSX	416	M	P416KSX					

431	M	P431KSX	Volvo Olympian YN2RC16Z4	Alexander Royale	BC49/27D	1996
432	M	P432KSX	Volvo Olympian YN2RC16Z4	Alexander Royale	BC49/27D	1996
433	M	P433KSX	Volvo Olympian YN2RC16Z4	Alexander Royale	BC49/27D	1996

501-505 — Dennis Trident Alexander ALX400 N51/25D 1999

501	C	T501SSG	503	C	T503SSG	504	C	T504SSG	505	C	T505SSG
502	C	T502SSG								

506-515 — Dennis Trident Plaxton President N49/30F 1999

506	C	T506SSG	509	C	T509SSG	512	C	V512ESC	514	C	V514ESC
507	C	T507SSG	510	C	T510SSG	513	C	V513ESC	515	C	V515ESC
508	C	T508SSG	511	C	V511ESC					

516-538 — Dennis Trident Plaxton President N45/26F* 1999 *516-29 are N45/30F

516	C	V516ESC	522	C	V522ESC	528	C	V528ESC	534	L	V534ESC
517	C	V517ESC	523	C	V523ESC	529	C	V529ESC	535	L	V535ESC
518	C	V518ESC	524	C	V524ESC	530	C	V530ESC	536	L	V536ESC
519	C	V519ESC	525	C	V525ESC	531	C	V531ESC	537	L	V537ESC
520	C	V520ESC	526	C	V526ESC	532	L	V532ESC	538	L	V538ESC
521	C	V521ESC	527	C	V527ESC	533	L	V533ESC			

539-549 — Dennis Trident Plaxton President NC45/27F* 1999-2000 *546-9 are NC45/26F *539-41 are NC45/29F

539	L	V539ESC	542	L	V542ESC	545	L	V545ESC	548	L	W548RSG
540	L	V540ESC	543	L	V543ESC	546	L	W546RSG	549	L	W549RSG
541	L	V541ESC	544	L	V544ESC	547	L	W547RSG			

551-598 — Dennis Trident Plaxton President N45/28F 2000

551	L	W551RSG	564	L	W564RSG	577	L	W577RSG	588	L	X588USC
552	L	W552RSG	566	L	W566RSG	578	L	X578USC	589	L	X589USC
553	L	W553RSG	567	L	W567RSG	579	L	X579USC	591	L	X591USC
554	L	W554RSG	568	L	W568RSG	581	L	X581USC	592	L	X592USC
556	L	W556RSG	569	L	W569RSG	582	L	X582USC	593	L	X593USC
557	L	W557RSG	571	L	W571RSG	583	L	X583USC	594	L	X594USC
558	L	W558RSG	572	L	W572RSG	584	L	X584USC	595	L	X595USC
559	L	W559RSG	573	L	W573RSG	585	L	X585USC	596	L	X596USC
561	L	W561RSG	574	L	W574RSG	586	L	X586USC	597	L	X597UKS
562	L	W562RSG	575	L	W575RSG	587	L	X587USC	598	L	X598USC
563	L	W563RSG	576	L	W576RSG					

599	M	SN51AYO	Dennis Trident	Plaxton President	N45/27D	2001
600	M	SN51AYP	Dennis Trident	Plaxton President	N45/27D	2001

601-628 — Dennis Trident Plaxton President N47/27D* 2001 *601-5 are N45/29F

601	C	SN51AXF	608	C	SN51AXR	615	C	SN51AXY	622	M	SN51AYF
602	C	SN51AXG	609	C	SN51AXS	616	M	SN51AXZ	623	M	SN51AYG
603	C	SN51AXH	610	C	SN51AXT	617	M	SN51AYA	624	M	SN51AYH
604	C	SN51AXJ	611	C	SN51AXU	618	M	SN51AYB	625	M	SN51AYJ
605	C	SN51AXK	612	C	SN51AXV	619	M	SN51AYC	626	M	SN51AYK
606	C	SN51AXO	613	C	SN51AXW	620	M	SN51AYD	627	M	SN51AYL
607	C	SN51AXP	614	C	SN51AXX	621	M	SN51AYE	628	M	SN51AYM

Dennis Tridents with Plaxton President bodywork formed the main delivery from 1999. Several carry a special livery for route 100 that connects the airport with the city centre. Seen in that scheme is 662, SN04AAE, which is fitted with additional luggage space for the service. *Richard Walter*

629-700   Dennis Trident   Plaxton President   N51/32F*   2002-04   *Seating varies

629	M	SN53AVU	647	C	SK52OHG	665	M	SN04AAK	683	M	SN04ADU
630	M	SN53AVV	648	C	SK52OHH	666	M	SN04AAU	684	M	SN04ADV
631	M	SN53AVW	649	C	SK52OHJ	667	M	SN04AAV	685	M	SN04ADX
632	M	SN53AVX	650	C	SK52OHL	668	M	SN04AAX	686	M	SN04ADZ
633	M	SN53AVZ	651	C	SK52OHN	669	M	SN04AAY	687	M	SN04AEA
634	M	SK52OHT	652	M	SK52OHO	670	M	SN04AAZ	688	M	SN04AEB
635	C	SK52OGT	653	M	SK52OHP	671	M	SN04ABF	689	M	SN04AEC
636	C	SK52OGU	654	M	SK52OHR	672	M	SN04ABK	690	M	SN53AED
637	C	SK52OGV	655	M	SK52OHS	673	M	SN04ABU	691	M	SN53AEE
638	C	SK52OGW	656	M	SN04AEV	674	M	SN04ABV	692	M	SN53AEF
639	C	SK52OGX	657	M	SN04AEW	675	M	SN04ABX	693	M	SN53AEG
640	C	SK52OGY	658	M	SN04AEX	676	M	SN04ABZ	694	M	SN53AEJ
641	C	SK52OGZ	659	M	SN04AEY	677	M	SN04ACJ	695	M	SN53AEK
642	C	SK52OHA	660	M	SN04AEZ	678	M	SN04ACU	696	M	SN53AEL
643	C	SK52OHB	661	M	SN04AFA	679	M	SN04ACV	697	M	SN53AEM
644	C	SK52OHC	662	M	SN04AAE	680	M	SN04ACX	698	M	SN53AEP
645	C	SK52OHD	663	M	SN04AAF	681	M	SN04ACY	699	M	SN53AET
646	C	SK52OHE	664	M	SN04AAJ	682	M	SN04ACZ	700	M	SN53AEU

701-750   Volvo B7TL   Wrightbus Eclipse Gemini   N48/33F   2005-06

701	L	SN55BJX	714	L	SN55BKX	727	L	SN55BMZ	739	L	SN55BNX
702	L	SN55BJY	715	L	SN55BKY	728	L	SN55BNA	740	L	SN55BNY
703	L	SN55BJZ	716	L	SN55BKZ	729	L	SN55BNB	741	L	SN55BNZ
704	L	SN55BKA	717	L	SN55BLF	730	L	SN55BND	742	L	SN55BOF
705	L	SN55BKD	718	L	SN55BLJ	731	L	SN55BNE	743	L	SN55BOH
706	L	SN55BKE	719	L	SN55BLK	732	L	SN55BNF	744	L	SN55BOJ
707	L	SN55BKF	720	L	SN55BLV	733	L	SN55BNJ	745	L	SN55BOU
708	L	SN55BKG	721	L	SN55BLX	734	L	SN55BNK	746	L	SN55BOV
709	L	SN55BKJ	722	L	SN55BLZ	735	L	SN55BNL	747	L	SN55BPE
710	L	SN55BKK	723	L	SN55BMO	736	L	SN55BNO	748	L	SN55BPF
711	L	SN55BKL	724	L	SN55BMU	737	L	SN55BNU	749	L	SN55BPK
712	L	SN55BKU	725	L	SN55BMV	738	L	SN55BNV	750	L	SN55BPO
713	L	SN55BKV	726	L	SN55BMY						

The Scottish Bus Handbook

Route 26 is a high-frequency route that crosses the city of Edinburgh from east to west, operating both day and night. All buses terminate at Clerwood in the west of the city through the centre and some journeys carrying on to Tranent in the east, although many journeys are truncated on the eastern side. A special livery is carried for this route, as shown here on 684, SN04ADV, parked at the Clerwood terminus. *Mark Doggett*

800-871

Leyland Olympian ON2R56C13Z4 Alexander RH   B51/30D   1990-91

800	L	G800GSX	818	L	G818GSX	836	L	J836TSC	854	C	J854TSC
801	L	G801GSX	819	L	G819GSX	837	L	J837TSC	855	C	J855TSC
802	L	G802GSX	820	L	G820GSX	838	C	J838TSC	856	C	J856TSC
803	L	G803GSX	821	L	G821GSX	839	C	J839TSC	857	C	J857TSC
804	L	G804GSX	822	L	G822GSX	840	C	J840TSC	858	C	J858TSC
805	L	G805GSX	823	L	G823GSX	841	C	J841TSC	859	C	J859TSC
806	L	G806GSX	824	L	G824GSX	842	C	J842TSC	860	M	J860TSC
807	L	G807GSX	825	L	G825GSX	843	C	J843TSC	861	M	J861TSC
808	L	G808GSX	826	L	G826GSX	844	C	J844TSC	862	M	J862TSC
809	L	G809GSX	827	L	G827GSX	845	C	J845TSC	863	M	J863TSC
810	L	G810GSX	828	L	G828GSX	846	C	J846TSC	864	M	J864TSC
811	L	G811GSX	829	L	G829GSX	847	C	J847TSC	865	M	J865TSC
812	L	G812GSX	830	L	G830GSX	848	C	J848TSC	866	M	J866TSC
813	L	G813GSX	831	L	G831GSX	849	C	J849TSC	867	M	J867TSC
814	L	G814GSX	832	L	G832GSX	850	C	J850TSC	868	M	J868TSC
815	L	G815GSX	833	L	G833GSX	851	C	J851TSC	869	M	J869TSC
816	L	G816GSX	834	L	G834GSX	852	C	J852TSC	870	M	J870TSC
817	L	G817GSX	835	L	G835GSX	853	C	J853TSC	871	M	J871TSC

872-894

Leyland Olympian ON2R56C13Z4 Alexander RH   B51/30D   1992-93*   *675 is B47/30F

872	M	K872CSF	878	M	K878CSF	884	M	K884CSF	890	M	K890CSF
873	M	K873CSF	879	M	K879CSF	885	M	K885CSF	891	M	K891CSF
874	M	K874CSF	880	M	K880CSF	886	M	K886CSF	892	M	K892CSF
875	E	K875CSF	881	M	K881CSF	887	M	K887CSF	893	M	K893CSF
876	M	K876CSF	882	M	K882CSF	889	M	K889CSF	894	M	K894CSF
877	M	K877CSF	883	M	K883CSF						

As in the English capital, Routemasters in Edinburgh are now confined to tourist services. Lothian operates guided tours of the Scottish capital using this type and other appropriate vehicles. Seen in Regent Road is 9, VLT242, which carries MacTours red and cream livery. *Billy Nicol*

950-983   Volvo Olympian YN2RC16Z4   Alexander RH   B51/30D   1994

950	C	L950MSC	959	C	L959MSC	968	C	L968MSC	976	C	L976MSC
951	C	L951MSC	960	C	L960MSC	969	C	L969MSC	977	C	L977MSC
952	C	L952MSC	961	C	L961MSC	970	r	L970MSC	978	C	L978MSC
953	C	L953MSC	962	C	L962MSC	971	C	L971MSC	979	C	L979MSC
954	C	L954MSC	963	C	L963MSC	972	C	L972MSC	980	C	L980MSC
955	C	L955MSC	964	C	L964MSC	973	C	L973MSC	981	C	L981MSC
956	C	L956MSC	965	C	L965MSC	974	C	L974MSC	982	C	L982MSC
957	C	L957MSC	966	C	L966MSC	975	C	L975MSC	983	C	L983MSC
958	C	L958MSC	967	C	L967MSC						

Special event buses:

595	C	JSX595T	Leyland Atlantean AN68A/1R	Alexander AL	B45/30D	1979
665	C	ASC665B	Leyland Titan PD3/6	Alexander E	B41/29F	1964
667	C	GSC667X	Leyland Olympian ONTL11/1R	Alexander RH	B47/28D	1982
777	C	C777SFS	Leyland Olympian ONTL11/2R	Eastern Coach Works	B51/33D	1985
801	C	ESF801C	Leyland Atlantean PDR1/1	Alexander A	B43/31F	1966

Previous registrations:

803DYE	10CLT, EDS221A	JSJ748	VLT80
858DYE	858DYE, WLT727	LST873	CEO952, TRN662A
28231(GBG)	J3660(GBJ)	WLT371	WLT371, EDS281A
JSJ746	VLT90	YSL334	J5567(GBJ), 7493(GBG), 12523(GBG)
JSJ747	VLT84		

Depot codes: C Central; E Edinburgh Tours; L Longstone; M Marine; T MacTours; ER/TR winter storage; u reserve.
On order: 75 Volvo B7TL with Wrightbus Gemini bodywork.

M-LINE

M-Line International Coaches Ltd, The Coach House, Riverbank, Alloa, FK10 1NT

Reg	Chassis	Body	Layout	Year	History
MDX540	Volvo B10M-56	Plaxton Viewmaster IV	C53F	1982	Philip, Dunfermline, 1996
EKA156Y	MCW Metrobus DR102/29	Alexander RH	B43/33F	1982	Classic, Annfield Plain, 2005
OFS676Y	Leyland Olympian ONTL11/2R	Eastern Coach Works	B50/31D	1982	Lothian Buses, 2000
MTU118Y	Leyland Olympian ONLXB/1R	Eastern Coach Works	B45/32F	1983	Arriva Fox County, 2002
AEF229Y	Leyland Olympian ONLXB/1R	Eastern Coach Works	B45/32F	1983	UK North, Manchester, 2003
FUM473Y	Leyland Olympian ONLXB/1R	Eastern Coach Works	B45/32F	1983	?, 2005
VRN830Y	Leyland Olympian ONLXB/1R	Eastern Coach Works	B45/32F	1983	Burnley & Pendle, 2003
B21TVU	Dennis Dominator DDA1003	Northern Counties	B43/32F	1984	Stagecoach, 2005
B22TVU	Dennis Dominator DDA1003	Northern Counties	B43/32F	1984	Stagecoach, 2005
B30TVU	Dennis Dominator DDA1003	Northern Counties	B43/32F	1984	Stagecoach, 2005
B908TVR	Dennis Dominator DDA1003	Northern Counties	B43/32F	1984	Stagecoach, 2004
NIL3416	Volvo B10M-61	Van Hool Alizée	C51F	1984	Mason, Bo'ness, 2005
E307EVW	Scania N112DRB	Alexander RH	B47/31F	1988	Black Prince, Morley, 2005
E89VWA	Neoplan Skyliner N122/3	Neoplan	C57/20CT	1988	Mason. Bo'ness, 2004
XIL6561	Volvo B10M-60	Jonckheere	C51F	1990	Clarkson, Barrow, 2005
Y804GDV	Volvo B10M-62	Caetano Enigma	C53F	2001	Bus Eireann, 2005
FE51RFJ	Iveco EuroRider 391E.12.35	Beulas Stergo ε	C51FT	2001	Mason, Bo'ness, 2005
SH03XBE	Ford Transit	Ford	M14	2003	

Previous registrations:

E89VWA	E89VWA, IJI336, PNR723	SJI8112	E515KNV
MDX540	LYM178X, USU644, NSC801X	XIL6561	G145MNH, UCE636
NIL3416	B298YSZ, YBK159	Y904GDV	?

Five Olympians are used by M-Line for school contracts, including former Lothian Buses OFS676Y, which retains its centre door. Recent arrivals for these services are Dennis Dominators supplied new to Greater Manchester Buses. *Phillip Stephenson*

McCOLL'S COACHES

McColl's Coaches Ltd, Ballagan Garage, Stirling Road, Balloch, G87 8RT

NEO832R	Leyland National 11351A/1R (Volvo)		B49F	1977	Lothian Buses, 2004
FTN702W	Leyland National NL116L11/1R		B49F	1981	Go-Ahead Northern, 2004
ROX644Y	MCW Metrobus DR102/27	MCW	B43/30F	1982	Travel West Midlands, 2005
CBZ9062	Volvo B10M-61	Van Hool Alizée	C49FT	1982	Taylor, Widnes, 2002
PIW6962	DAF MB200	Jonckheere Jubilee	C49FT	1984	Britton, Artigarvan, 2003
A686UOE	MCW Metrobus DR102/27	MCW	B43/30F	1984	Travel West Midlands, 2002
A694UOE	MCW Metrobus DR102/27	MCW	B43/30F	1984	Travel West Midlands, 2003
A703UOE	MCW Metrobus DR102/27	MCW	B43/30F	1984	Travel West Midlands, 2002
A766WVP	MCW Metrobus DR102/27	MCW	B43/30F	1984	Travel West Midlands, 2003
A768WVP	MCW Metrobus DR102/27	MCW	B43/30F	1984	Travel West Midlands, 2003
A114WVP	MCW Metrobus GR133/1	MCW	B43/30F	1984	Travel West Midlands, 2003
B774AOC	MCW Metrobus DR102/27	MCW	B43/30F	1984	Travel West Midlands, 2003
B777AOC	MCW Metrobus DR102/27	MCW	B43/30F	1984	Travel West Midlands, 2002
B852OSB	Dennis Dorchester SDA810	Plaxton Paramount 3500	C55F	1985	Highland Council, 2005
B810AOP	MCW Metrobus DR102/27	MCW	B43/30F	1985	Travel West Midlands, 2003
B820AOP	MCW Metrobus DR102/27	MCW	B43/30F	1985	Travel West Midlands, 2002
B825AOP	MCW Metrobus DR102/27	MCW	B43/30F	1985	Travel West Midlands, 2003
B826AOP	MCW Metrobus DR102/27	MCW	B43/30F	1985	Travel West Midlands, 2003
B848AOP	MCW Metrobus DR102/27	MCW	B43/30F	1985	Travel West Midlands, 2003
B852AOP	MCW Metrobus DR102/27	MCW	B43/30F	1985	Travel West Midlands, 2003
B853AOP	MCW Metrobus DR102/27	MCW	B43/30F	1985	Travel West Midlands, 2005
B858AOP	MCW Metrobus DR102/27	MCW	B43/30F	1985	Travel West Midlands, 2003
B864DOM	MCW Metrobus DR102/27	MCW	B43/30F	1985	Travel West Midlands, 2003
B867DOM	MCW Metrobus DR102/27	MCW	B43/30F	1985	Travel West Midlands, 2003
B884DOM	MCW Metrobus DR102/27	MCW	B43/30F	1985	Travel West Midlands, 2002
D935NDA	MCW Metrobus DR102/59	MCW	B43/30F	1986	Travel West Midlands, 2003
D947NDA	MCW Metrobus DR102/59	MCW	B43/30F	1986	Travel West Midlands, 2003
D954NDA	MCW Metrobus DR102/59	MCW	B43/30F	1986	Travel West Midlands, 2003
E987VUK	MCW Metrobus DR102/64	MCW	B43/30F	1988	Travel West Midlands, 2003
G118KUB	Mercedes-Benz 811D	Optare StarRider	B26F	1989	Scotways, Glasgow, 2003
G262TSL	Mercedes-Benz 709D	Alexander Sprint	B23F	1990	Stagecoach Western, 2003
G285TSL	Mercedes-Benz 709D	Alexander Sprint	B23F	1990	Stagecoach Western Buses, 2001

Although twenty years old, many of the Metrobuses acquired from West Midlands Travel have recently been refurbished. Now carrying an all-white paint scheme, A114WVP is seen heading out of Paisley to take up a school duty. *Bob Downham*

One of two Leyland Nationals that remain with McColls is FTN702W, seen here in Helensburgh while heading for Clydebank. *Murdoch Currie*

G756SRB	Scania N113CRB	Alexander PS	B51F	1990	City of Nottingham, 2005
K104OGB	Ford Transit	Advanced	M16	1992	Blythswood, Glasgow, 2002
L388BGA	Mercedes-Benz 709D	Eurocoach	B23F	1994	Avondale, Greenock, 2001
TXI4242	Volvo B12MT	Jonckheere Mistral 70	C44FT	1996	Bebb, Llantwit Fardre, 2000
MUD490	Volvo B10M-62	Jonckheere Mistral 50	C53F	1997	
P221EJW	Mercedes-Benz 811D	Marshall C16	B27F	1997	Travel West Midlands, 2003
P223EJW	Mercedes-Benz 811D	Marshall C16	B27F	1997	Travel West Midlands, 2003
P224EJW	Mercedes-Benz 811D	Marshall C16	B27F	1997	Travel West Midlands, 2003
P232EJW	Mercedes-Benz 811D	Marshall C16	B27F	1997	Travel West Midlands, 2005
P255RUM	Mercedes-Benz Vario 0810	Plaxton Beaver 2	B27F	1997	Travel West Midlands, 2005
P256RUM	Mercedes-Benz Vario 0810	Plaxton Beaver 2	B27F	1997	Travel West Midlands, 2005
P257RUM	Mercedes-Benz Vario 0810	Plaxton Beaver 2	B27F	1997	Travel West Midlands, 2005
P259RUM	Mercedes-Benz Vario 0810	Plaxton Beaver 2	B27F	1997	Travel West Midlands, 2005
W514PSF	Mercedes-Benz Vario 0814	Plaxton Beaver 2	BC31F	2000	
SF04RHJ	TransBus Dart 10.1m	TransBus Pointer	N34F	2004	
SF04RHK	TransBus Dart 10.1m	TransBus Pointer	N34F	2004	
SF04RHU	TransBus Dart 10.1m	TransBus Pointer	N34F	2004	

Previous registrations:

B852OSB	B409DSB, VLT204, B979EGG, VLT206		NEO832R	NEO832R, YXI3751
CBZ9062	STT603X		PIW6962	A374UNH
L388BGA	94D2017		TXI4242	P23TTX
MUD490	R952RCH			

Depots: Stirling Road, Balloch and Dalquhurn Ins Est, Renton, Alexandria

McDADE'S TRAVEL

McDade Travel Ltd, John Henry Road, Bothwell Park Ind Est, Uddingston, G71 7EJ

Reg	Chassis	Body	Type	Year	History
LDC84P	Daimler Fleetline CRG6LX	Northern Counties	B43/31F	1976	Lumley, Speke, 1989
PAU195R	Daimler Fleetline CRG6LX	Northern Counties	B47/33F	1976	P&O Lloyd, Bagillt, 1995
WDA680T	Leyland Fleetline FE30AGR	Park Royal	B43/33F	1979	Stuarts, Dukinfield, 1997
VEF151Y	Leyland Fleetline FE30AGR	Northern Counties	B43/31F	1982	Stagecoach Transit, 1999
YAJ154Y	Leyland Fleetline FE30AGR	Northern Counties	B43/31F	1982	Stagecoach Transit, 1999
CWR505Y	Leyland Olympian ONLXB/1R	Eastern Coach Works	B45/32F	1982	Rennie, Dunfermline, 2005
SIL1075	Leyland Olympian ONLXB/1R	Eastern Coach Works	B45/32F	1982	Stephenson, Rochford, 2003
AEF228Y	Leyland Olympian ONLXB/1R	Eastern Coach Works	B45/32F	1983	UK North, Manchester, 2003
OSN852Y	Volvo-Ailsa B55-10	Northern Counties	B48/36F	1983	Irvine, Law, 2002
OSN857Y	Volvo-Ailsa B55-10	Northern Counties	B48/36F	1983	Irvine, Law, 2002
2396FH	DAF MB200	Van Hool Alizée	C48FT	1983	Adkins, Upper Boddington, 1997
B811YTC	Leyland Tiger TRCTL11/3LZ	Wadham Stringer Vanguard	BC68F	1985	Woottens, Chesham, 2003
SIL7566	Volvo B10M-62	Van Hool Alizée	C53F	1985	Skills, Nottingham, 2005
JBZ4910	DAF MB200	Caetano Algarve	C49FT	1986	Go West, King's Lynn, 1997
E359NEG	Volvo B10M-61	Plaxton Paramount 3500 III	C53DL	1988	Patterson, Birmingham, 2001
G872SKE	Peugeot-Talbert Pullman	Talbot	B22F	1989	Ashton, Port Glasgow, 1997
PIL7835	Volvo B10M-60	Caetano Algarve II	C49FT	1993	Smith, Ashington, 2002
SIL1075	Volvo B10M-62	Jonckheere Deauville 45	C46FT	1995	Excalibur, Nunhead, 2003
N469SPA	Mercedes-Benz 709D	Alexander Sprint	B27FL	1995	Arriva Southern Counties, 2003
N839LGA	Mercedes-Benz 709D	Wadham Stringer Wessex II	B16FL	1995	
N840LGA	Mercedes-Benz 709D	Wadham Stringer Wessex II	B16FL	1995	
N841LGA	Mercedes-Benz 709D	Wadham Stringer Wessex II	B16FL	1995	
N843LGA	Mercedes-Benz 709D	Wadham Stringer Wessex II	B16FL	1995	
N78LGD	Mercedes-Benz 709D	Wadham Stringer Wessex II	B16FL	1995	
N79LGD	Mercedes-Benz 709D	Wadham Stringer Wessex II	B16FL	1995	
N81LGD	Mercedes-Benz 709D	Wadham Stringer Wessex II	B16FL	1995	
N638LGG	Mercedes-Benz 709D	Wadham Stringer Wessex II	B16FL	1995	
N639LGG	Mercedes-Benz 709D	Wadham Stringer Wessex II	B16FL	1995	
N640LGG	Mercedes-Benz 709D	Wadham Stringer Wessex II	B16FL	1995	
N642LGG	Mercedes-Benz 709D	Wadham Stringer Wessex II	B16FL	1995	
N965LHS	Mercedes-Benz 709D	Wadham Stringer Wessex II	B16FL	1995	
N966LHS	Mercedes-Benz 709D	Wadham Stringer Wessex II	B16FL	1995	
YJ04KWJ	Optare Solo M850	Optare	N29F	2004	
BU51AYL	Mercedes-Benz Sprinter 614	Crest	C24FL	2001	
BU51AYM	Mercedes-Benz Sprinter 614	Excel	M16L	2001	
MX54PJU	Mercedes-Benz Sprinter 616CDi	Univ	BC22F	2004	
SF55BKA	Mercedes-Benz Vario 0814	Plaxton Beaver 2	BC29FL	2005	

Previous registrations:

2396FH	FHJ84Y		SIL1075	M623ORJ
B811YTC	37KC52		SIL7566	M435ECS, KSK953
JBZ4910	C465PAH		TSO29X	TSO29X, SIL1075
PIL7835	K595VBC			

McDade's Travel operates a mix of double-deck buses for school contracts, coaches and minibuses fitted with access for wheelchairs for special needs services. Fleet colours are shown on Jonckheere Deauville M623ORJ, seen in Blackpool in September 2005.
Bob Downham

MacEWAN'S COACH SERVICES

J N MacEwan, Johnfield, Amisfield Town, Dumfries, DG1 3LS

Reg	Chassis	Body	Seating	Year	History
GFM882	Bristol L6A	Eastern Coach Works	B35F	1948	Allisons, Dunfermline, 1990
571BWT	AEC Reliance 2MU3RA	Duple	C41F	1962	preservation, 2002
MFR41P	Leyland Leopard PSU4C/2R	Alexander AY	B45F	1976	Stevensons, 1996
MFR125P	Leyland Leopard PSU4C/2R	Alexander AYS	B45F	1976	Stevensons, 1996
MFR126P	Leyland Leopard PSU4C/2R	Alexander AYS	B45F	1976	Edinburgh Transport, 1996
TSJ77S	Leyland Leopard PSU3D/4R	Alexander AY	B53F	1978	Wealden, Five Oak Green, 1997
AHN391T	Leyland Leopard PSU3E/4R	Plaxton Supreme III Express	C53F	1979	Reynolds, Watford, 1995
PGA833V	Leyland Leopard PSU3F/4R	Alexander AT	BC49F	1980	Enterprise & Silver Dawn, 1996
WDS323V	Leyland Leopard PSU3F/4R	Alexander AT	BC49F	1980	Fairline Coaches, Glasgow, 2002
GSO89V	Leyland Leopard PSU3E/4R	Alexander AYS	B49F	1980	Stonehouse Coaches, 2001
LFJ848W	Bristol LHS6L	Eastern Coach Works	B35F	1980	Moffat & Williamson, Gauldry, 1994
LFJ849W	Bristol LHS6L	Eastern Coach Works	B35F	1980	Golden Coaches, Llandow, 1995
LFJ850W	Bristol LHS6L	Eastern Coach Works	B35F	1980	Moffat & Williamson, Gauldry, 1994
NTT573W	Bedford VAS5	Plaxton PJK	C29F	1981	Gospel, Hucknall, 1997
SYJ961X	Bedford YMQ	Plaxton Supreme V	C45F	1982	Bysiau G&M, Lampeter, 2004
A375BDL	Bedford YNT	Duple Laser	C53F	1983	Glover, Ashbourne, 2004
ROX641Y	MCW Metrobus DR102/27	MCW	B43/30F	1983	Travel West Midlands, 2005
A752WVP	MCW Metrobus DR102/27	MCW	B43/30F	1984	Travel West Midlands, 2005
B885DOM	MCW Metrobus DR102/27	MCW	B43/30F	1985	Travel West Midlands, 2005
B500MPY	Leyland-DAB Tiger Cub	DAB / Eastern Coach Works	B46F	1985	Jim Stones, Leigh, 2002
CLZ1838	DAF MB200	Plaxton Paramount	C53F	1985	Thornewill, Derby, 1999
F747TRE	Freight Rover Sherpa	PMT Bursley	BC16F	1989	Rainbow, Dunkerswell, 1990
LIL8970	Volvo B10M-60	Plaxton Paramount 3500 III	C53F	1989	Dodds, Ashington, 2002
J947MFT	Dennis Dart 9.8m	Wright HandyBus	B40F	1992	Dart Buses, Paisley, 2001
K766DAO	Volvo B10M-55	Alexander PS	B49F	1993	Stagecoach, 2005
K788DAO	Volvo B10M-55	Alexander PS	B49F	1993	Stagecoach, 2005
K851RBB	Optare MetroRider MR07	Optare	BC28F	1993	Arriva North East, 2002
K852RBB	Optare MetroRider MR07	Optare	BC28F	1993	Arriva North East, 2002
K477SSM	Mercedes-Benz 709D	Dormobile Routemaker	B29F	1993	
K478SSM	Mercedes-Benz 709D	Dormobile Routemaker	B29F	1993	
M291OUR	Iveco 480.10.21	Wadham Stringer Vanguard II	B47F	1994	Travel de Courcey, Coventry, 2003
M804ASM	Mercedes-Benz 814D	Autobus Classique 2	C33F	1995	
M578BSM	Mercedes-Benz 709D	Alexander Sprint	B29F	1995	
N209FSM	Mercedes-Benz 709D	Plaxton Beaver	B29F	1996	
N210FSM	Mercedes-Benz 709D	Plaxton Beaver	B29F	1996	
N114DWE	Mercedes-Benz 709D	Plaxton Beaver	BC24FL	1996	Stonehouse Coaches, 2005

Two Scania L94s with Wrightbus Axcess Floline bodies operatre for MacEwans. Preparing to depart from Edinburgh on a return journey home to Dumfries is YP02AAZ. *Mark Doggett*

MacEwan's now operates one of the Scania N113DRBs with East Lancs bodywork purchased from stock. These were the last of the normal-height Scania chassis and all feature high-back seating. T399OWA is seen arriving in Dumfries on an afternoon service from Edinburgh. *Bob Downham*

N317DAG	LDV Convoy	Jubilee	M16	1996	NE Lincolnshire CC, 2004
N706FSM	Ford Transit VE6	Crystals Challenger	B20F	1996	
N117FSM	Scania K113CRB	Van Hool Alizée HE	C49FT	1996	
P630FTV	Volvo B10M-62	Jonckheere Mistral 50	C53FT	1997	Delta, Stockton, 2003
P385XGG	Mercedes-Benz 814D	Plaxton Beaver	B27F	1997	Dickson, Erskine, 2003
R102HUA	Optare MetroRider MR11	Optare	B28F	1997	Henderson Travel, Hamilton, 2004
P536PUB	Mercedes-Benz Vario 0810	Autobus Classique	B31F	1997	Stonehouse Coaches, 2001
R26USM	Mercedes-Benz Vario 0810	Plaxton Beaver	B33F	1998	
S48KSM	Ford Transit VE6	Crystals Challenger	B20F	1998	
T399OWA	Scania N113DRB	East Lancs	BC47/31F	1999	Dunn-Line, Nottingham, 2003
T131ARE	Mercedes-Benz Sprinter 614	Minibus Options	BC14F	1999	D&G, Kingstone, 2005
T136ARE	Mercedes-Benz Sprinter 614	Minibus Options	BC14F	1999	D&G, Kingstone, 2005
V829GGA	Mercedes-Benz Vario 0814	Plaxton Beaver 2	B31F	1999	Collinson, Stonehouse, 2003
W137OSM	Mercedes-Benz Vario 0810	Plaxton Beaver 2	B31F	2000	
W158WTA	Scania L94IB	Irizar Intercentury 12.32	C49FT	2000	Bus Eireann, 2004
Y11EAD	MAN 18.310	Caetano Montana	C53F	2002	Alec Head, Lutton, 2004
Y111EAD	MAN 18.310	Caetano Montana	C53F	2002	Alec Head, Lutton, 2004
Y138TVV	Mercedes-Benz Sprinter 311CDi AVC		M16	2000	Bowe, Salford, 203
KU02YUL	Mercedes-Benz Vario 0814	Plaxton Beaver 2	B31F	2002	Stonehouse Coaches, 2003
KU02YUN	Mercedes-Benz Vario 0814	Plaxton Beaver 2	B31F	2002	Stonehouse Coaches, 2003
YP02AAY	Scania L94UB	Wrightbus Axcess Floline	N43F	2002	Rapsons, 2003
YP02AAZ	Scania L94UB	Wrightbus Axcess Floline	N43F	2002	Rapsons, 2003
SK52UTT	TransBus Dart SLF 8.8m	TransBus Pointer MPD	N27F	2002	HAD, Shotts, 2004
SK52UTU	TransBus Dart SLF 8.8m	TransBus Pointer MPD	N27F	2002	HAD, Shotts, 2004
SA03YDB	Mercedes-Benz Vario 0814	TransBus Beaver 2	BC33F	2003	
SJ04MFV	Mercedes-Benz Vario 0814	TransBus Beaver 2	BC33F	2004	

Previous registrations:

B332LSA	B332LSA, TSV722	M291OUR	M291OUR, MJI2368
B500MPY	B500MPY, B1BUS	W158WTA	?
CLZ1838	B627JRC	WDS323V	GSO84V
LIL8970	F325DCL		

Depots: Johnfield, Amisfield Town; Catherinefield Ind Est, Heathall, Dumfries and Ae Bridge, Parkgate, Dumfries

McGILL'S

McGill's Bus Service Ltd, 99 Earnhill Road, Larkfield Ind Est, Greenock, PA16 0AQ

L733MWW	Optare MetroRider MR15	Optare	B31F	1993	On loan from Arriva NE & Scotland
L736PUA	Optare MetroRider MR15	Optare	B31F	1993	On loan from Arriva NE & Scotland
N501KCD	Dennis Dart 9.8m	Marshall C37	B40F	1995	Brighton & Hove, 2004
N502KCD	Dennis Dart 9.8m	Marshall C37	B40F	1995	Brighton & Hove, 2004
N503KCD	Dennis Dart 9.8m	Marshall C37	B40F	1995	Brighton & Hove, 2004
N504KCD	Dennis Dart 9.8m	Marshall C37	B40F	1995	Brighton & Hove, 2004
N506KCD	Dennis Dart 9.8m	Marshall C37	B40F	1995	Brighton & Hove, 2004
N508KCD	Dennis Dart 9.8m	Marshall C37	B40F	1995	Brighton & Hove, 2004
N511KCD	Dennis Dart 9.8m	Marshall C37	B40F	1995	Brighton & Hove, 2004
N513KCD	Dennis Dart 9.8m	Marshall C37	B40F	1995	Brighton & Hove, 2004
N516KCD	Dennis Dart 9.8m	Marshall C37	B40F	1995	Brighton & Hove, 2004
N517KCD	Dennis Dart 9.8m	Marshall C37	B40F	1995	Brighton & Hove, 2004
N518KCD	Dennis Dart 9.8m	Marshall C37	B40F	1995	Brighton & Hove, 2004
N519KCD	Dennis Dart 9.8m	Marshall C37	B40F	1995	Brighton & Hove, 2004
N752LUS	Mercedes-Benz 709D	UVG CitiStar	B29F	1996	On loan from Arriva NE & Scotland
N228MUS	Mercedes-Benz 709D	Marshall C19	B29F	1996	On loan from Arriva NE & Scotland
N254PGD	Mercedes-Benz 709D	Marshall C19	B29F	1996	On loan from Arriva NE & Scotland
N256PGD	Mercedes-Benz 709D	Marshall C19	B29F	1996	On loan from Arriva NE & Scotland
N258PGD	Mercedes-Benz 709D	Marshall C19	B29F	1996	On loan from Arriva NE & Scotland
P526UGA	Mercedes-Benz 711D	Marshall C19	B29F	1996	On loan from Arriva NE & Scotland
V110ESF	Mercedes-Benz 711D	Marshall C19	B29F	1996	Clan Coaches, Kyle, 2004

In 2003 McGill's placed eight SB120s in service on Greenock Town services. DAF Bus became part of VDL in 2001, and the VDL name applied from 2003, although as can be seen in this view of SP53JXK, these are probably the last to display DAF Bus names. *Bob Downham*

One of many Marshall-bodied Darts now working for McGills is N517KCD seen in Greenock. More than half the batch of Brighton & Hove's type is now in service in the company's white, blue and gold livery. *Bob Downham*

T52JBA	Dennis Dart SLF	Plaxton Pointer 2	N39F	1998	Harte, Greenock, 2005
T53JBA	Dennis Dart SLF	Plaxton Pointer 2	N36F	1999	Harte, Greenock, 2005
T517EUB	Volvo B10M-62	Plaxton Première 350	C49FT	1999	WA Shearings, 2005
T520EUB	Volvo B10M-62	Plaxton Première 350	C49FT	1999	WA Shearings, 2005
T401JSL	Volvo B10M-62	Van Hool T9 Alizée	C53F	1999	Docherty Midland, Auchterarder, '06
W600SOU	Volvo B10M-62	Van Hool T9 Alizée	C53F	2000	Southern Coaches, Barrhead, 2006
SA52EXD	Dennis Dart SLF 10.1m	Plaxton Pointer 2	N37F	2002	
SG52XMO	Dennis Dart SLF 10.1m	Plaxton Pointer 2	N37F	2002	
SG52XMP	Dennis Dart SLF 10.1m	Plaxton Pointer 2	N37F	2002	
SG52XMR	Dennis Dart SLF 10.1m	Plaxton Pointer 2	N37F	2002	
SG52XMK	Dennis Dart SLF 10.1m	Plaxton Pointer 2	N37F	2002	
SG52XML	Dennis Dart SLF 10.1m	Plaxton Pointer 2	N37F	2002	
SP53KGE	VDL Bus SB120	Wrightbus Cadet 2	N39F	2003	
SP53KGG	VDL Bus SB120	Wrightbus Cadet 2	N39F	2003	
SP53KGJ	VDL Bus SB120	Wrightbus Cadet 2	N39F	2003	
SP53KGK	VDL Bus SB120	Wrightbus Cadet 2	N39F	2003	
SP53JXJ	VDL Bus SB120	Wrightbus Cadet 2	N39F	2003	
SP53JXK	VDL Bus SB120	Wrightbus Cadet 2	N39F	2003	
SP53JXL	VDL Bus SB120	Wrightbus Cadet 2	N39F	2003	
SP53JXM	VDL Bus SB120	Wrightbus Cadet 2	N39F	2003	
SN05HDA	ADL Dart 10.1m	ADL Pointer	N37F	2005	
SN05HCX	ADL Dart 10.1m	ADL Pointer	N37F	2005	
SN05HCY	ADL Dart 10.1m	ADL Pointer	N37F	2005	
SN05HCZ	ADL Dart 10.1m	ADL Pointer	N37F	2005	

Previous registrations:

T52JBA	T52JBA, IIB1618		T401JSL	T77JDS
T53JBA	T53JBA, IIB7633			

MACKIE'S

J L Mackie, 40 Glasshouse Loan, Alloa, FK10 1PE

DLS520Y	Ward Dalesman C12-640	Plaxton Paramount 3200	C53F	1983	
B496MFS	Leyland Tiger TRCTL11/3R	Plaxton Paramount 3500	C53F	1985	
F774JYS	Volvo B10M-55	Duple 300	B53F	1989	Hutchinson, Overtown, 2003
G864RNC	Volvo B10M-60	Van Hool Alizée	C53F	1989	Glen Coaches, Port Glasgow, 2001
J498VMS	Ward Dalesman C12-640	Willowbrook Crusader	C53F	1991	
J612XHL	Dennis Dart 9m	Plaxton Pointer	B34F	1991	London Central, 2000
K433OKH	Dennis Dart 9m	Plaxton Pointer	B34F	1992	Metroline, Harrow, 2002
PFG362	Volvo B10M-60	Van Hool Alizée	C53F	1992	Hutchison, Overtown, 1997
YBL526	Volvo B10M-60	Van Hool Alizée	C53F	1992	Hutchison, Overtown, 1997
K620DMS	Volvo B10M-60	Van Hool Alizée	C53F	1993	
490SVX	Volvo B10M-62	Jonckheere Deauville 45	C53F	1995	Docherty's, Auchterarder, 2004
SL8417	Volvo B10M-62	Jonckheere Deauville 45	C55F	1994	Allisons, Dunfermline, 1998
YFS438	Volvo B10M-62	Van Hool Alizée HE	C53F	1994	
N620DMS	Volvo B10M-62	Jonckheere Deauville 45	C53F	1996	Long, Salsburgh, 1999
SL8207	Volvo B10M-62	Caetano Algarve 2	C49FT	1998	Whytes, Newmachar, 2002
XSV270	Volvo B10M-62	Caetano Algarve 2	C49FT	1998	Whytes, Newmachar, 2002
FJ04ETY	Volvo B7RLE	Wrightbus Eclipse Urban	N44F	2004	Volvo demonstrator, 2004
LS04OSL	Volvo B7RLE	Wrightbus Eclipse Urban	N44F	2004	
SL04OLS	Volvo B7RLE	Wrightbus Eclipse Urban	N44F	2004	
SL54OSL	Volvo B7RLE	Wrightbus Eclipse Urban	N44F	2005	
SN05EOV	VDL Bova Futura FHD12.340	VDL Bova	C57F	2005	
SN05EOW	VDL Bova Futura FHD12.340	VDL Bova	C57F	2005	

Special event vehicles:

SL9483	Bedford SB5	Duple	C41F	1964	Halley, Sauchie, 1984

Previous registrations:

490SVX	M407XSL, 7067ED, JD3164	SL8207	R549MSS
B496MFS	SL8207	SL8417	L6LJA
DLS520Y	CLS709Y, YFS438, WSC785Y, SL8417	XSV270	R551MSS
G864RNC	G864RNC, BAZ7914	YBL526	J20BUS
N620DMS	N936RBC, RJI1890, TSV956,	YFS438	L424LLS, SL8852
PFG362	J19BUS		

The timeless style of the Van Hool Alizée is seen on Mackie's of Alloa YBL526 pictured while awaiting time at Ibrox Park. *Philip Stephenson*

McKENDRY

AAW McKendry, 100 Straiton Road, Straiton, Loanhead, EH20 9NP

OFV21X	Leyland Olympian ONLXB/1R	Eastern Coach Works	B45/32F	1982	Burnley & Pendle, 2003
HIL8441	Volvo B10M-61	Jonckheere Jubilee	C51FT	1987	Charlie's, Edinburgh, 2002
MIL6548	Volvo B10M-61	Plaxton Paramount 3500 III	C51FT	1987	St Andrew's Executive, 2002
LCZ1890	Scania K93CRB	Van Hool Alizée	C53F	1990	Appleby Coaches, 2001
J34MKB	Volvo B10M-60	Plaxton Excalibur	C49FT	1992	Merseybus, Liverpool, 1999
K544RJX	DAF SB3000DKV585	Van Hool Alizée	C49FT	1993	North Kent Express, 2000
BUI5220	Scania K113CRB	Van Hool Alizée HE	C49FT	1994	Linburg, Catley, 2004
M358LFX	Scania K113CRB	Van Hool Alizée HE	C46FT	1995	Dorset Travel Services, 2002
N554SJF	Volvo B10M-62	Jonckheere Mistral 50	C51FT	1996	Clarkes of London, 2005
P316UHS	Dennis Javelin 12m	Marcopolo Explorer	BC69F	1997	Ashall, Manchester, 2005
P337CEP	Volvo B10M-62	Caetano Algarve 2	C48FT	1997	Diamond, Morriston, 2002
R83YVU	LDV Convoy	LDV	M16	1998	
R598EAB	Scania K113CRB	Van Hool Alizée	C57F	1998	Aston, Worcester, 2003
W272MKY	Scania K124IB	Irizar Century 12.32	C49FT	2001	
SW52FCF	Ford Transit	Ford	M16	2002	, 2004

Previous registrations:

BUI5220	L29ABB, 4672NT	MIL6548	E671CNS, AIA9000
HIL8441	E694NNH	R598EAB	R598EAB, RDU4
LCZ1890	G949WFE, UJV489, G649WFE		

Depot: Ramsay Colliery, Engine Road, Loanhead
Web: www.mckendrycoaches.co.uk

Blackpool Illuminations are still an attraction for many residents in the central Scottish towns. Seen on a visit during the 2005 season is McKendry's HIL8441, a Volvo B10M with Jonckheere bodywork. *Bob Downham*

McKINDLESS GROUP

McKindless Bus Co Ltd; M McKindless, 101 Main Street Newmains, ML2 9BG

NML600E	AEC Routemaster 2R2RH	Park Royal	B40/32R	1967	London United, 2004
EJR122W	Leyland Atlantean AN68A/2R	Alexander AL	B49/37F	1980	Wilson, Stonehaven, 2002
GYE469W	MCW Metrobus DR101/14	MCW	B43/28D	1981	Arriva London, 2005
GYE530W	MCW Metrobus DR101/14	MCW	B43/28D	1981	Arriva London, 2005
GYE544W	MCW Metrobus DR101/14	MCW	B43/28D	1981	Arriva London, 2001
KYV652X	MCW Metrobus DR101/14	MCW	B43/28D	1981	Arriva London, 2005
KYV661X	MCW Metrobus DR101/14	MCW	B43/28D	1981	Arriva London, 2005
KYV682X	MCW Metrobus DR101/14	MCW	B43/28D	1981	Arriva London, 2005
KYV702X	MCW Metrobus DR101/14	MCW	B43/28D	1981	Arriva London, 2001
KYV714X	MCW Metrobus DR101/14	MCW	B43/28D	1981	Arriva London, 2005
KYV721X	MCW Metrobus DR101/14	MCW	B43/28D	1981	Arriva London, 2005
KYV732X	MCW Metrobus DR101/14	MCW	B43/28D	1981	Arriva London, 2005
KYV752X	MCW Metrobus DR101/14	MCW	B43/28D	1982	Arriva London, 2005
KYV765X	MCW Metrobus DR101/14	MCW	B43/28D	1982	Arriva London, 2005
KYV772X	MCW Metrobus DR101/14	MCW	B43/28D	1982	Arriva London, 2005
KYV773X	MCW Metrobus DR101/14	MCW	B43/28D	1982	Arriva London, 2005
KYV798X	MCW Metrobus DR101/14	MCW	B43/28D	1982	Arriva London, 2005
KSU317	Volvo B10M-61	Plaxton Viewmaster IV	C49FT	1982	Phillips, Rushington, 2003
POG524Y	MCW Metrobus DR102/27	MCW	B43/30F	1983	Thorpe, Perivale, 2005
A729YFS	Leyland Olympian ONTL11/2R	Eastern Coach Works	B51/32D	1983	Lothian Buses, 2001
A730YFS	Leyland Olympian ONTL11/2R	Eastern Coach Works	B51/32D	1983	Lothian Buses, 2001
A731YFS	Leyland Olympian ONTL11/2R	Eastern Coach Works	B51/32D	1983	Lothian Buses, 2001
A700UOE	MCW Metrobus DR102/27	MCW	B43/30F	1983	Thorpe, Perivale, 2005
A939SUL	MCW Metrobus DR101/16	MCW	B43/28D	1983	Arriva London, 2001
A777RUG	Volvo B10M-61	Plaxton Paramount 3500	C53F	1984	Go-Well, Motherwell, 2005
A980SYF	MCW Metrobus DR101/17	MCW	B43/31F	1984	London United, 2000
A990SYF	MCW Metrobus DR101/17	MCW	B43/31F	1984	London United, 2000
B109WUL	MCW Metrobus DR101/17	MCW	B43/28D	1984	Arriva London, 2001
B121WUL	MCW Metrobus DR101/17	MCW	B43/28D	1984	Arriva London, 2005
B129WUL	MCW Metrobus DR101/17	MCW	B43/28D	1984	Arriva London, 2005
B131WUL	MCW Metrobus DR101/17	MCW	B43/28D	1984	Arriva London, 2001
B133WUL	MCW Metrobus DR101/17	MCW	B43/28D	1984	Arriva London, 2001
B154WUL	MCW Metrobus DR101/17	MCW	B43/28D	1985	Arriva London, 2001
B159WUL	MCW Metrobus DR101/17	MCW	B43/28D	1985	Metroline, Harrow, 2001
B164WUL	MCW Metrobus DR101/17	MCW	B43/28D	1985	Arriva London, 2001
B281WUL	MCW Metrobus DR101/17	MCW	B43/31F	1985	Arriva London, 2001
B291WUL	MCW Metrobus DR101/17	MCW	B43/28D	1985	Arriva London, 2001
B293WUL	MCW Metrobus DR101/17	MCW	B43/28D	1985	Arriva London, 2001
B296WUL	MCW Metrobus DR101/17	MCW	B43/31F	1985	Arriva London, 2001
B297WUL	MCW Metrobus DR101/17	MCW	B43/31F	1985	Arriva London, 2001

One of the many Metrobuses now operated by McKindless is GYE544W, seen in Stockwell Street in Glasgow while heading for Hamilton. The McKindless Metrobuses were latterly used by Arriva London and have arrived over the last several years. *Billy Nicol*

The last remaining Lynx with McKindless is G44VME, seen here in Motherwell while operating route 56 from Shotts to Motherwell. New to the Maidstone municipal operation it later joined Arriva. *Phillip Stephenson*

B298WUL	MCW Metrobus DR101/17	MCW	B43/28D	1985	Arriva London, 2001
B299WUL	MCW Metrobus DR101/17	MCW	B43/28D	1985	Arriva London, 2001
B303WUL	MCW Metrobus DR101/17	MCW	B43/28D	1985	Arriva London, 2001
B875DOM	MCW Metrobus DR102/27	MCW	B43/28D	1985	Thorpe, Perivale, 2005
C406BUV	MCW Metrobus DR101/17	MCW	B43/28D	1985	Arriva London, 2005
TJI3143	Volvo B10M-61	Plaxton Paramount 3500	C53F	1987	Galloway, Harthill, 2001
RIL9868	DAF SB220	Optare Delta	B49F	1989	Stanwell Buses, 2000
G44VME	Leyland Lynx LX2R11C15Z4	Leyland Lynx	B49F	1989	Hall, Kennoway, 2000
G935MYG	DAF SB220	Optare Delta	B49F	1990	City Solutions, Walsall, 2004
SIL1816	DAF SB3000	Van Hool Alizée	C51FT	1990	Hogg, Glasgow, 2000
G512VYE	Dennis Dart 8.5m	Duple Dartline	B21F	1990	London United, 2004
JDZ2401	Dennis Dart 9m	Wright HandyBus	B36F	1990	Stanwell Buses, 2000
JDZ2403	Dennis Dart 9m	Wright HandyBus	B36F	1990	Stanwell Buses, 2000
JDZ2404	Dennis Dart 9m	Wright HandyBus	B36F	1990	Stanwell Buses, 2000
JDZ2410	Dennis Dart 9m	Wright HandyBus	B36F	1990	Stanwell Buses, 2000
JDZ2411	Dennis Dart 9m	Wright HandyBus	B36F	1990	Stanwell Buses, 2000
JDZ2412	Dennis Dart 9m	Wright HandyBus	B36F	1990	Stanwell Buses, 2000
VIL4589	MAN 11.190	Optare Vecta	B41F	1991	Dunn-Line, Nottingham, 2003
H102THE	Dennis Dart 8.5m	Reeve Burgess Pointer	B28F	1991	London United, 2000
H103THE	Dennis Dart 8.5m	Reeve Burgess Pointer	B28F	1991	London United, 2000
H105THE	Dennis Dart 8.5m	Reeve Burgess Pointer	B28F	1991	London United, 2000
H106THE	Dennis Dart 8.5m	Reeve Burgess Pointer	B28F	1991	London United, 2000
H107THE	Dennis Dart 8.5m	Reeve Burgess Pointer	B28F	1991	London United, 2000
H108THE	Dennis Dart 8.5m	Reeve Burgess Pointer	B28F	1991	London United, 2000
H109THE	Dennis Dart 8.5m	Reeve Burgess Pointer	B28F	1991	London United, 2000
H110THE	Dennis Dart 8.5m	Reeve Burgess Pointer	B28F	1991	London United, 2000
H114THE	Dennis Dart 8.5m	Reeve Burgess Pointer	B28F	1991	London United, 2000
H611TKU	Dennis Dart 8.5m	Reeve Burgess Pointer	B28F	1991	London United, 2000
J118HGF	Dennis Dart 9m	Reeve Burgess Pointer	B35F	1991	Metrobus, Crawley, 2004
J122HGF	Dennis Dart 9m	Reeve Burgess Pointer	B35F	1991	Metrobus, Crawley, 2004
J224HGY	Dennis Dart 9m	Plaxton Pointer	B35F	1991	Metrobus, Crawley, 2004
J156GAT	Dennis Dart 8.5m	Plaxton Pointer	B28F	1991	London United, 2000
J158GAT	Dennis Dart 8.5m	Plaxton Pointer	B24F	1991	London United, 2000
J609XHL	Dennis Dart 9m	Plaxton Pointer	B34F	1991	Wilson, Gourock, 2004
J611XHL	Dennis Dart 9m	Plaxton Pointer	B34F	1991	Wilson, Gourock, 2004

The Scottish Bus Handbook

Trent was a keen operator of the Optare Delta which was built on a DAF SB220 chassis. Time has shown this chassis to have been particularly successful with many operators retaining the model for longer than planned. Seen in McKindless' colours is K338FAL. *Phillip Stephenson*

J613XHL	Dennis Dart 9m	Plaxton Pointer	B34F	1991	Wilson, Gourock, 2004
J605KCU	Dennis Dart 9.8m	Wright HandyBus	B40F	1991	Go-Ahead Northern, 2001
J608KCU	Dennis Dart 9.8m	Wright HandyBus	B40F	1991	Go-Ahead Northern, 2001
J614KCU	Dennis Dart 9.8m	Wright HandyBus	B40F	1991	Go-Ahead Northern, 2001
YIB4337	DAF SB220	Optare Delta	B49F	1991	Trent Buses, 2001
YIB9500	DAF SB220	Optare Delta	B49F	1991	Trent Buses, 2001
J319BVO	DAF SB220	Optare Delta	B49F	1991	Trent Buses, 2001
J324BVO	DAF SB220	Optare Delta	B49F	1992	Trent Buses, 2001
J325BVO	DAF SB220	Optare Delta	B49F	1992	Trent Buses, 2001
J626KCU	Dennis Dart 9.8m	Wright HandyBus	B40F	1992	Go-Ahead Northern, 2001
J629KCU	Dennis Dart 9.8m	Wright HandyBus	B40F	1992	Go-Ahead Northern, 2001
J634KCU	Dennis Dart 9.8m	Wright HandyBus	B40F	1992	Go-Ahead Northern, 2001
J945MFT	Dennis Dart 9.8m	Wright HandyBus	B40F	1992	Go-Ahead Northern, 2001
J946MFT	Dennis Dart 9.8m	Wright HandyBus	B40F	1992	Go-Ahead Northern, 2001
YIB7073	Volvo B10M-60	Plaxton Première 350	C48FT	1992	Wray's, Harrogate, 2001
YIB5488	Volvo B10M-60	Plaxton Première 350	C48FT	1992	Bakers, Biddulph, 2001
YIB4528	Volvo B10M-60	Plaxton Première 350	C48FT	1992	Titterington, Blencowe, 2004
K327FAL	DAF SB220	Optare Delta	B48F	1992	Trent Buses, 2002
K328FAL	DAF SB220	Optare Delta	B48F	1992	Trent Buses, 2002
K330FAL	DAF SB220	Optare Delta	B48F	1992	Trent Buses, 2002
K336FAL	DAF SB220	Optare Delta	B48F	1992	Trent Buses, 2002
K337FAL	DAF SB220	Optare Delta	B48F	1992	Trent Buses, 2002
K338FAL	DAF SB220	Optare Delta	B48F	1992	Trent Buses, 2002
K339FAL	DAF SB220	Optare Delta	B48F	1992	Trent Buses, 2002
K342FAL	DAF SB220	Optare Delta	B48F	1992	Trent Buses, 2002
K621PGO	Dennis Dart 9m	Plaxton Pointer	B35F	1992	Metrobus, Crawley, 2004
K622PGO	Dennis Dart 9m	Plaxton Pointer	B35F	1992	Metrobus, Crawley, 2004
K889BRW	Volvo B10M-60	Plaxton Première 320	C53F	1992	Alec Head, Lutton, 2005
52GYY	Volvo B10M-60	Plaxton Première 320	C53F	1993	Alec Head, Lutton, 2005
JIL5144	Volvo B10M-60	Plaxton Première 320	C50F	1993	Helms, Bootle, 2003
JIL5145	Volvo B10M-60	Plaxton Première 320	C53F	1993	ABC Coachlines, Bootle, 2003
K97SAG	Dennis Dart 9m	Plaxton Pointer	B28F	1993	London United, 2002
K98SAG	Dennis Dart 9m	Plaxton Pointer	B28F	1993	London United, 2002
K102SAG	Dennis Dart 9m	Plaxton Pointer	B28F	1993	London United, 2002
K103SAG	Dennis Dart 9m	Plaxton Pointer	B28F	1993	London United, 2002
K104SAG	Dennis Dart 9m	Plaxton Pointer	B28F	1993	London United, 2002

An integral low-floor product from Optare was the Excel of which just under of six hundred were built. WIL9228 was one new to Stanwell Buses in London before entering service in Scotland. It is seen operating route 41 that connects Hamilton with Lanark. *Bob Downham*

K105SAG	Dennis Dart 9m	Plaxton Pointer	B28F	1993	London United, 2002
K106SAG	Dennis Dart 9m	Plaxton Pointer	B28F	1993	London United, 2002
K210SAG	Dennis Dart 9m	Plaxton Pointer	B28F	1993	London United, 2002
K21CDW	Dennis Dart 8.5m	Wright HandyBus	B29F	1993	Stagecoach, 2004
K983CBO	Dennis Dart 8.5m	Wright HandyBus	B29F	1993	2Travel, Swansea, 2004
K991CBO	Dennis Dart 8.5m	Wright HandyBus	B29F	1993	Stagecoach, 2004
K994CBO	Dennis Dart 8.5m	Wright HandyBus	B29F	1993	Stagecoach, 2004
L101SDY	Dennis Javelin 11m	Plaxton Première Interurban	BC47F	1994	Blazefield, Harrogate, 2005
L141BFV	Dennis Javelin 11m	Plaxton Première Interurban	BC47F	1994	Blazefield, Harrogate, 2005
L151WAG	Dennis Dart 9m	Plaxton Pointer	BC34F	1993	Arriva London, 2005
L152WAG	Dennis Dart 9m	Plaxton Pointer	B34F	1993	Arriva London, 2005
L154WAG	Dennis Dart 9m	Plaxton Pointer	B34F	1993	Arriva London, 2005
L155WAG	Dennis Dart 9m	Plaxton Pointer	B34F	1993	Arriva London, 2005
L156WAG	Dennis Dart 9m	Plaxton Pointer	B34F	1993	Arriva London, 2005
L157WAG	Dennis Dart 9m	Plaxton Pointer	B34F	1993	Arriva London, 2005
L158WAG	Dennis Dart 9m	Plaxton Pointer	B34F	1993	Arriva London, 2005
L160XRH	Dennis Dart 9m	Plaxton Pointer	B28F	1994	London United, 2004
L162XRH	Dennis Dart 9m	Plaxton Pointer	B28F	1994	London United, 2004
L164XRH	Dennis Dart 9m	Plaxton Pointer	B28F	1994	London United, 2004
L165YAT	Dennis Dart 9m	Plaxton Pointer	B28F	1994	London United, 2004
L166YAT	Dennis Dart 9m	Plaxton Pointer	B28F	1994	London United, 2004
L167YAT	Dennis Dart 9m	Plaxton Pointer	B28F	1994	London United, 2004
L168YAT	Dennis Dart 9m	Plaxton Pointer	B28F	1994	London United, 2004
L169YAT	Dennis Dart 9m	Plaxton Pointer	B28F	1994	London United, 2004
M507ALP	MAN 11.190	Optare Vecta	B42F	1995	Metroline, Harrow, 2002
WIL9201	Dennis Lance 11m	Berkhof 2000	N33D	1995	Menzies, Heathrow, 2003
WIL9202	Dennis Lance 11m	Berkhof 2000	N33D	1995	Menzies, Heathrow, 2003
WIL9203	Dennis Lance 11m	Berkhof 2000	N33D	1995	Menzies, Heathrow, 2003
WIL9204	Dennis Lance 11m	Berkhof 2000	N33D	1995	Menzies, Heathrow, 2003
WIL9205	Dennis Lance 11m	Berkhof 2000	N33D	1995	Menzies, Heathrow, 2003
WIL9206	Dennis Lance 11m	Berkhof 2000	N33D	1995	Menzies, Heathrow, 2003
WIL9207	Dennis Lance 11m	Berkhof 2000	N33D	1995	Menzies, Heathrow, 2003
WIL9208	Dennis Lance 11m	Berkhof 2000	N33D	1995	Menzies, Heathrow, 2003
WIL9218	Dennis Lance 11m	Berkhof 2000	N33D	1995	Menzies, Heathrow, 2003
WIL9220	Dennis Lance 11m	Berkhof 2000	N33D	1995	Menzies, Heathrow, 2003
N22DTS	Volvo B10M-60	Plaxton Première 350	C44FT	1995	Dunn-Line, Nottingham, 2003
P422JDT	Dennis Javelin GX 12m	Plaxton Première 320	C49FT	1996	Aldershot Coaches, 2003

P718RYL	Dennis Dart SLF 10m	Plaxton Pointer 2	N36F	1996	Go-Ahead London, 2004
P721RYL	Dennis Dart SLF 10m	Plaxton Pointer 2	N36F	1996	Go-Ahead London, 2004
P723RYL	Dennis Dart SLF 10m	Plaxton Pointer 2	N36F	1996	Go-Ahead London, 2004
P730RYL	Dennis Dart SLF 10m	Plaxton Pointer 2	N36F	1996	Go-Ahead London, 2004
P336JND	Volvo B6LE	Alexander ALX200	N36F	1997	Burnley & Pendle, 2005
P340JND	Volvo B6LE	Alexander ALX200	N36F	1997	Burnley & Pendle, 2005
P349JND	Volvo B6LE	Alexander ALX200	N36F	1997	Burnley & Pendle, 2005
WIL9223	Optare Excel L1000	Optare	N36F	1997	London United, 2003
WIL9224	Optare Excel L1000	Optare	N36F	1997	London United, 2003
WIL9225	Optare Excel L1000	Optare	N36F	1997	London United, 2003
WIL9226	Optare Excel L1000	Optare	N36F	1997	London United, 2003
WIL9227	Optare Excel L1000	Optare	N36F	1997	London United, 2003
WIL9228	Optare Excel L1000	Optare	N36F	1997	London United, 2003
YBZ1462	Optare Excel L1150	Optare	N45F	1997	East Yorkshire, 2003
YBZ6469	Optare Excel L1150	Optare	N45F	1997	East Yorkshire, 2003
YBZ7531	Optare Excel L1150	Optare	N45F	1997	East Yorkshire, 2003
R114RLY	Dennis Dart SLF 10m	Plaxton Pointer 2	N36F	1997	Metroline, Harrow, 2006
R116RLY	Dennis Dart SLF 10m	Plaxton Pointer 2	N36F	1997	Metroline, Harrow, 2006
R178VLA	Dennis Dart SLF 10m	Plaxton Pointer 2	N36F	1997	Metroline, Harrow, 2006
R183VLA	Dennis Dart SLF 10m	Plaxton Pointer 2	N36F	1997	Metroline, Harrow, 2006
R86JAR	Dennis Dart SLF 10m	Marshall Capital	N37F	1997	Isle of Man Transport, 2004
R681OYS	Dennis Dart SLF 10m	Marshall Capital	N37F	1997	Isle of Man Transport, 2004
R682OYS	Dennis Dart SLF 10m	Marshall Capital	N37F	1997	Isle of Man Transport, 2004
R691OYS	Dennis Dart SLF 10m	Marshall Capital	N37F	1997	Isle of Man Transport, 2004
R692OYS	Dennis Dart SLF 10m	Marshall Capital	N37F	1997	Isle of Man Transport, 2004
R694OYS	Dennis Dart SLF 10m	Marshall Capital	N37F	1997	Isle of Man Transport, 2004
R797OYS	Dennis Dart SLF 10m	Marshall Capital	N37F	1997	Isle of Man Transport, 2004
R798OYS	Dennis Dart SLF 10m	Marshall Capital	N37F	1997	Isle of Man Transport, 2004
R809OYS	Dennis Dart SLF 10m	Marshall Capital	N37F	1997	Isle of Man Transport, 2004
R817OYS	Dennis Dart SLF 10m	Marshall Capital	N37F	1997	Isle of Man Transport, 2004

Special event vehicle:

YDL318	Bristol Lodekka FS6G	Eastern Coach Works	B33/27R	1962	preservation, 2002

Previous registrations:

52GYY	L53GNY
A777RUG	VDV534, A997RUB, 6857WA
H611TKU	H611TKU, WLT931
J122HGF	CMN9H
J118HGF	CMN10H
JIL5144	K847HUM, K88ABC
JIL5145	K848HUM, K888ABC
K21CDW	NDZ3133
K210SAG	K210SAG, ALM2B
K621PGO	CMN106L
K622PGO	CMN107L
K889BRW	K889BRW, 7195BY
K983CBO	NDZ3138
K991CBO	NDZ3147
K994CBO	NDZ3155
K996CBO	NDZ3144
R86JAR	DMN17R
R681OYS	DMN23R
R682OYS	DMN
R691OYS	DMN21R
R692OYS	DMN36R
R694OYS	DMN35R
R797OYS	DMN34R
R798OYS	DMN33R
R809OYS	DMN28R
R817OYS	DMN29R
RIL9868	F551SHX, A5LBR

SIL1816	G990KJX
TJI3143	E919EAY
VIL4589	H846UUA
WIL9201	M192UAN
WIL9202	M957SDP
WIL9203	M189UAN
WIL9204	M198UAN
WIL9205	M182UAN
WIL9206	M181UAN
WIL9207	M188UAN
WIL9208	M967SDP
WIL9218	M958SDP
WIL9220	M187UAN
WIL9223	P151BUG
WIL9224	P152BUG
WIL9225	P153BUG
WIL9226	P154BUG
WIL9227	P156BUG
WIL9228	P157BUG
YBZ1462	R278EKH
YBZ6469	R279EKH
YBZ7531	R281EKH
YIB4337	J307BVO
YIB4528	J711CWT
YIB5488	J720CWT, 7820WA, J720EUA
YIB7073	J717CWT, FBZ4780
YIB9500	J308BVO

Depots: Main Street, Newmains; Quay Road North, Rutherglen; Nuneaton Street, Glasgow and McKindless Business Park, Wishaw.
Web: www.mckindlessgroup.co.uk

MARBILL

Marbill Coach Services Ltd, Mains Garage, Mains Road, Beith, KA15 2AP

CSL612V	Ailsa B55-10 Mk II	Alexander RV	B44/34F	1980	Tayside, 1997
OFS671Y	Leyland Olympian ONTL11/2R	Eastern Coach Works	B50/36F	1983	Lothian Buses, 2001
OFS672Y	Leyland Olympian ONTL11/2R	Eastern Coach Works	B50/36F	1983	Lothian Buses, 2001
OFS677Y	Leyland Olympian ONTL11/2R	Eastern Coach Works	B50/36F	1983	Lothian Buses, 2001
OFS685Y	Leyland Olympian ONTL11/2R	Eastern Coach Works	B50/36F	1983	Lothian Buses, 2001
OFS686Y	Leyland Olympian ONTL11/2R	Eastern Coach Works	B50/36F	1983	Lothian Buses, 2001
OFS687Y	Leyland Olympian ONTL11/2R	Eastern Coach Works	B50/36F	1983	Lothian Buses, 2001
OFS688Y	Leyland Olympian ONTL11/2R	Eastern Coach Works	B50/36F	1983	Lothian Buses, 2001
OFS692Y	Leyland Olympian ONTL11/2R	Eastern Coach Works	B50/36F	1983	Lothian Buses, 2001
OFS694Y	Leyland Olympian ONTL11/2R	Eastern Coach Works	B50/36F	1983	Lothian Buses, 2001
OFS695Y	Leyland Olympian ONTL11/2R	Eastern Coach Works	B50/36F	1983	Lothian Buses, 2001
OFS696Y	Leyland Olympian ONTL11/2R	Eastern Coach Works	B50/31D	1983	Lothian Buses, 2001
OFS697Y	Leyland Olympian ONTL11/2R	Eastern Coach Works	B50/31D	1983	Lothian Buses, 2001
OFS699Y	Leyland Olympian ONTL11/2R	Eastern Coach Works	B50/31D	1983	Lothian Buses, 2001
OFS700Y	Leyland Olympian ONTL11/2R	Eastern Coach Works	B50/31D	1983	Lothian Buses, 2001
A715YFS	Leyland Olympian ONTL11/2R	Eastern Coach Works	B51/35F	1983	Lothian Buses, 2001
A716YFS	Leyland Olympian ONTL11/2R	Eastern Coach Works	B51/35F	1983	Lothian Buses, 2001
A718YFS	Leyland Olympian ONTL11/2R	Eastern Coach Works	B50/36F	1983	Lothian Buses, 2001
A722YFS	Leyland Olympian ONTL11/2R	Eastern Coach Works	B50/36F	1983	Lothian Buses, 2001
A723YFS	Leyland Olympian ONTL11/2R	Eastern Coach Works	B51/35F	1983	Lothian Buses, 2001
A724YFS	Leyland Olympian ONTL11/2R	Eastern Coach Works	B51/35F	1983	Lothian Buses, 2001
A732YFS	Leyland Olympian ONTL11/2R	Eastern Coach Works	B51/36F	1983	Lothian Buses, 2001
A733YFS	Leyland Olympian ONTL11/2R	Eastern Coach Works	B52/36F	1983	Lothian Buses, 2001
A735YFS	Leyland Olympian ONTL11/2R	Eastern Coach Works	B51/35F	1983	Lothian Buses, 2001
B762GSC	Leyland Olympian ONTL11/2R	Eastern Coach Works	B51/35F	1986	Lothian Buses, 2003
B763GSC	Leyland Olympian ONTL11/2R	Eastern Coach Works	B51/35F	1986	Lothian Buses, 2003
C775SFS	Leyland Olympian ONTL11/2R	Eastern Coach Works	B51/35F	1986	Lothian Buses, 2001
E915NAC	Leyland Tiger TRBTL11/2RP	Plaxton Derwent II	BC69F	1988	Travel West Midlands, 1998
E916NAC	Leyland Tiger TRBTL11/2RP	Plaxton Derwent II	BC69F	1988	Travel West Midlands, 1998
E917NAC	Leyland Tiger TRBTL11/2RP	Plaxton Derwent II	BC69F	1988	Travel West Midlands, 1998
E918NAC	Leyland Tiger TRBTL11/2RP	Plaxton Derwent II	BC69F	1988	Travel West Midlands, 1998
F335RWK	Leyland Tiger TRBTL11/2RP	Plaxton Derwent II	BC69F	1988	Travel West Midlands, 1998
F336RWK	Leyland Tiger TRBTL11/2RP	Plaxton Derwent II	BC69F	1988	Travel West Midlands, 1998
F337RWK	Leyland Tiger TRBTL11/2RP	Plaxton Derwent II	BC69F	1988	Travel West Midlands, 1998
F338RWK	Leyland Tiger TRBTL11/2RP	Plaxton Derwent II	BC69F	1988	Travel West Midlands, 1998
H149SKU	Volvo B10M-55	Plaxton Derwent II	BC69F	1990	Travel West Midlands, 2000
H150SKU	Volvo B10M-55	Plaxton Derwent II	BC69F	1990	Travel West Midlands, 2000
H151SKU	Volvo B10M-55	Plaxton Derwent II	BC69F	1990	Travel West Midlands, 2000
H152SKU	Volvo B10M-55	Plaxton Derwent II	BC69F	1990	Travel West Midlands, 2000
H153SKU	Volvo B10M-55	Plaxton Derwent II	BC69F	1990	Travel West Midlands, 2000

Marbill operates several Leyland Olympians that were latterly used by Lothian, their principal use now being on an extensive network of school services. Many have had their central doors disabled, similar to OFS687Y, seen here. *Billy Nicol*

H154SKU	Volvo B10M-55	Plaxton Derwent II	BC69F	1990	Travel West Midlands, 2000
H155SKU	Volvo B10M-55	Plaxton Derwent II	BC69F	1990	Travel West Midlands, 2000
H156SKU	Volvo B10M-55	Plaxton Derwent II	BC69F	1990	Travel West Midlands, 2000
H157SKU	Volvo B10M-55	Plaxton Derwent II	BC69F	1990	Travel West Midlands, 2000
H158SKU	Volvo B10M-55	Plaxton Derwent II	BC69F	1990	Travel West Midlands, 2000
H159SKU	Volvo B10M-55	Plaxton Derwent II	BC69F	1990	Travel West Midlands, 2000
K667NGB	Mercedes-Benz 609D	Made-to-Measure	C24F	1992	
GJI926	Mercedes-Benz 811D	Dormobile Routemaker	B33F	1994	
GJI627	Volvo B9M	Van Hool Alizée HE	C40FT	1995	Cygnus, Paisley, 2004
2154K	Volvo B9M	Van Hool Alizée HE	C38F	1995	
XRY278	Volvo B10M-62	Van Hool Alizée HE	C55F	1995	
N993KUS	Mercedes-Benz 410D	Deansgate	M16L	1995	
BJI6863	Volvo B10M-62	Van Hool Alizée HE	C49FT	1998	
Y989TSD	Volvo B10M-62	Van Hool T9 Alizée	C49FT	2001	
Y991TSD	Volvo B10M-62	Van Hool T9 Alizée	C49FT	2001	
SA02RYZ	Volvo B12M	Van Hool T9 Alizée	C57F	2002	
SA02RZB	Volvo B12M	Van Hool T9 Alizée	C55F	2002	
SA02UHW	Mercedes-Benz Vario 0814	Plaxton Cheetah	C33F	2002	
SJ03AOR	Volvo B12B	Van Hool T9 Alicron	C49FT	2003	
SF03AWC	Volvo B12B	Van Hool T9 Alicron	C49FT	2003	
SF03ABV	Volvo B7R	Plaxton Profile 70	BC70F	2003	
SF03ABX	Volvo B7R	Plaxton Profile 70	BC70F	2003	
SJ03BZL	Volvo B7R	Plaxton Profile 70	BC70F	2003	
SF04LLD	Mercedes-Benz 0815DT	Sitcar Beluga	C33F	2004	
SF54HFT	Volvo B7R	Plaxton Profile 70	BC70F	2004	
SF54HFU	Volvo B7R	Plaxton Profile 70	BC70F	2004	
SF05KWM	Volvo B7R	Plaxton Profile 70	BC70F	2005	
SF05KWN	Volvo B7R	Plaxton Profile 70	BC70F	2005	
SF05KWO	Volvo B7R	Plaxton Profile 70	BC70F	2005	

Previous registrations:

2154K	XSV270, M821YSC		GJI627	M75FGG, 2367AT
BJI6863	R591USJ		HJI565	LSK503, M831HNS, M5END
GJI926	L857WDS		XRY278	M760GGE

Delivered to Marbill in 2003 were three Plaxton Profile vehicles. These Profile 70 variants feature 3+2 high-back seating and are intended for school contracts. One of these, SF03ABX, is shown. *Billy Nicol*

MAYNES

Maynes Coaches Ltd, Cluny Garage, 4 March Road West, Buckie, AB56 4BU

YSU990	Volvo B10M-62	Caetano Algarve 2	C51F	1997	Whytes, Newmachar, 2001
R555GSM	Volvo B10M-62	Caetano Algarve 2	C53F	1998	
M17YNE	Mercedes-Benz Vito 108D	Mercedes-Benz	M8	2000	
MM03GSM	Mercedes-Benz Vario 0814	Plaxton Cheetah	C33F	2003	
CM03GSM	Volvo B7R	Plaxton Prima	C57F	2003	
HM03GSM	Volvo B7R	Plaxton Prima	C57F	2003	
RM03GSM	Volvo B7R	Plaxton Prima	C57F	2003	
KM03GSM	Volvo B12M	Van Hool T9 Alizée	C53F	2003	
7MCB	Mercedes-Benz Vario 0815	Sitcar Beluga	C27F	2004	
MM04GSM	Mercedes-Benz Vario 0814	Plaxton Cheetah	C33F	2004	
DM04GSM	VDL Bova Futura FHD12.340	VDL Bova	C49FT	2004	
GM04GSM	VDL Bova Futura FHD12.340	VDL Bova	C49FT	2004	
SM04GSM	VDL Bova Futura FHD12.340	VDL Bova	C49FT	2004	
KM04GSM	Volvo B12B	Van Hool T9 Alicron	C53F	2004	
MM54GSM	Mercedes-Benz Sprinter 614	Onyx	C24F	2005	
HM05GSM	Mercedes-Benz Sprinter 815	Sitcar Beluga	C33F	2005	
RM05GSM	Mercedes-Benz Sprinter 815	Sitcar Beluga	C33F	2005	
DM05GSM	Volvo B12B	Van Hool T9 Alicron	C53F	2005	
KM05GSM	Volvo B12B	Van Hool T9 Alicron	C53F	2005	
MM05GSM	Volvo B12B	Van Hool T9 Alicron	C53F	2005	
SM05GSM	MAN 18-310	Marcopolo Viaggio II 330	C57F	2005	
CM05GSM	MAN 18-310	Marcopolo Viaggio II 330	BC70F	2005	
SM06GSM	MAN 18-310	Marcopolo Viaggio II 330	BC70F	2006	
DM06GSM	Volvo B12B	Van Hool T9 Alicron	C49FT	2006	
GM06GSM	Volvo B12B	Van Hool T9 Alicron	C49FT	2006	
KM06GSM	Volvo B12B	Van Hool T9 Alicron	C49FT	2006	
MM06GSM	Volvo B12B	Van Hool T9 Alicron	C49FT	2006	

Special event vehicles:

KKN752	Bedford OB	Duple Vista	C29F	1948	Burton, Alfreton, 1997
PUF249M	Ford R1114	Duple Dominant	C49F	1974	Bluebird Buses, 1996

Previous registrations:

		MM54GSM	SF54CCA
KKN752	KSU362	YSU990	P684DRS

Web: www.maynes.co.uk

MILLPORT MOTORS

Millport Motors Ltd, 16 Bute Terrace, Millport, Isle of Cumbrae, KA28 0BA

GGE173T	Leyland National 10351A/1R		B41F	1979	Strathclyde, 1987
L910JRN	Dennis Dart 9m	East Lancs EL2000	B34F	1994	LocalLink, Bishop's Stortford, 2005
N804GRV	Dennis Dart 9.8m	UVG UrbanStar	B40F	1996	Wealden, Five Oak Green, 1997
P743HND	Dennis Dart SLF	Plaxton Pointer 2	N39F	1996	Pete's Travel, West Bromwich, 1999

Depot: Crawford Street, Millport

The Scottish Bus Handbook

Maynes of Buckie has built up an interesting collection of 'GSM' index marks since the introduction of the new system of marks in 2001. One of several Volvo B12Bs with Van Hool T9 Alicron bodywork is KM04GSM, seen here in Leyland while operating a tour for David Urquhart Travel. *Bob Downham*

The small operation of Millport Motors contains a UVG-bodied Dennis Dart, N804GRV. The bus is seen in Millport during the summer of 2005. *Murdoch Currie*

MOFFAT & WILLIAMSON

Moffat & Williamson Ltd, Main Road, Gauldry, Newport-on-Tay, DD6 8RQ

C771OCN	MCW Metrobus DR102/55	MCW	B46/31F	1986	Go-Ahead Northern, 2002
C778OCN	MCW Metrobus DR102/55	MCW	B46/31F	1986	Go-Ahead Northern, 2002
121ASV	Volvo B9M	Plaxton Paramount 3200 III	C38FT	1988	Berkeley, Paulton, 1999
J48SNY	Leyland Tiger TRCL10/3ARZM	Plaxton 321	BC70F	1991	Watts, Old Tupton, 2002
BSK790	Volvo B9M	Plaxton Paramount 3200 III	C44F	1992	Capital, West Drayton, 2000
L23WGA	MAN 11.190	Optare Vecta	B41F	1993	MacEwan, Amisfield Town, 2003
L106YGD	MAN 11.190	Optare Vecta	B41F	1994	MacEwan, Amisfield Town, 2003
L670PWT	MAN 11.190	Optare Vecta	B41F	1994	MacEwan, Amisfield Town, 2003
L82RHL	Dennis Javelin 12m	Wadham Stringer Vanguard II	BC70F	1994	MoD, 2003
WUH704	Dennis Javelin 12m	Wadham Stringer Vanguard II	BC70F	1994	MoD, 2003
M498XSP	Mercedes-Benz 709D	Mellor	B27F	1995	
M303YWE	Dennis Javelin 12m	Wadham Stringer Vanguard II	BC70F	1995	MoD, 2003
M304YWE	Dennis Javelin 12m	Wadham Stringer Vanguard II	BC70F	1995	MoD, 2003
M760ASL	Dennis Javelin 12m	Wadham Stringer Vanguard II	BC70F	1995	MoD, 2003
M783ASL	Dennis Javelin 12m	Wadham Stringer Vanguard II	BC70F	1995	MoD, 2003
M788ASL	Dennis Javelin 12m	Wadham Stringer Vanguard II	BC70F	1995	MoD, 2003
M796ASL	Dennis Javelin 12m	Wadham Stringer Vanguard II	BC70F	1995	MoD, 2003
M802ASL	Dennis Javelin 12m	Wadham Stringer Vanguard II	BC70F	1995	MoD, 2004
M808ASL	Dennis Javelin 12m	Wadham Stringer Vanguard II	BC70F	1995	MoD, 2004
M814ASL	Dennis Javelin 12m	Wadham Stringer Vanguard II	BC70F	1995	MoD, 2004
M823ASL	Dennis Javelin 12m	Wadham Stringer Vanguard II	BC70F	1995	MoD, 2004
N790EES	Dennis Javelin 12m	Wadham Stringer Vanguard II	BC70F	1995	MoD, 2004
N702FLN	MAN 11.190	Optare Vecta	B41F	1995	Metroline, Harrow, 2001
YBK159	Volvo B12T	Van Hool Astrobel	C53/14CT	1995	Bakers, Weston-super-Mare, 2001
N86FHL	Dennis Javelin 10m	Wadham Stringer Vanguard III	BC47F	1995	MoD, 2003
N87FHL	Dennis Javelin 10m	Wadham Stringer Vanguard II	BC57F	1995	MoD, 2003
FSU373	Volvo B10M-62	Van Hool Alizée HE	C49FT	1996	Amport & District, 2002
FSU374	Volvo B10M-62	Van Hool Alizée HE	C54F	1996	Tellings-Golden Miller, 2002
FSU375	Volvo B10M-62	Van Hool Alizée HE	C49FT	1996	Amport & District, 2002
122ASV	Volvo B10M-62	Plaxton Première 350	C57F	1996	Tellings-Golden Miiller, 2000
R166GNW	DAF SB3000	Ikarus Blue Danube	C53F	1997	Cropper, Kirkstall, 2005
BSK791	Mercedes-Benz Vario 0814	Plaxton Cheetah	C29F	1998	Elcock Reisen, Telford, 2003
FSU371	Volvo B10M-62	Plaxton Première 350	C53F	1998	
FSU394	Volvo B10M-62	Plaxton Excalibur	C49FT	1998	
FSU372	Volvo B10M-62	Plaxton Excalibur	C49FT	1998	
S718MGB	Mercedes-Benz Sprinter 412D	Onyx	M16	1998	
S2HMC	Volvo B7R	Plaxton Prima	C55F	1998	Stephenson, Tolthorpe, 2005
T645JWB	Dennis Javelin 12m	Plaxton Première 320	BC70F	1998	Myall, Bassingbourne, 2004
T675ASN	Volvo B10M-62	Plaxton Excalibur	C49FT	1999	

The German-built MAN chassis have attempted to break into the British market on several occasions in recent years, the Optare Vecta being one example. It was launched in 1991 with one hundred and thirty midibuses being built. L106YGB was new to Hutchinson's in 1994 and is now with Moffat & Williamson, seen here in Glenrothes.
Bob Downham

T676ASN	Volvo B10M-62	Plaxton Excalibur	C49FT	1999	
W877VGT	Volvo B10M-62	Plaxton Panther	C48FT	2000	Epsom Coaches, 2002
W878VGT	Volvo B10M-62	Plaxton Panther	C53FT	2000	Epsom Coaches, 2002
X2JPT	Volvo B7TL	East Lancs Vyking	N47/29F	2000	JPTravel, Middleton, 2004
Y396PSP	Volvo B10M-62	Plaxton Paragon	C57F	2001	
YK51ADZ	LDV Convoy	Crest	M16	2001	
YR02ZMO	Volvo B10M-62	Plaxton Paragon	C49FT	2002	
ST52GZN	Volvo B12M	Plaxton Panther	C53F	2003	Logan, Dunloy, 2005
YN03WXH	Volvo B10M-62	Plaxton Paragon	C49FT	2003	
SP53HDD	Mercedes-Benz Vario 0814	Plaxton Cheetah	C33F	2004	
YN04WTV	Volvo B10M-62	Plaxton Panther	C49FT	2004	
MX54KYG	Optare Solo M850	Optare	N31F	2004	
SP54AHX	Mercedes-Benz Vario 0814	Plaxton Beaver 2	B33F	2004	
YN54WCM	Volvo B7R	Plaxton Prima	C57F	2004	
SP54FML	Volvo B7R	Plaxton Profile 70	BC70F	2005	
SP54FMM	Volvo B7R	Plaxton Profile 70	BC70F	2005	
YK05CDE	Optare Solo M850	Optare	N31F	2005	
YK05CDF	Optare Solo M850	Optare	N31F	2005	
SP55EEF	Mercedes-Benz Vario 0814	Plaxton Cheetah	C33F	2005	
SP06EBJ	Mercedes-Benz Vario 0814	Plaxton Cheetah	C29F	2006	
MX06ACZ	Optare Solo M850	Optare	N27F	2006	
MX06ADO	Optare Solo M850	Optare	N27F	2006	
-06	Volvo B12M	Plaxton Panther	C53F	2006	

Previous registrations:

121ASV	E593UHS	M760ASL	94RN07
122ASV	N30GTA	M783ASL	EC48AA
BSK790	J331LLK	M788ASL	EC49AA
BSK791	R650XAW	M796ASL	EC47AA
FSU371	R153SSN	M802ASL	EC46AA
FSU372	R155SSN	M808ASL	00RN45
FSU374	N80TGM	M814ASL	EC50AA
FSU375	HSK648, N471PYS	M823ASL	00RN44
FSU393	M808ASL	N86FHL	ES15AA
FSU394	F154SSN	N87FHL	M964CGS
FSU395	M823ASL	N790EES	N634AYC
L82RHL	00RN38	WUH704	EC44AA
M303YWE	EC43AA	YBK159	M414VYD
M304YWE	EC51AA		

Depots: Boston Road, Glenrothes and Old Station Yard, St Fort, Wormit
Web: www.moffat-williamson.co.uk

Following the sale of many of its own buses the MoD policy is now to hire in coaches when required. Many Dennis Javelins and Volvo B10Ms have been sold. Wadham Stringer Vanguard II-bodywork, refurbished with 3+2 seating is now common across Britain and M796ASL is shown in Moffat & Williamson colours.
Bob Downham

MUNRO's of JEDBURGH

Munro's of Jedburgh Ltd, Oakvale Garage, Bongate, Jedburgh, TD8 6DU

Fleet	Reg	Chassis	Body	Seating	Year	Notes
	OBZ6976	DAF MB230	Van Hool Alizée	C51F	1990	Whippet, Bournemouth, 2000
	G931MYG	DAF SB220	Optare Delta	B49F	1990	London Westlink, 2000
	J500BCS	Mercedes-Benz 709D	Made to Measure	BC19F	1992	
494	J494NBD	Van hool T815	Van Hool Alizée	C55F	1992	
955	J955SBU	Dennis Dart 10.1m	Northern Counties Paladin	B37F	1992	Woodcock, Ferrybridge, 2002
972	J972OGV	DAF SB3000	Van Hool Alizée	C53F	1992	
235	K235AHG	DAF SB3000	Van Hool Alizée	C49FT	1992	Tyrer's, Nelson, 2005
515	K515RJX	DAF SB3000	Van Hool Alizée	C49FT	1992	Partner, Normanton, 2005
523	K523RJX	DAF SB3000	Van Hool Alizée	C49FT	1992	
546	K546RJX	DAF SB3000	Van Hool Alizée	C49FT	1992	
631	M631RCP	DAF SB3000	Van Hool Alizée	C51FT	1994	Wood, Barnsley, 2002
	M901NKS	Mercedes-Benz 814D	Plaxton Beaver	BC33F	1994	
432	T432EBD	Mercedes-Benz Vario 0814	Plaxton Beaver 2	B29F	1994	Western Isles Council, 2005
435	T435EBD	Mercedes-Benz Vario 0814	Plaxton Beaver 2	B29F	1994	Western Isles Council, 2005
794	T794TWX	DAF SB220	Ikarus Citibus 481	N43F	1999	
470	T549HNH	Dennis Dart SLF 8.8m	Plaxton Pointer MPD	N26F	1999	Armchair, London, 2002
463	X463UKS	Dennis Dart SLF 10.7m	Alexander ALX200	NC43F	2000	
464	X464UKS	Dennis Dart SLF 10.7m	Alexander ALX200	NC43F	2000	
465	X465UKS	Dennis Dart SLF 10.7m	Alexander ALX200	NC43F	2000	
466	X466UKS	Dennis Dart SLF 10.7m	Alexander ALX200	NC43F	2000	
688	Y668BKS	Mercedes-Benz Vario 0814	Autobus Nouvelle	C33F	2001	
D1	YN51HBF	LDV Convoy	Jaycas	M16	2001	
D2	YN51HCJ	LDV Convoy	Jaycas	M16	2001	
D3	YN51HCK	LDV Convoy	Jaycas	M16	2001	
468	SK51AYC	Dennis Dart SLF 8.8m	Plaxton Pointer MPD	N26F	2002	
469	SK51AYD	Dennis Dart SLF 8.8m	Plaxton Pointer MPD	N26F	2002	
C1	MK52UGJ	Mercedes-Benz Sprinter 614	Crest	BC20F	2002	
C2	MK52UHG	Mercedes-Benz Sprinter 614	Crest	BC20F	2002	
C3	MK52OKX	Mercedes-Benz Sprinter 614	Crest	BC20F	2002	
C4	MX03OBG	Mercedes-Benz Sprinter 614	Crest	BC20F	2003	
C5	MK03OCB	Mercedes-Benz Sprinter 614	Crest	BC20F	2003	
301	VU52UEA	Optare Solo M920	Optare	N33F	2002	
302	VU52UEB	Optare Solo M920	Optare	N33F	2002	
303	VU52UEC	Optare Solo M920	Optare	N33F	2002	
501	YR03UMR	Optare Excel L1180	Optare	N41F	2003	Optare demonstrator, 2004
502	YN53WZJ	Optare Excel L1180	Optare	N41F	2002	Optare demonstrator, 2004
503	VO53OVA	Optare Excel L1180	Optare	N41F	2004	
504	VO53OVB	Optare Excel L1180	Optare	N41F	2004	
401	MX55WDS	Plaxton Primo 7.9m	Plaxton	N27F	2006	
402	MX55WDT	Plaxton Primo 7.9m	Plaxton	N27F	2006	
	AE06HBP	MAN 14.220	MCV Evolution	N43	2006	

Previous registrations:

ESK834	D572MVR	OBZ6976	G235SEC
ESK847	E375HSH		

Munro's operates four Optare Excel buses which comprise the final pair to enter service and a pair of demonstrators. Seen in Edinburgh, 504, YO53OVB was pictured arriving on an afternoon journey from Jedburgh on route 29.
Bob Downham

NICOLL

M W Nicoll Hirers (Laurencekirk) Ltd, Laurencekirk Business Park, Aberdeen Road, Laurencekirk, Aberdeen, AB30 1EY

FBV912Y	Volvo B10M-61	Duple Laser	C49FT	1983	Cotter, Morecambe, 1986
B220WEU	Leyland Tiger TRCTL11/3RH	Duple Laser 2	C51F	1984	Butler, Kirkby-in-Ashfield, 2004
A5MWN	Volvo B10M-61	Van Hool Alizée	C53F	1986	Pride of the Clyde, Glasgow, 1998
A12MWN	Volvo B10M-61	Van Hool Alizée	C53F	1986	Pride of the Clyde, Glasgow, 1998
E173FRA	Volvo B10M-61	Van Hool Alizée	C53F	1987	Sharpe, Scarrington, 2005
E996FRA	Volvo B10M-61	Van Hool Alizée	C53F	1987	Sharpe, Scarrington, 2005
A15MWN	Volvo B10M-61	Van Hool Alizée	C53F	1987	Park's of Hamilton, 1992
A19MWN	Volvo B10M-60	Van Hool Alizée	C53F	1989	Walker, Neilston, 2000
H242TSS	Mercedes-Benz 410D	Devon Conversions	M15	1990	
A17MWN	Setra S210 H	Setra	C32FT	1990	Turner & Rugg, Edinburgh, 1991
A20MWN	Volvo B10M-60	Van Hool Alizée	C53F	1991	Shearings, 1998
L155UEM	Mercedes-Benz 709D	Alexander Sprint	B25F	1993	Greenbus, Darlington, 2005
L156UEM	Mercedes-Benz 709D	Alexander Sprint	B25F	1993	Greenbus, Darlington, 2005
M102WKA	Mercedes-Benz 709D	Alexander Sprint	BC23F	1994	Greenbus, Darlington, 2005
M104WKA	Mercedes-Benz 709D	Alexander Sprint	BC23F	1994	Greenbus, Darlington, 2005
M158WWM	Mercedes-Benz 709D	Alexander Sprint	B25F	1994	Greenbus, Darlington, 2005
P127FRS	Toyota Coaster HZB50R	Caetano Optimo IV	C21F	1997	
S137JSO	Mercedes-Benz Vario 0814	Plaxton Beaver 2	B25F	1998	
N10CLL	Mercedes-Benz 310D	Whitacre	M13	1998	
V501FSF	Mercedes-Benz Vario 0614	Onyx	BC24F	2000	
V502FSF	Mercedes-Benz Vario 0614	Onyx	BC24F	2000	
W462RSX	Mercedes-Benz Sprinter 413cdi	Onyx	M16	2000	
W463RSX	Mercedes-Benz Vario 0814	Plaxton Beaver 2	BC33F	2000	
W464RSX	Mercedes-Benz Vario 0614	Onyx	BC24F	2000	
X675USX	Mercedes-Benz Vario 0814	Plaxton Cheetah	C33F	2001	
SN51WYC	Mercedes-Benz Vario 0614	Onyx	BC24F	2002	
YL02FKZ	Optare Solo M920	Optare	N31F	2002	
SK02VCG	Mercedes-Benz Vario 0814	KVC	BC24F	2002	
SK02VCL	Mercedes-Benz Vario 0814	KVC	BC24F	2002	
SK52OCO	Mercedes-Benz Vario 0814	Plaxton Cheetah	C33F	2002	
SL52AFZ	Mercedes-Benz Sprinter 413cdi	KVC	M16	2002	
SL52AKN	Mercedes-Benz Sprinter 413cdi	KVC	M16	2002	
N33CLL	Mercedes-Benz Sprinter 413cdi	KVC	M16	2004	
N1CLL	VDL Bova Futura FHD12.340	Bova	C55F	2005	
N2CLL	VDL Bova FHD 12.340	Bova Futura	C55F	2005	
N3CLL	Volvo B12M	Van Hool T9 Alizée	C53F	2006	

Previous registrations:
E173FRA	E311OPR, JBZ551, UXI476	E996FRA	E310OPR, UXI551, BHZ122

Munro's operates five Dennis Darts with Alexander ALX200 bodywork that feature high-back seating. Seen in Galashiels while operating a morning service to Kelso is 64, X464UKS.
Bob Downham

PARK'S of HAMILTON

Parks of Hamilton (Coach Hirers) Ltd, 14 Bothwell Road, Hamilton, ML3 0AY
Trathens Travel Services, 18 Walkham Business Park, Burrington Way, Plymouth, PL5 3LS

LSK870	Volvo B10MT	Van Hool Astrobel	C12/6FT	1985	Deeble, Darley Ford, 1995
LSK612	Volvo B12T	Van Hool Astrobel	C10/6CT	1985	
LSK613	Volvo B12T	Van Hool Astrobel	C10/6CT	1993	
LSK611	Volvo B12T	Van Hool Astrobel	C10/6CT	1994	
LSK812	Volvo B12T	Van Hool Astrobel	C10/6CT	1995	
LSK814	Volvo B12T	Van Hool Astrobel	C10/6CT	1995	
LSK511	Volvo B12T	Van Hool Astrobel	C57/14CT	1997	
LSK512	Volvo B12T	Van Hool Astrobel	C57/14CT	1997	
LSK473	Volvo B12T	Van Hool Astrobel	C57/14CT	1998	
LSK481	Volvo B12T	Van Hool Astrobel	C57/14CT	1998	
LSK498	Volvo B12T	Van Hool Astrobel	C57/14CT	1998	
LSK499	Volvo B12T	Van Hool Astrobel	C57/14CT	1998	
LSK510	Irisbus EuroRider 397E.12.35	Beulas Stergo ε	C49FT	2001	
LSK513	Irisbus EuroRider 397E.12.35	Beulas Stergo ε	C49FT	2001	
LSK514	Irisbus EuroRider 397E.12.35	Beulas Stergo ε	C49FT	2001	
YN51XMU	Neoplan Skyliner N122/3	Neoplan	C57/14FT	2001	
YN51XMV	Neoplan Skyliner N122/3	Neoplan	C57/14FT	2001	
YN51XMW	Neoplan Skyliner N122/3	Neoplan	C57/14FT	2001	
YN51XMX	Neoplan Skyliner N122/3	Neoplan	C57/14FT	2002	
YN51XMK	Neoplan Skyliner N122/3	Neoplan	C57/14FT	2002	
YN51XML	Neoplan Skyliner N122/3	Neoplan	C57/14FT	2002	
YN51XMZ	Neoplan Skyliner N122/3	Neoplan	C57/14FT	2002	
YN51XNC	Neoplan Skyliner N122/3	Neoplan	C57/14FT	2002	
YN51XND	Neoplan Skyliner N122/3	Neoplan	C57/14FT	2002	
YN51XNE	Neoplan Skyliner N122/3	Neoplan	C57/14FT	2002	
YN51XMH	Neoplan Skyliner N122/3	Neoplan	C57/14FT	2002	
YN51XMJ	Neoplan Skyliner N122/3	Neoplan	C57/14FT	2002	
LSK614	Volvo B12T	Jonckheere Monaco	C10/6CT	2002	
LSK615	Volvo B12T	Jonckheere Monaco	C10/6CT	2002	
KSK981	Volvo B12T	Jonckheere Monaco	C57/14CT	2002	
KSK982	Volvo B12T	Jonckheere Monaco	C57/14CT	2002	
KSK983	Volvo B12T	Jonckheere Monaco	C57/14CT	2002	
KSK984	Volvo B12T	Jonckheere Monaco	C57/14CT	2002	
KSK985	Volvo B12T	Jonckheere Monaco	C57/14CT	2002	
KSK986	Volvo B12T	Jonckheere Monaco	C57/14CT	2002	
SG03ZJH	Volvo B12M	Jonckheere Mistral 50	C53F	2003	
SG03ZES	Volvo B12M	Jonckheere Mistral 50	C53F	2003	
SG03ZEV	Volvo B12M	Jonckheere Mistral 50	C53F	2003	

Claiming to be Scotland's Driving Force, Park's black and gold livery is impressive. The fleet comprises Volvo and Neoplan products that are replaced while still young. Eight double-deck Jonckheere Monaco coaches were supplied in 2002, represented by KSK982, seen in Blackpool.
Bob Downham

SG03ZCR	Volvo B12M	Jonckheere Mistral 50	C53F	2003
SG03ZCH	Volvo B12M	Jonckheere Mistral 50	C53F	2003
SG03ZEX	Volvo B12M	Jonckheere Mistral 50	C53F	2003
SG03ZCC	Volvo B12M	Jonckheere Mistral 50	C53F	2003
SG03ZCB	Volvo B12M	Jonckheere Mistral 50	C53F	2003
SG03ZEY	Volvo B12M	Jonckheere Mistral 50	C53F	2003
SG03ZBM	Volvo B12M	Jonckheere Mistral 50	C53F	2003
SG03ZEZ	Volvo B12M	Jonckheere Mistral 50	C53F	2003
SG03ZJD	Volvo B12M	Plaxton Paragon	C53F	2003
SG03ZBH	Volvo B12M	Plaxton Paragon	C53F	2003
SG03ZJF	Volvo B12M	Plaxton Paragon	C53F	2003
SG03ZHS	Volvo B12M	Plaxton Paragon	C53F	2003
SG03ZJA	Volvo B12M	Plaxton Paragon	C53F	2003
SG03ZJB	Volvo B12M	Plaxton Paragon	C53F	2003
SG03ZJC	Volvo B12M	Plaxton Paragon	C53F	2003
SG03ZEP	Volvo B12M	Plaxton Paragon	C53F	2003
LSK503	Volvo B12M	VDL Jonckheere Mistral 50	C49FT	2004
LSK504	Volvo B12M	VDL Jonckheere Mistral 50	C49FT	2004
LSK505	Volvo B12M	VDL Jonckheere Mistral 50	C49FT	2004
LSK506	Volvo B12M	VDL Jonckheere Mistral 50	C49FT	2004
LSK507	Volvo B12M	VDL Jonckheere Mistral 50	C49FT	2004
LSK508	Volvo B12M	VDL Jonckheere Mistral 50	C49FT	2004
LSK871	Volvo B12M	VDL Jonckheere Mistral 50	C53F	2004
LSK872	Volvo B12M	VDL Jonckheere Mistral 50	C53F	2004
LSK873	Volvo B12M	VDL Jonckheere Mistral 50	C53F	2004
LSK874	Volvo B12M	VDL Jonckheere Mistral 50	C53F	2004
LSK875	Volvo B12M	VDL Jonckheere Mistral 50	C53F	2004
LSK876	Volvo B12M	VDL Jonckheere Mistral 50	C53F	2004
LSK877	Volvo B12M	VDL Jonckheere Mistral 50	C53F	2004
LSK878	Volvo B12M	VDL Jonckheere Mistral 50	C53F	2004
LSK879	Volvo B12M	VDL Jonckheere Mistral 50	C53F	2004
LSK500	Volvo B12M	VDL Jonckheere Mistral 50	C53F	2004
2HW	Volvo B12B	VDL Jonckheere Mistral 50	C53F	2005
HSK641	Volvo B12B	VDL Jonckheere Mistral 50	C49FT	2005
HSK642	Volvo B12B	VDL Jonckheere Mistral 50	C49FT	2005
HSK643	Volvo B12B	VDL Jonckheere Mistral 50	C49FT	2005
HSK644	Volvo B12B	VDL Jonckheere Mistral 50	C49FT	2005
HSK645	Volvo B12B	VDL Jonckheere Mistral 50	C49FT	2005
HSK646	Volvo B12B	VDL Jonckheere Mistral 50	C49FT	2005
HSK647	Volvo B12B	VDL Jonckheere Mistral 50	C49FT	2005
HSK648	Volvo B12B	VDL Jonckheere Mistral 50	C49FT	2005
HSK649	Volvo B12B	VDL Jonckheere Mistral 50	C49FT	2005
HSK650	Volvo B12B	VDL Jonckheere Mistral 50	C49FT	2005
KSK950	Volvo B12B	VDL Jonckheere Mistral 50	C53F	2005
KSK951	Volvo B12B	VDL Jonckheere Mistral 50	C53F	2005
KSK952	Volvo B12B	VDL Jonckheere Mistral 50	C53F	2005
KSK953	Volvo B12B	VDL Jonckheere Mistral 50	C53F	2005
LSK501	Volvo B12B	VDL Jonckheere Mistral 50	C53F	2005
LSK502	Volvo B12B	VDL Jonckheere Mistral 50	C53F	2005
LSK830	Volvo B12B	VDL Jonckheere Mistral 50	C53F	2005
LSK831	Volvo B12B	VDL Jonckheere Mistral 50	C53F	2005
LSK832	Volvo B12B	VDL Jonckheere Mistral 50	C53F	2005
LSK835	Volvo B12B	VDL Jonckheere Mistral 50	C53F	2005
LSK839	Volvo B12B	VDL Jonckheere Mistral 50	C53F	2005
LSK844	Volvo B12B	VDL Jonckheere Mistral 50	C53F	2005
LSK845	Volvo B12B	VDL Jonckheere Mistral 50	C53F	2005
HSK651	Volvo B12M	VDL Jonckheere Mistral 50	C53F	2006
HSK652	Volvo B12M	VDL Jonckheere Mistral 50	C53F	2006
HSK653	Volvo B12M	VDL Jonckheere Mistral 50	C53F	2006
HSK654	Volvo B12M	VDL Jonckheere Mistral 50	C53F	2006
HSK655	Volvo B12M	VDL Jonckheere Mistral 50	C53F	2006
HSK656	Volvo B12M	VDL Jonckheere Mistral 50	C53F	2006
HSK657	Volvo B12M	VDL Jonckheere Mistral 50	C53F	2006
HSK658	Volvo B12M	VDL Jonckheere Mistral 50	C53F	2006
HSK659	Volvo B12M	VDL Jonckheere Mistral 50	C53F	2006
HSK660	Volvo B12M	VDL Jonckheere Mistral 50	C53F	2006
LSK444	Volvo B12M	VDL Jonckheere Mistral 50	C53F	2006
LSK555	Volvo B12M	VDL Jonckheere Mistral 50	C53F	2006
12HM	Volvo B12M	VDL Jonckheere Mistral 50	C53F	2006
2WR	Volvo B12M	VDL Jonckheere Mistral 50	C53F	2006
2HAN	Volvo B12M	VDL Jonckheere Mistral 50	C53F	2006
3HWS	Volvo B12M	VDL Jonckheere Mistral 50	C53F	2006
1RWM	Volvo B12M	VDL Jonckheere Mistral 50	C53F	2006

Each year Park's vehicle intake is allocated the sequential cherished index marks from new, the marks being replaced with standard numbers just prior to sale. While Volvo have been the main chassis supplier to the company for many years, current bodywork is provided by Jonckheere, the member of Dutch VDL Groep based in Belgium. KSK950 was one of the 2003 intake of Volvo B12Ms that have just been allocated SG03 plates in preparation for disposal as the 2006 intake arrives. *Bob Downham*

2RWM	Volvo B12M	VDL Jonckheere Mistral 50	C53F	2006
3RWM	Volvo B12M	VDL Jonckheere Mistral 50	C53F	2006
15RWM	Volvo B12M	VDL Jonckheere Mistral 50	C53F	2006
SF06MFM	Volvo B12M	VDL Jonckheere Mistral 50	C53F	2006
SF06MFN	Volvo B12M	VDL Jonckheere Mistral 50	C53F	2006
KSK954	Volvo B12M	Plaxton Panther	C53FL	2006
KSK976	Volvo B12M	Plaxton Panther	C53FL	2006
KSK977	Volvo B12M	Plaxton Panther	C53FL	2006
KSK978	Volvo B12M	Plaxton Panther	C53FL	2006
KSK979	Volvo B12M	Plaxton Panther	C53FL	2006
KSK980	Volvo B12M	Plaxton Panther	C53FL	2006
LSK483	Volvo B12M	Plaxton Panther	C53FL	2006
LSK495	Volvo B12M	Plaxton Panther	C53FL	2006
LSK496	Volvo B12M	Plaxton Panther	C53FL	2006
LSK497	Volvo B12M	Plaxton Panther	C53FL	2006

Previous registrations:

290WE	B418CGG	SG03ZCR	HSK651
LSK499	R264OFJ	SG03ZEP	KSK980
LSK500	SF04SSZ	SG03ZES	2WR
LSK511	P926KYC	SG03ZEV	3RWM
LSK512	P927KYC	SG03ZEX	HSK656
LSK611	LSK831	SG03ZEY	HSK659
LSK612	LSK832	SG03ZEZ	KSK948
LSK613	L977KDT	SG03ZHS	KSK976
SG03ZBH	LSK495	SG03ZJA	KSK977
SG03ZBM	HSK660	SG03ZJB	KSK978
SG03ZBS	HSK655	SG03ZJC	KSK979
SG03ZCC	HSK657	SG03ZJD	LSK483
SG03ZCH	HSK652	SG03ZJF	LSK497

Depots: Forest Street, Blantyre, Bothwell Road, Hamilton and Burrington Way Ind Est, Plymouth
Web: www.parks.co.uk

PRENTICE

DR & MG Prentice; R Prentice and D Prentice, 2D Hospital Road, Haddington, EH41 3BH

MFS444P	Bedford YRQ	Plaxton Supreme IV	C45F	1975	preservation, 2003
IIL4595	Volvo B10M-60	Van Hool Alizée	C53F	1990	
B12DPC	Volvo B10M-60	Van Hool Alizée	C48FT	1985	National Holidays, 2001
N18SCP	Mercedes-Benz 609D	Crystals	BC23F	1996	Flying Scotsman, Paisley, 2002
VIL4714	Mercedes-Benz 614D	Anderson	BC24F	1998	Pride of the Clyde, P Glasgow, 2001
S4DPC	Dennis Javelin 12m	Plaxton Première 320	C53F	1998	
WSU982	Dennis Javelin 12m	Plaxton Première 320	C53F	1998	Mackay, Dornoch, 2005
B10DPC	Volvo B10M-60	Van Hool T9 Alizée	C46FT	1998	Shearings, 2005
B10MDP	Volvo B10M-60	Van Hool T9 Alizée	C51F	1999	Southern, Barrhead, 2005
JSU550	Mercedes-Benz Vario 0814	Plaxton Cheetah	C33F	2000	McNee, Ratho, 2003
Y556KSC	Mercedes-Benz Vario 0814	Plaxton Beaver 2	BC33F	2001	
Y557KSC	Mercedes-Benz Vario 0814	Plaxton Beaver 2	BC33F	2001	
SC02DPC	Mercedes-Benz Vario 0814	Plaxton Cheetah	C33F	2002	
SN54FNL	Mercedes-Benz Vario 0814	KVC	C29F	2004	
PH54PCH	Mercedes-Benz Vario 0814	KVC	C29F	2004	

Previous registrations:

B10MDP	T100SOU	N18SCP	N327MHS
B10DPC	R913YBA		
B12DPC	N313DYA, N261PYS	PH54PCH	SN54FNL
IIL4595	G342HSC, HIL8647, G720FSJ, B10PPC	S4DPC	S913BSF
JSU550	W512PSF	VIL4714	R458VSD
MFS444P	IIL4595, MFS444P	WSU982	T14HCT

Depot: Hospital Road, Haddington

Pictured in Edinburgh is B10MDP, a Volvo B10M with classic Van Hool Alizée bodywork, which was new to Shearings. While the service between Haddington and Edinburgh airport was withdrawn in 2004, Prentice's local service through Gifford, numbered 123, continues and uses the minibus fleet. *Bob Downham*

PRENTICE WESTWOOD

Prentice Westwood Ltd, Coach Depot, West Calder, EH55 8PW

TJT196X	Leyland Olympian ONLXB/1R	Marshall	B47/31F	1980	Trustline, Hundon, 2001
A705YFS	Leyland Olympian ONTL11/2R	Eastern Coach Works	B51/35F	1983	Lothian Buses, 2000
A706YFS	Leyland Olympian ONTL11/2R	Eastern Coach Works	B51/35F	1983	Lothian Buses, 2000
A709YFS	Leyland Olympian ONTL11/2R	Eastern Coach Works	B51/35F	1983	Lothian Buses, 2000
B759GSC	Leyland Olympian ONTL11/2R	Eastern Coach Works	B51/32D	1984	HAD, Shotts, 2004
B760GSC	Leyland Olympian ONTL11/2R	Eastern Coach Works	B51/32D	1984	HAD, Shotts, 2004
755ABL	Volvo B10M-61	Van Hool Alizée	C53F	1984	Penman, Glasgow, 2001
RIA5991	Volvo B10M-61	Van Hool Alizée	C53F	1984	Renman, Glasgow, 2001
JIL8208	Leyland Tiger TRCTL11/3LZ	Wadham Stringer Vanguard	B70F	1985	MoD (37KC11), 2000
FLZ7953	Leyland Tiger TRCTL11/3LZ	Wadham Stringer Vanguard	B70F	1985	MoD (37KC54), 2000
C788SFS	Leyland Olympian ONTL11/2R	Eastern Coach Works	B51/32D	1985	Lothian Buses, 2004
C789SFS	Leyland Olympian ONTL11/2R	Eastern Coach Works	B51/32D	1985	Lothian Buses, 2004
C790SFS	Leyland Olympian ONTL11/2R	Eastern Coach Works	B51/32D	1985	Lothian Buses, 2004
240BBU	Volvo B10M-61	Van Hool Alizée HE	C57F	1986	Campbell, Clydebank, 2003
NIL2266	Neoplan Skyliner N122/3	Neoplan	C59/18CT	1987	Cedric's, Wivenhoe, 2001
E452SON	MCW Metrobus DR102/63	MCW	B45/30F	1987	Arriva North West, 1992
E453SON	MCW Metrobus DR102/63	MCW	B45/30F	1987	Arriva North West, 1992
E455SON	MCW Metrobus DR102/63	MCW	B45/30F	1987	Arriva North West, 1992
E342RSC	Setra S215 H	Setra	C49FT	1988	Hamiltons, Uxbridge, 2001
CBZ4622	Volvo B10M-61	Caetano Algarve	C53F	1988	Earnside, Glenfaig, 2001
YIJ351	Volvo B10M-61	Duple 300	BC59F	1988	Go-Goodwin, Eccles, 2001
NCH868	Volvo B10M-60	Jonckheere Deauvile	C51FT	1988	Bradshaw, Heywood, 2002
DLZ4298	Volvo B10M-60	Van Hool Alizée	C53F	1989	White, Keady, 2001
VSV632	Volvo B10M-60	Van Hool Alizée	C48FT	1989	Brown, Edinburgh, 2005
YIL8799	Volvo B10M-61	Caetano Algarve	C57F	1990	Chalkwell, Sittingbourne, 2005
138ASV	Volvo B10M-60	Van Hool Alizée	C53F	1990	Wilson's, Carnwath,1999
828EWB	Volvo B10M-60	Van Hool Alizée	C53FT	1990	Wilson's, Carnwath,1999

The Bova Futura has retained the 'pregnant coach' appearance since it was first launched. Four currently operate with Prentice Westwood, including 383DVF seen on a visit to the Lathalmond spring transport event.
Bob Downham

New for the 2006 season is another Volvo B12B for Prentice Westwood with Berkhof Axial bodywork. SN06AEF illustrates the Axial variant with air intakes for the rear-engined B12B and this model is fitted with a central toilet, fridge drinks facility and satellite navigation.

SIL7058	Mercedes-Benz 709D	Olympus	BC24F	1990	St Andrews Coaches, 2002
YSV607	Neoplan Skyliner N122/3	Neoplan	C55/22CT	1990	Graham, Kilkeith, 2004
FLZ6854	Volvo B10M-60	Ikarus Blue Danube	C53F	1991	Swanbrook, Cheltenham,1995
YRR436	Neoplan Skyliner N122/3	Neoplan	C55/22CT	1992	Moffat & Williamson, Gauldry, 2001
PIL2162	Volvo B10M-60	Jonckheere Deauville	C53F	1993	Classic, Anfield Plain, 2003
NGH456	Volvo B10M-60	Jonckheere Deauville	C51FT	1993	Shamrock, Pontypridd, 2003
PIL7834	Volvo B10M-60	Caetano Algarve 2	C49FT	1993	Simpson, Rosehearty, 2003
367NHA	Volvo B10M-60	Caetano Algarve 2	C53F	1993	Reliant, Heather, 2003
OJU106	Volvo B10M-62	Plaxton Première 350	C49FT	1993	Smith, Wouldham, 2004
M308BAV	Volvo B10M-62	Plaxton Première 350	C57F	1994	Dalybus, Standish, 2006
YSV608	Volvo B10M-62	Caetano Algarve 2	C51F	1994	Reliance, Heather, 2004
LSU689	Volvo B10M-62	Caetano Algarve 2	C53F	1995	Reliance, Heather, 2003
OUR610	Mercedes-Benz 609D	Olympus	C24F	1995	Waverley Travel, 2000
WNB604	Volvo B12T	Van Hool Astrobel	C57/14DT	1996	Trathens, Plymouth, 2002
JSV440	DAF SB3000	Van Hool Alizée	C49FT	1996	Reliance, Heather, 2003
ONR314	Volvo B10M-62	Jonckheere Mistral 50	C49FT	1998	Brown, Edinburgh, 2002
383OVF	Bova Futura FHD12.340	Bova	C49FT	1999	
81CBK	Volvo B12T	Jonckheere Monaco	C57/14CT	2000	Patterson, 2004
YSV125	Volvo B10M-62	Plaxton Première 320	C49FT	2000	Wallace Arnold, 2005
USY858	Volvo B10M-62	Plaxton Première 320	C49FT	2000	Wallace Arnold, 2005
UO6929	Bova Futura FHD12.370	Bova	C49FT	2000	Maynes of Buckie, 2002
DSU355	Mercedes-Benz Vario 0815	Sitcar Beluga	C27F	2001	Maynes of Buckie, 2003
SJ53CUU	Volvo B7R	Plaxton Prima	BC70F	2003	Pride of the Clyde, 2005
SJ53CUV	Volvo B7R	Plaxton Prima	BC70F	2003	Pride of the Clyde, 2005
36RP	Bova Futura FHD12.340	Bova	C49FT	2003	
SN04GNJ	VDL Bova Futura FHD12.340	VDL Bova	C49FT	2004	
SN05FBE	VDL Bova Futura FHD13.340	VDL Bova	C49FT	2005	
SN06AEF	Volvo B12M	VDL Berkhof Axial 50	C51FT	2006	

The Neoplan Skyliner has proved a popular double-deck coach, and is used across Britain on private hire, National Express services as well as trans-European services, especially to Spain. Seen at work in Edinburgh in Prentice Westwood colours is YSV607.

Previous registrations:

36RP	SF03AXJ	NGH456	P98VGD
81CBK	?, VSV632	NIL2266	E600WDV
138ASV	G341HSC, HIL8646	ONR314	R359KSG
240BBU	D564MVR, GIL683, D781OSJ,	ONR610	M687KPO
	... BJI6863, PIL6351, D453EKS	OUJ106	M31TRR
367NHA	K103UFP	OUJ969	S573KJF
383DVF	S919CSX	PIL2162	K919UBB
570PRR	P685DRS	PIL7894	K594VBC
755ABL	A194MNE	RIA5991	A190MNE
828EWB	G339HSC, NIL1509	RPP734	S769JUG
CBZ4622	E747HJF, WSV490, E747HJF	UO6929	W222GSM
DLZ4298	F171RJF, DLZ4298, F171RJF	SIL7058	H643YDS, RAM39Y, H643YDS
DSU355	Y500GSM, Y767TSJ	TDZ4787	D801SGB
E342RSC	E492GPX, 3553PH, E492BPK, JSV440	USY858	W657FVM
E756ODF	E112HFH, A5ALP	VSV632	?
FLZ6854	H132JFH, RPP734	WNB604	N708CYC
FLZ7953	B153YWS	YIJ351	F775JYS
JIL8208	B101YWS	YIL8799	G347GSD, 187NKN
JSV440	N505CVM, REU18, N720HKU	YRR436	J2DTS, YBK159, J120NJR
LSU689	M3OCLA, REL135	YSV125	W653FVM
LUI7857	TGD761W, ONR314	YSV607	H882AVK
NCH868	F905YNV	YSV608	N94HSJ

Web: www.prenticewestwoodcoaches.co.uk

The Scottish Bus Handbook

PRIDE OF THE CLYDE

Pride of the Clyde Coaches Ltd, 1 Bellhaven Street, Port Glasgow, PA14 5DG

ECS883V	Leyland Fleetline FE30AGR	Northern Counties	B43/29F	1979	Marbill, Beith, 1999
GTO303V	Leyland Fleetline FE30AGR	Northern Counties	B43/29F	1980	Clydeside Buses, 1997
WSD212V	Leyland Fleetline FE30AGR	Northern Counties	B43/29F	1980	Clydeside Buses, 1997
WSD216V	Leyland Fleetline FE30AGR	Northern Counties	B43/29F	1980	Clydeside Buses, 1997
HSR37X	Volvo Ailsa B55-10	Alexander RV	B48/36F	1981	Travel Tayside, 2000
HSR43X	Volvo Ailsa B55-10	Alexander RV	B48/36F	1981	Travel Tayside, 2000
HSR49X	Volvo Ailsa B55-10	Alexander RV	B48/36F	1981	Travel Tayside, 2000
HSR50X	Volvo Ailsa B55-10	Alexander RV	B48/36F	1981	Travel Tayside, 2000
D702EES	Dodge S56	Alexander AM	B23F	1987	Travel Tayside, 2000
NDZ7937	Neoplan Skyliner N122/3	Neoplan	C57/20CT	1988	Silver Choice, East Kilbride, 1996
SJI2765	Neoplan Skyliner N122/3	Neoplan	C57/20CT	1988	Burns, Tarves, 2003
FXU355	Neoplan Skyliner N122/3	Neoplan	C57/20CT	1992	Patterson, Seahouses, 2005
L512LNR	Mazda E2200	Howletts	M15	1994	Waddell, Lochwinnoch, 1998
M827HNS	Volvo B10M-62	Van Hool Alizée HE	C53F	1995	Park's of Hamilton, 1998
M983HNS	Volvo B10M-62	Van Hool Alizée HE	C53F	1995	Park's of Hamilton, 1998
M984HNS	Volvo B10M-62	Van Hool Alizée HE	C53F	1995	Park's of Hamilton, 1998
N469PYS	Volvo B10M-62	Van Hool Alizée HE	C53F	1996	Park's of Hamilton, 1999
N517PYS	Volvo B10M-62	Van Hool Alizée HE	C53F	1996	Park's of Hamilton, 1999
P224YGG	Volvo B10M-62	Van Hool Alizée HE	C53F	1997	Flight's, Birmingham, 2001
P225YGG	Volvo B10M-62	Van Hool Alizée HE	C53F	1997	Flight's, Birmingham, 2001
R339RRA	Volvo Citybus B10M-50	East Lancs	BC45/35F	1997	City of Nottingham, 2005
R886YOM	LDV Convoy	LDV	M16	1998	Horton, Blairmore, 2003

Previous registrations:

FXU355	J449NTT		NDZ7937	E469YWJ
M827HNS	LSK499		P224YGG	KSK949
M983HNS	LSK505		P225YGG	LSK555, LSK496
M984HNS	LSK509		SJI2765	E472YWJ, SEL123, E499CTU
N469PYS	HSK642		WDS212V	GTO46V
N517PYS	LSK835		WDS216V	GTO308V

Pride of the Clyde operates three Neoplan Skyliners including NDZ7937 seen at rest in Blackpool.
Bob Downham

PUMA

A Morrin, 60 Clydeholm Road, Whiteinch, Glasgow, G14 0QQ

F61RFS	MCW MetroRider MF150/98	MCW	B25F	1988	Dolan, Barrhead, 2001
NDZ3146	Dennis Dart 8.5m	Wright HandyBus	B29F	1993	Stagecoach Fife, 2003
K103OMW	Dennis Dart	Plaxton Pointer	B33F	1993	Laws, Tetbury, 2004
M771TFS	Mercedes-Benz 709D	Alexander Sprint	B25F	1994	Stagecoach, 2005
M318RSO	Mercedes-Benz 709D	Alexander Sprint	B25F	1994	Stagecoach, 2005
N996CCC	Mercedes-Benz 709D	Alexander Sprint	B27F	1995	Arriva Cymru, 2002
N997CCC	Mercedes-Benz 709D	Alexander Sprint	B27F	1995	Arriva Cymru, 2002
N799FSD	Mercedes-Benz 709D	Wadham Stringer Wessex	B28FL	1995	Marbill, Beith, 2001
N801FSD	Mercedes-Benz 709D	Wadham Stringer Wessex	B24FL	1995	Marbill, Beith, 2001
N208GCS	Mercedes-Benz 709D	Wadham Stringer Wessex	B28FL	1995	Marbill, Beith, 2001

Puma is represented by Dennis Dart NDZ3146, an example with Wright HandyBus bodywork latterly in use with Stagecoach. The bus is seen in service in Govan. *Mark Doggett*

The Scottish Bus Handbook

RAPSONS

Highland Country - Rapsons - Peaces - Shalders

Rapsons Coaches Ltd, 1 Seafield Road, Inverness, IV1 1TN

1	SH	HRO2Y	Mercedes-Benz Vario 0814	Plaxton Beaver 2	B32F	1997	Pete's. W Bromwich. 2005
2	K	KKZ5534	Mercedes-Benz Vario 0814	Buscraft	C35F	1996	Smith, Ledbury, 2005
3	SH	WIB7085	Mercedes-Benz Vario 0814	Plaxton Beaver 2	B33F	1998	?, 2005
4	K	PIL6829	Mercedes-Benz Vario 0814	Plaxton Beaver 2	B27F	1997	Jones, Rhosllanerchrugog, 05
6	SH	YJ05XOA	Optare Solo M920	Optare	N31F	2005	
7	I	YJ05XOB	Optare Solo M950	Optare	N31F	2005	
8	P	YJ05XOC	Optare Solo M950	Optare	N31F	2005	
9	A	YJ05XOD	Optare Solo M950	Optare	N31F	2005	
10	A	YJ05XOE	Optare Solo M950	Optare	N31F	2005	
11	I	YJ05XOF	Optare Solo M1020	Optare	N35F	2005	
12	I	YJ05XOG	Optare Solo M1020	Optare	N35F	2005	
13	K	YJ05XOH	Optare Solo M990	Optare	N35F	2005	
14	K	YJ05XOK	Optare Solo M990	Optare	N35F	2005	
15	K	YJ05XOM	Optare Solo M920	Optare	N29F	2005	
16	K	YJ05XOL	Optare Solo M920	Optare	N31F	2005	
35	T	K504NST	Mercedes Benz 811D	Wright NimBus	B31F	1993	Highland Country, 1999
36	K	K247MOS	Toyota Coaster HDB30R	Caetano Optimo II	C21F	1993	Peace, Kirkwall, 1999
37	K	M487WAS	Mercedes Benz 811D	Alexander Sprint	B33F	1995	Highland Country, 1999
38	I	M623WAS	Mercedes Benz 811D	Alexander Sprint	B33F	1995	Highland Bus & Coach, 1999
39	K	N11JDP	Ford Transit VE6	Ford	M14	1995	Peace, Kirkwall, 1999
40	FW	P111JDP	Ford Transit VE6	Ford	M14	1996	Peace, Kirkwall, 1999
41	I	P677VJS	Mercedes Benz 814D	Wadham Stringer Wessex	BC25F	1996	Highland Bus & Coach, 1999
43	P	P343JAS	Mercedes Benz 814D	Wadham Stringer Wessex	BC24F	1996	Highland Country, 1999
44	I	KSU674	Optare Metrorider MR15	Optare	B32F	1996	Highland Country, 1999
45	A	P905DST	Optare Metrorider MR15	Optare	B32F	1996	Highland Country, 1999
46	I	YSU882	Optare Metrorider MR15	Optare	B32F	1996	Highland Country, 1999
47	FW	P907DST	Optare Metrorider MR	Optare	B32F	1996	Highland Country, 1999
48	FW	T133AST	Optare Metrorider MR17	Optare	B29F	1999	Highland Country, 1999
53	P	P611RGB	Mercedes Benz 711D	Adamson	BC24F	1996	Highland Country, 1999
54	T	P612RGB	Mercedes Benz 711D	Adamson	BC24F	1996	Highland Country, 1999
55	T	P166LSC	Mercedes Benz 609D	Onyx	BC24F	1996	Highland Country, 1999
60	KY	G710HOP	Mercedes-Benz 709D	Carlyle	B25F	1990	Travel West Midlands, 2000
66	I	H166WWT	Optare Metrorider MR03	Optare	B26F	1991	Chalkwell, Sittingbourne, 2000
71	K	K314YKG	Mercedes Benz 811D	Wright TS303	B33F	1992	Stagecoach Red & White, 2001
72	K	K316YKG	Mercedes Benz 811D	Wright TS303	B33F	1992	Stagecoach Red & White, 2001
73	I	J414PRW	Mercedes Benz 811D	Wright TS303	B33F	1991	Stagecoach Red & White, 2002
75	P	W691NST	Mercedes Benz Vario 0814	Plaxton Beaver 2	BC33F	2000	Nicolson, Borve, 2002
76	I	W692NST	Mercedes Benz Vario 0814	Plaxton Beaver 2	BC33F	2000	Nicolson, Borve, 2002
77	I	K310YKG	Mercedes Benz 811D	Wright TS303	B33F	1992	Stagecoach Red & White, 2001
78	K	L35OKV	Mercedes Benz 811D	Wright TS303	B33F	1993	Arriva Cymru, 2002
79	K	N108WRC	Mercedes Benz 811D	Plaxton Beaver	B30F	1995	City of Nottingham, 2002
80	K	N101WRC	Mercedes Benz 811D	Plaxton Beaver	B30F	1995	City of Nottingham, 2002
81	I	N102WRC	Mercedes Benz 811D	Plaxton Beaver	B30F	1995	City of Nottingham, 2002
82	K	N109WRC	Mercedes Benz 811D	Plaxton Beaver	B30F	1995	City of Nottingham, 2002
83	KY	N103WRC	Mercedes Benz 811D	Plaxton Beaver	B30F	1995	City of Nottingham, 2002
84	I	N106WRC	Mercedes Benz 811D	Plaxton Beaver	B30F	1995	City of Nottingham, 2002
85	T	M243JHB	Mercedes Benz 811D	Plaxton Beaver	B31F	1994	EST Bus, Llandow, 2002
86	T	K325YKG	Mercedes Benz 811D	Wright	B33F	1993	Stagecoach Red & White, 2002
87	I	S751SCJ	Mercedes Benz Vario 814D	Plaxton Beaver 2	B31F	1998	Bromyard Omnibus, 2002
88	T	T993PFH	Toyota Coaster BB50R	Caetano Optimo IV	C21F	1999	David, Minchinhampton, 2004
98	T	YK04KWH	Optare Solo M920	Optare	N26F	2004	*Operated for Highland Council*
99	K	YN03UYJ	Optare Alero AL3	Optare	N14F	2003	*Operated for Orkney I Council*
133	T	DOC36V	Leyland National 2 NL116L11/1R [DAF]		B50F	1980	Highland Country, 1999
140	SH	TGD759W	Volvo B58-61	Van Hool Alizée	C50F	1981	Rosie, St Margaret's Hope, '05
141	SH	NST61Y	Bedford YNT	Plaxton Paramount 3200	C53F	1983	Rosie, St Margaret's Hope, '05
144	SH	C663EHU	Volvo B10M-61	Duple Laser	C55F	1986	Rosie, St Margaret's Hope, '05
164	T	MBZ6454	Volvo B10M-61	East Lancashire (1991)	B55F	1985	Green Triangle, Lostock 2000
165	KY	HIL7467	Volvo B10M-61	East Lancashire (1991)	B55F	1983	Green Triangle, Lostock 2000
167	KY	C55HOM	Volvo Citybus YV31MEC	Alexander P	B50F	1986	Travel West Midlands, 2000
168	KY	C56HOM	Volvo Citybus YV31MEC	Alexander P	B50F	1986	Travel West Midlands, 2000
169	KY	C57HOM	Volvo Citybus YV31MEC	Alexander P	B50F	1986	Travel West Midlands, 2000
170	KY	C58HOM	Volvo Citybus YV31MEC	Alexander P	B50F	1986	Travel West Midlands, 2000

While the number of Leyland Nationals in the Rapson's fleet has reduced, three examples remain. Number 182, KRE278P, is seen at its home town of Fort William and was new to National Bus subsidiary PMT. *Bob Downham*

171	KY	C59HOM	Volvo Citybus YV31MEC	Alexander P	B50F	1986	Travel West Midlands, 2000
175	T	B857XYR	Volvo B10M-61	East Lancs EL2000 (1991)	B49F	1985	Arriva The Shires, 2002
176	T	B858XYR	Volvo B10M-61	East Lancs EL2000 (1991)	B49F	1985	Arriva The Shires, 2002
178	FW	B860XYR	Volvo B10M-61	East Lancs EL2000 (1991)	B49F	1985	Arriva The Shires, 2002
182	FW	KRE278P	Leyland National 11351/1R (Volvo)		B52F	1976	Lothian Buses, 2003
183	T	KHT121P	Leyland National 11351/1R (Volvo)		B52F	1977	Lothian Buses, 2003
196	FW	J610KCU	Dennis Dart 9.8m	Wright HandyBus	B40F	1991	Dennis's, Dukinfield, 2005
197	FW	J623KCU	Dennis Dart 9.8m	Wright HandyBus	B40F	1991	Dennis's, Dukinfield, 2005
198	A	N4SKY	Mercedes-Benz O405	Optare Prisma	B45F	1995	MacEwans, Amisfield Town, 03
199	I	M211YAS	Mercedes-Benz O405	Optare Prisma	B45F	1995	MacEwans, Amisfield Town, 03
200	I	P817EST	Dennis Dart 9.8m	Plaxton Pointer	B43F	1996	Nicolson, Borve, 2002
201	I	S388JPS	MAN 11.220	Marshall City	N36F	1999	Shalder, Scalloway, 1999
202	I	S389JPS	MAN 11.220	Marshall City	N36F	1999	Shalder, Scalloway, 1999
205	I	T132AST	Volvo B10BLE	Wright Renown	N45F	1999	Highland Bus & Coach, 1999
206	I	T134AST	Volvo B6BLE	Wright Crusader 2	N37F	1999	Highland Country, 1999
207	I	V32JST	Volvo B6BLE	Wright Crusader 2	N37F	1999	Shalder, Scalloway, 1999
208	I	W747NAS	Volvo B10BLE	Alexander ALX300	N44F	2000	
211	I	YP02AAZ	Scania L94UB	Wrightbus Solar	N43F	2002	
212	FW	JAZ9851	Optare Excel L1150	Optare	N45F	1997	East Yorkshire, 2002
213	FW	JAZ4632	Optare Excel L1150	Optare	N45F	1997	East Yorkshire, 2002
214	FW	JAZ9857	Optare Excel L1150	Optare	N45F	1997	East Yorkshire, 2002
215	I	X461UKS	Dennis Dart SLF	Alexander ALX200	NC43F	2000	Munro, Jedburgh, 2004
216	I	X462UKS	Dennis Dart SLF	Alexander ALX200	NC43F	2000	Munro, Jedburgh, 2004
217	I	X467UKS	Dennis Dart SLF	Alexander ALX200	NC43F	2000	Munro, Jedburgh, 2004
299	I	YJ04HLC	VDL Bus SB200	Wrightbus Commander 2	N44F	2004	
301	I	RAN645R	Bristol VRT/SL3/6LXB	Eastern Coach Works	B43/34F	1977	Highland Country, 1999
302	I	SAS859T	Leyland Fleetline FE30AGR	Eastern Coach Works	B43/32F	1978	Highland Bus & Coach, 1999
306	I	ECS882V	Leyland Fleetline FE30AGR	Northern Counties	B44/31F	1979	Highland Bus & Coach, 1999
307	A	BKE832T	Bristol VRT/SL3/6LXB	Eastern Coach Works	B43/31F	1979	Highland Country, 1999
308	I	HKM884V	Bristol VRT/SL3/6LXB	Eastern Coach Works	B43/31F	1980	Highland Country, 1999
311	CW	DSP928V	Volvo-Ailsa B55-10 Mk II	Alexander AV	B44/31F	1980	Highland Country, 1999
315	CW	DSP934V	Volvo-Ailsa B55-10 Mk II	Alexander AV	B44/31F	1980	Highland Country, 1999
323	T	NIL2734	Leyland Olympian ONTL11/2R	Eastern Coach Works	BC45/28F	1984	Highland Country, 1999
324	I	NIL2735	Leyland Olympian ONTL11/2R	Eastern Coach Works	BC45/28F	1985	Highland Country, 1999
325	A	FAO426V	Bristol VRT/SL3/6LXB	Eastern Coach Works	B43/31F	1980	Highland Bus & Coach, 1999

Carrying Scottish Citylink colours is Rapson's 643, R874RST, a Volvo B10M with Plaxton Première 320 bodywork. The 919 service links Fort William with Inverness. *Bob Downham*

326	T	KVF246V	Bristol VRT/SL3/6LXB	Eastern Coach Works	B43/31F	1980	Stagecoach Cambus, 2000
328	FW	PWY49W	Bristol VRT/SL3/6LXB	Eastern Coach Works	B43/31F	1981	Stagecoach Cambus, 2000
330	T	VAH280X	Bristol VRT/SL3/6LXB	Eastern Coach Works	B43/31F	1981	Stagecoach Cambus, 2000
351	FW	B803AOP	MCW Metrobus DR102/27	MCW	B43/30F	1984	Travel West Midlands, 2001
352	I	SHE306Y	Leyland Olympian ONLXB/1R	Eastern Coach Works	B45/32F	1982	Stagecoach East Midland, 2001
353	I	UDT312Y	Leyland Olympian ONLXB/1R	Eastern Coach Works	B45/32F	1983	Stagecoach East Midland, 2001
354	A	CWR510Y	Leyland Olympian ONLXB/1R	Eastern Coach Works	B45/32F	1982	Burgundycar, Bracknell, 2001
355	I	EEH905Y	Leyland Olympian ONLXB/1R	Eastern Coach Works	B45/32F	1983	Arriva Midlands North, 2001
356	FW	B742GSC	Leyland Olympian ONTL11/2R	Eastern Coach Works	B51/32F	1984	Lothian Buses, 2001
357	I	B743GSC	Leyland Olympian ONTL11/2R	Eastern Coach Works	B51/32F	1984	Lothian Buses, 2001
358	I	B744GSC	Leyland Olympian ONTL11/2R	Eastern Coach Works	B51/32F	1984	Lothian Buses, 2001
359	I	B745GSC	Leyland Olympian ONTL11/2R	Eastern Coach Works	B51/32F	1984	Lothian Buses, 2001
360	FW	C791SFS	Leyland Olympian ONTL11/2R	Eastern Coach Works	B51/32F	1985	Lothian Buses, 2004
361	FW	C794SFS	Leyland Olympian ONTL11/2R	Eastern Coach Works	B51/32F	1985	Lothian Buses, 2004
401	T	MIL9753	Volvo B10M-61	Plaxton Paramount 3500 III	C53F	1989	
402	K	HDZ5417	Volvo B58-56	Duple Dominant II Express	C53F	1980	Shalder, Scalloway, 1999
403	K	JAZ9858	Scania K93CRB	Plaxton Paramount 3200 III	C57F	1989	Highland Country, 1999
404	T	YAZ6428	Volvo B10M-61	Plaxton Paramount 3500 III	C53F	1989	Express Travel, Perth, 1993
405	T	G780CFA	Scania K93CRB	Plaxton Paramount 3200 III	C53F	1990	Highland Country, 1999
406	I	MIL9755	Volvo B10M-60	Plaxton Paramount 3500 III	C49FT	1990	Highland Country, 1999
408	K	JAZ9859	Volvo B10M-60	Plaxton Paramount 3500 III	C49FT	1990	Highland Country, 1999
410	T	G149YAS	Volvo B10M-60	Plaxton Paramount 3200 III	C53F	1990	Highland Country, 1999
411	ST	KPS701T	Bedford YLQ	Plaxton Supreme IV Express	C45F	1979	Shalder, Scalloway, 1999
413	K	JAZ9856	Scania K93CRB	Plaxton Paramount 3200 III	C57F	1989	Highland Country, 1999
414	T	KAZ2065	Volvo B10M-60	Van Hool Alizée	C46FT	1990	Wallace Arnold, 1995
416	K	RXW982	Volvo B10M-61	Plaxton Paramount 3200 III	C49FT	1987	Sansome, Southampton, 2002
419	ST	PVS20W	Bedford YLQ	Duple Dominant II	C35F	1980	Shalder, Scalloway, 1999
437	ST	JIL5809	Bedford YMP	Plaxton Paramount 3200	C45F	1983	Shalder, Scalloway, 1999
439	K	JAZ9850	Volvo B10M-61	Van Hool Alizée	C52FT	1984	Highland Country, 1999
441	P	JAZ9853	Volvo B10M-61	Van Hool Alizée	C52FT	1984	Highland Country, 1999
442	ST	A106MAC	Bedford YNT	Plaxton Paramount 3200	C53F	1984	Shalder, Scalloway, 1999
443	ST	A416SPS	Bedford YNT	Plaxton Paramount 3200	C53F	1983	Shalder, Scalloway, 1999
444	K	HDZ5427	Volvo B10M-61	Van Hool Alizée	C50FT	1984	Peace, Kirkwall, 1999
449	K	A157PKR	Volvo B10M-61	Plaxton Paramount 3200 II	C49F	1984	Mason, Bo'ness, 1996
450	T	JAZ9855	Volvo B10M-56	Plaxton Paramount 3200 II	C46FT	1986	Highland Country, 1999

The Bristol VR, once out of favour with the Scottish Bus Group, can still be found in some areas. At Thurso 330, VAH280X, is seen at rest between journeys. *Phillip Stephenson*

451	ST	B509YAT	Bedford YNT	Plaxton Paramount 3200 II	C53F	1985	Shalder, Scalloway, 1999
452	ST	C771FBH	Bedford YNV	Duple 320	C57F	1985	Shalder, Scalloway, 1999
454	I	D181TSB	Volvo B10M-60	Plaxton Paramount 3200 III	C55F	1986	Shalder, Scalloway, 1999
455	ST	TJI7192	Bedford YNT	Plaxton Paramount 3200 III	C53F	1987	Shalder, Scalloway, 1999
456	ST	D31RYB	Bedford YNT	Plaxton Paramount 3200 III	C53F	1987	Shalder, Scalloway, 1999
457	K	SJI1631	Bedford YNT	Plaxton Paramount 3200 III	C53F	1987	Peace, Kirkwall, 1999
459	I	D660XPS	Volvo B10M-61	Duple 320	C57F	1987	Shalder, Scalloway, 1999
460	T	KLZ2315	Volvo B10M-60	Plaxton Paramount 3200 III	C57F	1989	Shalder, Scalloway, 1999
461	T	F469WFX	Volvo B10M-60	Plaxton Paramount 3200 III	C53F	1989	Shalder, Scalloway, 1999
462	T	MIL9754	Volvo B10M-60	Plaxton Paramount 3500 III	C49FT	1990	Highland Country, 1999
463	T	MIL9756	Volvo B10M-60	Plaxton Paramount 3500 III	C49FT	1990	Highland Country, 1999
464	T	G253VPK	Volvo B10M-60	Plaxton Paramount 3500 III	C49FT	1990	Highland Country, 1999
467	KY	J75FPS	Volvo B10M-60	Plaxton Paramount 3200 III	C57F	1991	Shalder, Scalloway, 1999
468	KY	H410DPS	Volvo B10M-60	Plaxton Paramount 3200 III	C57F	1990	Shalder, Scalloway, 1999
471	KY	B450GCB	Volvo B10M-61	Van Hool Alizée	C49FT	1985	Highland Country, 1999
473	K	D451CNR	Bedford YNT	Duple 320	C53F	1987	Tebbett, South Kirkby, 2001
474	K	A446BGM	Bedford YNT	Plaxton Paramount 3200	C53F	1984	Shiel Buses, Acharacle, 2001
475	K	B460KRM	Bedford YMP	Plaxton Paramount 3200	C45F	1985	Rae, Whitehaven, 2002
476	K	C321PRM	Bedford YNT	Plaxton Paramount 3200 II	C53F	1986	Rae, Whitehaven, 2002
477	K	C322PRM	Bedford YNT	Plaxton Paramount 3200 II	C53F	1986	Rae, Whitehaven, 2002
478	K	E176TWW	Bedford YNT	Plaxton Paramount 3200	C57F	1988	Pierce, Maghull, 2002
479	K	A449HJF	Bedford YNT	Plaxton Paramount 3200	C53F	1984	Goldstraw, Cheadle, 2002
480	K	B193DVL	Bedford YNT	Plaxton Paramount 3200	C53F	1985	Goldstraw, Cheadle, 2002
481	K	C268XSC	Bedford Venturer YNV	Plaxton Paramount 3200 II	C53F	1985	Goldstraw, Cheadle, 2002
482	K	535LXB	Dennis Javelin 11m	Plaxton Première 320	C51F	1993	Centrebus, Leicester, 2004
483	K	550XBV	Dennis Javelin 11m	Plaxton Interurban	BC51F	1994	Burnley & Pendle, 2004
484	K	720RXJ	Dennis Javelin 11m	Plaxton Interurban	BC51F	1994	Burnley & Pendle, 2004
485	K	520PXR	Dennis Javelin 11m	Plaxton Interurban	BC51F	1995	Sovereign, Stevenage, 2004
486	K	700CWL	Dennis Javelin 11m	Plaxton Interurban	BC47F	1994	Sovereign, Stevenage, 2004
487	K	JAZ9852	Dennis Javelin 11m	Plaxton Interurban	BC47F	1993	Sovereign, Stevenage, 2004
488	P	G636WJS	Dennis Javelin 12m	Duple Dominant	B65F	1989	Nicholson, Borve, 2002
489	I	R849CJS	Dennis Javelin 12m	UVG S320	BC70F	1998	Nicholson, Borve, 2002
490	I	R412YWJ	Dennis Javelin 12m	Plaxton Première 320	BC70F	1998	Spring IT Training, 2002
491	I	FSU718	Dennis Javelin 12m	Plaxton Première 320	BC67F	1998	Spring IT Training, 2002
492	P	S690RWG	Dennis Javelin 12m	Plaxton Première 320	BC67F	1998	Spring IT Training, 2002

Carrying Highland names is the only Wright Renown body in the Rapson fleet. Built on a Volvo B10BLE chassis, it is seen in Inverness. *Phillip Stephenson*

493	P	SY51EZU	Dennis Javelin 12m	Plaxton Prima 70	BC70F	2002	
494	P	SY51EHT	Dennis Javelin 12m	Plaxton Prima 70	BC70F	2002	
495	FW	SY51EHU	Dennis Javelin 12m	Plaxton Prima 70	BC70F	2002	
496	KY	SY51EHZ	Dennis Javelin 12m	Plaxton Prima 70	BC70F	2002	
497	P	SY51EHV	Dennis Javelin 12m	Plaxton Prima 70	BC70F	2002	
498	T	SY51EHX	Dennis Javelin 12m	Plaxton Prima 70	BC70F	2002	
499	K	A615KRT	Bedford YNT	Plaxton Paramount 3200	C53F	1984	Minsterley Motors, 2002
501	P	F70DDA	Leyland Lynx LX2R11C15Z4R	Leyland	B49F	1989	Travel West Midlands, 2001
502	P	G83EOG	Leyland Lynx LX2R11C15Z4R	Leyland	B49F	1989	Travel West Midlands, 2001
504	A	G103EOG	Leyland Lynx LX2R11C15Z4R	Leyland	B49F	1989	Travel West Midlands, 2001
508	P	G111EOG	Leyland Lynx LX2R11C15Z4R	Leyland	B49F	1989	Travel West Midlands, 2001
515	P	G132EOG	Leyland Lynx LX2R11C15Z4R	Leyland	B49F	1989	Travel West Midlands, 2001
517	A	G150EOG	Leyland Lynx LX2R11C15Z4R	Leyland	B49F	1989	Travel West Midlands, 2001
524	P	G173EOG	Leyland Lynx LX2R11C15Z4R	Leyland	B49F	1989	Travel West Midlands, 2001
526	P	G176EOG	Leyland Lynx LX2R11C15Z4R	Leyland	B49F	1989	Travel West Midlands, 2001
531	A	G284EOG	Leyland Lynx LX2R11C15Z4R	Leyland	B49F	1990	Travel West Midlands, 2001
534	A	G289EOG	Leyland Lynx LX2R11C15Z4R	Leyland	B49F	1990	Travel West Midlands, 2001
540	K	UIJ412	Dennis Javelin 11m	Plaxton Interurban	BC47F	1993	Lancashire United, 2004
541	K	PDZ7762	Dennis Javelin 11m	Plaxton Interurban	BC51F	1994	Burnley & Pendle, 2005
542	A	YK05FEK	Dennis Javelin 12m	Plaxton Prima 70	BC70F	2005	
613	K	ESK930	Volvo B10M-62	Plaxton Première 350	C46FT	1993	
614	A	FSU797	Volvo B10M-62	Plaxton Première 350	C48FT	1993	
616	T	JAZ9854	Volvo B10M-62	Plaxton Première 350	C49FT	1992	Flights, Birmingham, 1997
617	T	OIL4570	Volvo B10M-62	Plaxton Première 350	C49FT	1992	Wallace Arnold, 1997
619	T	930GJF	Volvo B10M-60	Plaxton Expressliner	C53F	1993	Ambassador, 1998
620	I	OAF990	DAF SB3000DKV601	Van Hool Alizée	C53F	1993	Blackpool Buses, 1999
621	I	673EXA	DAF SB3000DKV601	Van Hool Alizée	C53F	1993	?, 1999
622	K	L500GSM	Dennis Javelin 10m	Berkhof Excellence 1000L	C35F	1994	Peace, Kirkwall, 1999
623	I	RIB8035	Volvo B10M-62	Jonckheere Deauville 45	C50F	1994	Wallace Arnold, 1998
624	T	(ESK934)	Volvo B10M-62	Plaxton Expressliner 2	C48FT	1995	
625	T	KLZ2316	Volvo B10M-62	Plaxton Première 350	C51FT	1995	
626	T	HDZ5407	Volvo B10M-62	Plaxton Première 350	C47FT	1995	Bebb, Llantwit Fardre, 1998
627	P	CXP742	Volvo B10M-62	Plaxton Première 320	C49FT	1994	Tyrer, Trawden, 1999
628	I	650GXJ	Volvo B10M-62	Plaxton Expressliner 2	C47FT	1995	
629	I	YBZ818	Volvo B10M-62	Plaxton Première 350	C48FT	1995	

The Scottish Bus Handbook

Loading in readiness to take the 15:45 to Kinlochleven is Rapson 495, SY51EHU, one of several Dennis Javelins with Plaxton Prima 70 bodywork. These high-capacity vehicles are used on the longer services.
Bob Downham

630	I	FSU331	Volvo B10M-62	Plaxton Première 350	C47FT	1995	
631	I	LIJ595	Setra S250 Special	Setra	C55F	1995	Scancoaches, N Acton, 1999
632	FW	IDZ828	Dennis Javelin 12m	Berkhof Excellence 1000	C51F	1996	Highland Country, 1999
633	FW	EUI656	Dennis Javelin 12m	Berkhof Excellence 1000	C49F	1996	Highland Country, 1999
634	I	KLZ858	Volvo B10M-62	Plaxton Expressliner 2	C49FT	1997	
635	I	900HKU	Volvo B10M-62	Plaxton Expressliner 2	C46FT	1997	
636	FW	IDZ636	Volvo B10M-62	Plaxton Expressliner 2	C51FT	1997	
637	FW	162EKH	Volvo B10M-62	Plaxton Première 350	C51F	1995	Cummer Commercials, 1997
638	I	540FFX	Volvo B10M-62	Jonckheere Mistral 50	C53FT	1997	
639	I	719CEL	DAF DE33WSSB3000	Van Hool Alizée	C50FT	1997	Davies Bros, Pencader, 1999
640	I	MIL5573	Volvo B10M-62	Jonckheere Mistral 50	C43F	1998	
641	I	NFL881	Volvo B10M-62	Plaxton Première 350	C50F	1998	
643	FW	R874RST	Volvo B10M-62	Plaxton Première 320	C55F	1998	
644	I	T131AST	Volvo B10M-62	Plaxton Première 320	C54FT	1999	
645	T	V943JST	Volvo B10M-62	Plaxton Première 350	C49FT	2000	
646	I	V944JST	Volvo B10M-62	Plaxton Première 350	C49FT	2000	
647	I	W743NAS	Volvo B10M-62	Plaxton Paragon	C50FT	2000	
648	I	XIJ602	Volvo B10M-62	Plaxton Paragon	C49FT	2000	
649	I	W745NAS	Volvo B10M-62	Plaxton Paragon	C49FT	2000	
650	I	444VNX	Volvo B10M-62	Plaxton Paragon	C49FT	2000	
651	I	GSU375	Volvo B10M-60	Jonckheere Deauville	C53F	1995	Abbots, Blackpool, 2001
652	T	MIL9752	Volvo B10M-60	Plaxton Paramount 3500 III	C51F	1989	
653	FW	Y285YST	Volvo B10M-62	Plaxton Excalibur	C49FT	2001	
654	I	KLZ2317	Volvo B10M-62	Plaxton Première 320	C49FT	2001	
655	I	X466XAS	Volvo B10M-62	Plaxton Première 320	C53F	2001	
656	I	318DHR	Volvo B10M-62	Plaxton Première 350	C48FT	1999	Wallace Arnold, 2001
657	I	LTU284	Volvo B10M-62	Plaxton Première 350	C48FT	1999	Wallace Arnold, 2001
658	T	T535EUB	Volvo B10M-62	Plaxton Première 350	C48FT	1999	Wallace Arnold, 2001
659	I	LTU284	Volvo B10M-62	Plaxton Première 350	C48FT	1999	Wallace Arnold, 2001
660	I	TFX966	Volvo B10M-62	Van Hool Alizée HE	C49FT	1996	Whitelaw, Stonehaven, 2002
662	I	448GWL	Volvo B10M-62	Van Hool Alizée HE	C46FT	1996	
663	P	KFO809	Dennis Javelin 12m	Plaxton Première 320	C50F	1998	Spring IT Training, 2003
664	P	WFO311	Dennis Javelin 12m	Plaxton Première 320	C50F	1998	Spring IT Training, 2002
665	FW	200UWX	Volvo B10M-60	Van Hool Alizée HE	C49F	1992	Kingdon, Tiverton, 2004
667	I	DSU707	Volvo B10M-62	Plaxton Paragon	C49FT	2001	Bebb, Llantwit Fardre, 2004
668	I	900RWX	Volvo B10M-62	Plaxton Paragon	C49FT	2001	Bebb, Llantwit Fardre, 2004
669	I	FN04JZR	Volvo B10M-62	Jonckheere Mistral 50	C49FT	2004	
670	I	FN04JZT	Volvo B10M-62	Jonckheere Mistral 50	C49FT	2004	
671	I	850RFX	Volvo B10M-62	Van Hool Alizée HE	C46FT	1996	Tellings-Golden Miller, 2003

Ancillary vehicle:

| 454 | I | KLZ2318 | Volvo B10M-60 | Plaxton Paramount 3200 III | TV | 1988 | Shalder, Scalloway, 1999 |

162EKH	95G955, M105VRA	JAZ9854	P229DBS
200UWX	J257NNC, 804TYA	JAZ9855	C330FSU, ESK983, 318DHR
318DHR	T536EUB	JAZ9856	F431GWG, 199PBS
444VNX	W746NAS	JAZ9857	P277NPH, NXI321
448GWL	J738CWT	JAZ9858	G803RNC
520PKR	M107CCD	JAZ9859	G813BPG
535LXB	L15BFV	JIL3391	ONV647Y, 3085EL, CHN587Y
540FFX	P648FST, 4234NT	JIL5809	XVN501Y
550XBV	L156BFV	JST224N	GFJ663N, JIL606, KKZ5534
650GXJ	N764CAS	J75FPS	J75FPS, KLZ2317
673EXA	J64GCX	K247MOS	K500WCM
700CWL	M951JBO	KAZ2065	H619UWR, NJS246, 1983NT
719CEL	R272FBX	KFO809	S494UAK
720RXJ	L158BFV	KKZ5534	P65HBG
850RFX	M90TGM	KLZ858	P491FAS
900HKU	P492FAS	KLZ2315	F828APS
930GJF	K65BKG	KLZ2316	M488WAS, ESK983
A157PKR	A157PKR, GAZ4632	KLZ2317	X465SAS, MXI694
A449HJF	A449HJF, GAZ6666	KLZ2318	D181TSB
A615KRT	A253SBM, 866NVU	KSU674	P904DST
B193DVL	B193DVL, PAZ9319, GAZ7227	LIJ595	M972NFU
B450GCB	B47UNB, XTW359, B450GCB, RIB8035	LTU284	T539EUB, ESK985
B857XYR	B857XYR, XIJ602	M211YAS	M926TYG, M6SKY
B858XYR	B858XYR, KXI424	MBZ6454	B572AVW, URY598
B859XYT	B859XYR, UIJ412	MIL6675	G810BPG
C268XSC	B885RMS, B977NSF	MIL9752	F437DUG, DSK558
CXP742	L9TCC	MIL9753	F306URU, ESK985, TRM144
D31RYB	D31RYB, PDZ7762	MIL9754	G251VPK
DSU707	X47CNY	MIL9755	G811BPG
ESK930	L592RST	MIL9756	G252VPK
ESK934	N139YST	MUY59X	PNT850X, GBB254
EUI656	N865XMO	NFL881	R872RST
FSU331	N906AAS	NIL2734	A507GPC, A12MTL, A260YEP
FSU718	R413YWJ	NIL2735	B693BPU
FSU797	L591RST, ESK986	NST61Y	HRO2Y
G149YAS	G512EFX, 3275RU, G264NUX, TFX966, MIL5573	OAF990	J26LRN, ESK981
G780CFA	G780CFA, JAZ9857	OIL4570	J737CWT, ESK932
		OSK620V	DOC36V
		P343JAS	JN90AA
GSU375	M307KRY	P677VJS	JN88AA
HDZ5407	M45KAX, 9637EL	P907DST	P907DST, FSU797
		PIL6829	P698HND
HDZ5417	MPS970W. FSU718	R412YWJ	R412YWJ, OFA990
		RIB8035	L947NWW, 3692NT
		RXW982	D783SGB, PSU630
		S690RNG	S690RNG, LTU284
		S751SCJ	S751SCJ, FSU797
HDZ5427	LTU284. A128TAS	SJI1631	D125VRM, 748COF, D410BDP
H410DPS	H410DPS, KLZ2316	T535EUB	T535EUB, TRM144
HIL7467	FUA387Y, 3408WY, NRV859Y	TFX966	N330RGB, 9396WW
HRO2Y	S593UPV	TGD759W	TGD759W, WNR536, WIB7085
IDZ636	P649FST	TJI7192	D676FWK, 9737VC, D523TUJ
IDZ828	N866XMO	TRM144	T535EUB
JAZ4632	P276NRH, OXI459	UIJ412	L153BFV
JAZ9850	A639EJS, 1983NT, A199PBS	V943JST	V943JST, TRM144
		WFO311	S495UAK
		WIB7085	R937AMB
JAZ9851	P275NRH, OXI413	XIJ602	W744NAS
JAZ9852	L144BFV	YAZ6428	G260UAS, 318HDR, ESK985
		YBZ818	N905AAS
JAZ9853	B217FJS	YSU882	P906DST

RENNIES

Rennie's of Dunfermline Ltd, Wellwood, Dunfermline, KY12 0PY

TPD108X	Leyland Olympian ONTL11/1R	Roe	B43/29F	1982	Beeston, Hadleigh, 2002
KYV756X	MCW Metrobus DR101/14	MCW	B43/28D	1982	Arriva Scotland West, 2002
NUW596Y	Leyland Titan TNLXB2RR	Leyland	B44/24F	1982	Stagecoach South, 2002
NUW600Y	Leyland Titan TNLXB2RR	Leyland	B44/28F	1982	Stagecoach North West, 2002
OHV697Y	Leyland Titan TNLXB2RR	Leyland	B44/24D	1983	Stagecoach North West, 2002
OHV721Y	Leyland Titan TNLXB2RR	Leyland	B44/28F	1983	Stagecoach London, 2002
OHV744Y	Leyland Titan TNLXB2RR	Leyland	B44/28F	1983	Stagecoach London, 2002
OHV771Y	Leyland Titan TNLXB2RR	Leyland	B44/28F	1983	Stagecoach London, 2002
OHV804Y	Leyland Titan TNLXB2RR	Leyland	B44/28F	1983	Stagecoach London, 2002
OHV805Y	Leyland Titan TNLXB2RR	Leyland	B44/28F	1983	Stagecoach London, 2002
OHV812Y	Leyland Titan TNLXB2RR	Leyland	B44/28F	1983	Stagecoach London, 2002
BHZ9546	Leyland Titan TNLXB2RR	Leyland	B44/27F	1983	Stagecoach London, 2001
A104OUG	Leyland Olympian ONTL11/1R	Northern Counties	B45/28F	1984	Millman Cs, Heathfield, 2003
A938SYE	Leyland Titan TNLXB2RR	Leyland	B44/26D	1984	Robinson, Leighton Buzzard, 2002
A648THV	Leyland Titan TNLXB2RR	Leyland	B44/33F	1984	Stagecoach West & Wales, 2002
B121WUV	Leyland Titan TNLXB2RR	Leyland	B44/26F	1984	Stagecoach South, 2002
B132WUL	MCW Metrobus DR101/17	MCW	B43/28D	1985	Arriva Scotland West, 2002
B209WUL	MCW Metrobus DR101/14	MCW	B43/28D	1985	Arriva Scotland West, 2002
E911KYR	Leyland Olympian ONLXB/1RH	Northern Counties	B43/30F	1987	Stagecoach, 2004
E919KYR	Leyland Olympian ONLXB/1RH	Northern Counties	B43/30F	1987	Stagecoach, 2004
E920KYR	Leyland Olympian ONLXB/1RH	Northern Counties	B43/30F	1987	Stagecoach, 2004
PIB9211	Volvo B10M-61	Jonckheere Jubilee	C51FT	1988	Croydon Circuit Coaches, 1991
IIL3504	Volvo B10M-60	Van Hool Alizée	C53F	1989	Stagecoach Bluebird, 2001
GDZ3363	Volvo B10M-60	Van Hool Alizée	C53F	1989	Stagecoach Bluebird, 2001
439BUS	Dennis Javelin 12m	Wadham Stringer Vanguard II	BC70F	1992	MoD, 2005
BHZ9543	Dennis Javelin 12m	Wadham Stringer Vanguard II	BC70F	1992	MoD, 2005
BHZ9545	Dennis Javelin 12m	Wadham Stringer Vanguard II	BC70F	1995	Stonehouse Coaches, 2006
LSK478	Volvo B10M-62	Jonckheere Deauville 50	C46FT	1995	TWH, Camberwell, 2002
LSK479	Volvo B10M-62	Jonckheere Deauville 50	C46FT	1995	TWH, Camberwell, 2002
BHZ9542	Dennis Javelin 12m	Wadham Stringer Vanguard II	BC70F	1995	MoD, 2005
BHZ9549	Dennis Javelin 12m	Wadham Stringer Vanguard II	BC70F	1995	MoD, 2004
NXX451	Dennis Javelin 12m	Wadham Stringer Vanguard II	BC70F	1995	Billy Mitchell, Plean, 2004
A16RNY	Dennis Javelin 12m	Caetano Algarve 2	C53F	1995	Lothian Buses, 2003
A19RNY	Dennis Javelin 12m	Caetano Algarve 2	C57F	1995	Lothian Buses, 2003
C12RNY	Dennis Javelin 12m	Caetano Algarve 2	C53F	1996	Lothian Buses, 2003
A17RNY	Dennis Javelin 12m	Caetano Algarve 2	C53F	1997	Lothian Buses, 2003

Newest of a selection of Leyland Titans operated by Rennies is B121WUV, seen here in Edinburgh.
Richard Walters

2004 saw the arrival of two less-common coaches into the Rennies fleet. These are the integral Mercedes-Benz Touro and FJ04ESU, a Volvo B12M with Sunsundegui Sideral 330 bodywork. The latter is the 3.5-metre version which contrasts with the 3.2-metre model both of which are assembled at the Spanish builder's facility in Alsasua. The current model, which looks similar, is the Sideral 2000. *Mark Doggett*

BHZ9548	Dennis Javelin 12m	UVG Cutlass	BC70F	1998	Billy Mitchell, Plean, 2004
CCZ5837	Volvo B10M-62	Jonckheere Mistral 50	C51FT	1998	Edinburgh Castle Coaches, 2005
XCD108	Iveco EuroRider 397E.12.35	Beulas Stergo ε	C48FT	1998	
C13RNY	Mercedes-Benz Sprinter 614	Autobus Classique	C24F	1999	Armstrong, Inverkeithing, 2002
PIJ601	Mercedes-Benz Sprinter 614	Onyx	C24F	1999	
NX03MVL	Mercedes-Benz Touro 1836RL	Mercedes-Benz	C49FT	2003	Evobus demonstrator, 2003
SN53BHD	LDV Convoy	LDV	M14	2003	
FJ04ESU	Volvo B12M	Sunsundegui Sideral 330	C49FT	2004	
BX04NCD	Mercedes-Benz Touro 1836RL	Mercedes-Benz	C49FT	2004	
SN04GFK	BMC Falcon 111	BMC	N35F	2004	
SN05FCU	BMC Falcon 111	BMC	N35F	2004	
SN05FCX	BMC Falcon 111	BMC	N35F	2005	
BX06NZU	Autosan Eagle	Autosan	BC67F	2006	
BX06NZV	Autosan Eagle	Autosan	BC67F	2006	

Previous registrations:

439BUS	75KK34		C12RNY	P76KSC
A16RNY	N75CSX		C13RNY	S584ACT
A17RNY	P78OSC		CCZ5837	98KK1562, R442LSC
A19RNY	N74BFS		GDZ3363	F555TMH, NSU132, F555TMH
B554ATX	B554ATX, BHZ9542		GSU343	L5BSL, L51LTF
BHZ9540	-		IIL3504	E626UNE, GIL2967, E937XSB
BHZ9541	-		K914SUS	75KK04
BHZ9542	EC57AA, N887HSX		LSK478	M627KVU
BHZ9543	K914SUS		LSK479	M624DRJ
BHZ9544	E214GNV, MJI2995, LSK479		NXX451	EC56AA, N94RGD
BHZ9545	75KK08, K966SUS		PIB9211	E698NNH
BHZ9546	A628THV		PIJ601	T807TSC
BHZ9547	-		XCD108	S107KJF
BHZ9548	R710TRV			
BHZ9549	CX47AA, M933ROS			

Web: www.renniesofdunfermline.co.uk

The Scottish Bus Handbook

RIVERSIDE

Riverside Transport Training Ltd, 15 Carlibar Road, Barrhead, G78 1AA

M354SDC	Mercedes-Benz 709D	Plaxton Beaver	B25F	1995	Metcalf, Sedgefield, 1996
N221MUS	Mercedes-Benz 709D	UVG CityStar	B29F	1996	
N779OGA	Mercedes-Benz 709D	UVG CityStar	B29F	1996	
N810PDS	Mercedes-Benz 811D	Marshall	B33F	1996	
N491FDT	Mercedes-Benz 709D	Plaxton Beaver	B27F	1996	Plaxton demonstrator, 1997
P478TGA	Mercedes-Benz 811D	UVG CityStar	B33F	1996	
P939YSB	Mercedes-Benz 709D	Plaxton Beaver	B29F	1997	
X109RGG	Dennis Dart SLF 8.8m	Plaxton Pointer MPD	N29F	2000	
SH51KJY	Dennis Dart SLF 8.8m	Plaxton Pointer MPD	N29F	2001	
PA51LEY	Dennis Dart SLF 10.7m	Plaxton Pointer 2	N37F	2001	
SA02UEX	Dennis Dart SLF 9.2m	Plaxton Pointer 2	N31F	2002	
SA02UEY	Dennis Dart SLF 9.2m	Plaxton Pointer 2	N31F	2002	
SA52GXO	Dennis Dart SLF 8.8m	Plaxton Pointer MPD	N29F	2002	
SF03YXP	Mercedes-Benz Vario 814D	TransBus Beaver 2	B29F	2003	
SF03YXR	Mercedes-Benz Vario 814D	TransBus Beaver 2	B29F	2003	
SF03ABU	TransBus Dart 10.7m	TransBus Pointer	N37F	2003	
SF04LHR	TransBus Dart 8.8m	TransBus Pointer	N29F	2004	

Riverside Transport operates a variety of lengths of Dennis Dart. Seen in Paisley while en route for Todholm is SF03ABU, a model built during TransBus ownership of the former Alexander factory in Falkirk. *Bob Downham*

ROWE & TUDHOPE

TC & G Rowe, West Hilhead, Weston Road, Kilmarnock, KA3 1PH

Reg	Chassis	Body	Seating	Year	History
TMS407X	Leyland Leopard PSU3G/4R	Alexander AYS	B49F	1982	Stagecoach Western, 1999
D713CSC	Leyland Tiger TRCTL11/2RH	Alexander P	B61F	1986	Stagecoach Fife, 2000
D518VSX	Leyland Tiger TRCTL11/3R	Alexander P	B61F	1987	Dart Buses, Paisley, 2002
D131UGB	Dennis Dorchester SDA811	Alexander TC	B69F	1987	Stagecoach Western, 2001
D216NCS	Dennis Dorchester SDA811	Alexander TC	B69F	1987	Stagecoach Western, 2001
D217NCS	Dennis Dorchester SDA811	Alexander TC	B69F	1987	Stagecoach Western, 2001
D218NCS	Dennis Dorchester SDA811	Alexander TC	B69F	1987	Stagecoach Western, 2001
D220NCS	Dennis Dorchester SDA811	Alexander TC	B69F	1987	Stagecoach Western, 2001
D221NCS	Dennis Dorchester SDA811	Alexander TC	B69F	1987	Stagecoach Western, 2001
VJI9410	Volvo B10M-61	Plaxton Paramount 3500 III	C57F	1987	Riddler's, Arbroath, 2005
G806JRH	Scania N113DRB	East Lancs	B51/27F	1989	Stonehouse Coaches, 2005
L704AGA	Mercedes-Benz 811D	Wadham Stringer Wessex II	B32FL	1992	
VJI9411	Volvo B10M-62	Jonckheere Deauville 45	C53F	1993	Swift, Barrhead, 2005
P376NSX	Ford Transit	Mayflower	M16	1997	, 2005
CJZ9222	Volvo B10M-62	Jonckheere Deauville 45	C51FT	1995	Bullick, Rathfriland, 2005
YBZ4427	Volvo B10M-62	Jonckheere Deauville 45	C53F	1995	Bullick, Rathfriland, 2005
VJI3002	Volvo B10M-62	Plaxton Première 350	C53F	1999	Bus Eireann, 2004
S617LRN	LDV Convoy	Jaycas	M16	1999	Owen, Paisley, 2005
W348WCS	Mercedes-Benz Vario O814	Plaxton Beaver 2	B31F	2000	
W349WCS	Mercedes-Benz Vario O814	Plaxton Beaver 2	B31F	2000	
VJI9412	Volvo B10M-62	Jonckheere Mistral 50	C53FT	2001	Park's of Hamilton, 2004
SJ03EHT	Mercedes-Benz Vario O814	TransBus Cheetah	C33F	2003	Mitchell, Plean, 2005
SF04HXM	Mercedes-Benz Vario O814	TransBus Beaver 2	BC33F	2004	

Previous registrations:

CJZ9222	M336KRY		
D131UGB	D219NCS, VLT73	VJI3002	T391UCH, 99D41322
D216NCS	D216NCS, WLT526	VJI9410	D804SGB, 4504RU
D217NCS	D217NCS, FSU737	VIJ9411	L746YGE, 1PSV, L942LBV, RIL2576
D218NCS	D218NCS, WLT415	VIJ9412	LSK509, Y201CDS
D220NCS	D220NCS, WLT447	VJI9413	-
D221NCS	D221NCS, WLT501	VJI9414	-
		YBV4427	M309KRY

Web: www.roseamdtudhope.com

Interesting vehicles owned by Rowe & Tudhope are six Dennis Dorchester buses with Alexander TC bodywork. All were new to Western Scottish and featured high-back seating which has now been replaced with 3+2 seating for school contracts. *Billy Nicol*

SCOTTISH TRAVEL

Scottish Travel - Wilson's Coaches

Flosshaul Ltd; R H Wilson, 15 Dellingburn Street, Greenock, PA15 4RN

Reg	Chassis	Body	Seating	Year	History
HSL660	AEC Routemaster RH2H1	Park Royal	O40/32R	1961	London United, 2005
JJD432D	AEC Routemaster R2RH/2	Park Royal	B40/32R	1967	London United, 2005
SMK697F	AEC Routemaster R2RH/2	Park Royal	B40/32R	1967	London United, 2005
C787GGB	Volvo B10M-61	Plaxton Paramount 3200	C57F	1985	Pride of the Clyde, Gourock, 2005
J615XHL	Dennis Dart 9m	Plaxton Pointer	B34F	1991	London Central, 2000
NDZ7925	Mercedes-Benz 811D	Wright NimBus	B26F	1993	Metroline, Harrow, 2000
K476FYN	Mercedes-Benz 811D	Wright NimBus	B26F	1993	Metroline, Harrow, 2000
M327TSF	Mercedes-Benz 709D	Alexander Sprint	B29F	1994	
M394KVR	Mercedes-Benz 709D	Alexander Sprint	B27F	1994	Arriva Cymru, 2003
M101WKA	Mercedes-Benz 709D	Alexander Sprint	B27F	1994	Arriva Midlands, 2003
M378EFD	Mercedes-Benz 709D	Alexander Sprint	B27F	1995	Arriva Midlands, 2003
M121YCM	Mercedes-Benz 709D	Alexander Sprint	B29F	1995	Arriva North West, 2003
M126YCM	Mercedes-Benz 709D	Alexander Sprint	B29F	1995	Arriva North West, 2003
M128YCM	Mercedes-Benz 709D	Alexander Sprint	B29F	1995	Arriva North West, 2003
N345OBC	Mercedes-Benz 709D	Alexander Sprint	B27F	1995	Arriva North West, 2003
N468SPA	Mercedes-Benz 709D	Alexander Sprint	B27F	1995	Arriva North West & Wales, 2005
N470SPA	Mercedes-Benz 709D	Alexander Sprint	B27F	1995	Arriva North West & Wales, 2005
N345OBC	Mercedes-Benz 709D	Alexander Sprint	B27F	1995	Arriva North West, 2003
P398FEA	Mercedes-Benz 709D	Alexander Sprint	B27F	1996	Arriva North West & Wales, 2005
P61HOJ	Mercedes-Benz Vario 0814	Alexander ALX100	BC29F	1997	Arriva North West & Wales, 2005
P675RWU	Dennis Dart SLF	Plaxton Pointer	N35F	1997	Dickson, Erskine, 2005
P691RWU	Dennis Dart SLF	Plaxton Pointer	N35F	1997	Henderson, Hamilton, 2005
P697RWU	Dennis Dart SLF	Plaxton Pointer	N35F	1997	, 2005
R719JGD	LDV Convoy	LDV	M16	1998	van, 2000
R531PJH	LDV Convoy	LDV	M16	1998	van, 2000
WIL9216	Dennis Dart SLF 10.7m	Plaxton Pointer 2	N37F	1999	Harte, Greenock, 2005
WIL9217	Dennis Dart SLF 10.7m	Plaxton Pointer 2	N37F	1999	Beatie, Renfrew, 2005
V7CTL	Mercedes-Benz Vario 0814	Plaxton Beaver 2	BC33F	2001	Red Lion, Blantyre, 2005
YJ55YGD	Optare Solo M850	Optare	N29F	2006	

Previous registrations:

HSL660	WLT891	WIL9216	S609HGD, IIB3728
V7CTL	SF51PWE	WIL9217	V800CBC

The connected operations of Wilson's and Scottish Travel employ a fleet dominated by the Mercedes-Benz minibus. M126YCM, seen here in Scottish Travel colours, was new to North Western prior to becoming Arriva North West. *Phillip Stephenson*

SHUTTLE BUSES

Shuttle Buses, 2 Caledonia House, Longford Avenue, Kilwinning, KA13 6EX

Reg	Chassis	Body	Seating	Year	History
875YYA	AEC Reliance 6U3ZR	Plaxton Supreme IV	C53F	1979	Ogden, St Helens, 1998
GSU551	Leyland Tiger TRCTL11/3R	Plaxton Paramount 3500	C53F	1983	Viscount Central, Burnley, 1998
GSU342	Leyland Tiger TRCTL11/2RH	Alexander TC	C49F	1985	T&E Docherty, Irvine, 2002
G757SRB	Scania N113CRB	Alexander PS	B58F	1989	City of Nottingham, 2003
G831RDS	Ford Transit VE6	Dormobile	BC20F	1990	
IUI9892	Mercedes-Benz 709D	Dormobile Routemaker	B29F	1990	Bridge Coaches, Paisley, 1997
J383GKH	Dennis Dart 8.5m	Plaxton Pointer	B28F	1992	Tanner, St Helens, 2004
K770AFS	Mercedes-Benz 814D	Plaxton Beaver	BC33F	1992	Whitestar, Neilston, 1996
P241WWX	Mercedes-Benz 611D	Mellor	B18F	1997	MB Leeds, 2004
S310KNW	Optare MetroRider MR17	Optare	B29F	1998	
S904DUB	Optare MetroRider MR17	Optare	BC31F	1998	Wilson's of Rhu, 2001
S515GGD	Ford Transit VE6	Ford	M14	1998	Manchester Minibuses, 2000
T337TVM	Dennis Dart SLF 8.8m	Plaxton Pointer MPD	N28F	1999	Jim Stones, Leigh, 2002
T902JTD	Dennis Dart SLF 8.8m	Plaxton Pointer MPD	N28F	1999	Jim Stones, Leigh, 2003
T56RJL	Mercedes-Benz Vario 0814	Autobus Classique Nouvelle 2	C33F	1999	Fairway, Kirkstall, 2002
X299DHF	Ford Transit	Ford	M14	1998	Manchester Minibuses, 2000
X311ABU	Mercedes-Benz Vario 0814	Plaxton Beaver 2	B31F	2000	
X704UKS	Dennis Dart SLF 8.8m	Plaxton Pointer MPD	N29F	2001	Stuarts, Carluke, 2005
SJ04FLA	Mercedes-Benz Vario 0614	Onyx	BC24F	2004	
N5SBL	Optare Solo M850	Optare	N20F	2004	
N6SBL	Optare Solo M850	Optare	N20F	2004	
N7SBL	Optare Solo M850	Optare	N20F	2004	
SF54CHK	Mercedes-Benz Sprinter 311cdi	Mercedes-Benz	M16	2004	
SP05AKK	Mercedes-Benz Sprinter 311cdi	Mercedes-Benz	M16	2005	
N3SBL	Optare Solo M920	Optare	N33F	2005	
N2SBL	Optare Solo M850	Optare	N280F	2006	

Previous registrations:

Reg	Previous		Reg	Previous
875YYA	DCH359T, HFF234, TKC833T		N6SBL	YJ54ZXV
IUI9892	H124YGG		N7SBL	YJ54ZXW
GSU342	B208FPS		S904DUB	S904DUB, N400RHU
GSU551	A201MFR		T337TVM	BUS1N
N5SBL	YJ54ZXU		T902JTD	BUS1T

Still providing active service for Shuttle Buses is AEC Reliance 875YYA. New in 1979 to Cartledge of Huthwaite, it carries a Plaxton Supreme IV body and is seen here on private hire work in Glasgow. *Billy Nicol*

SLAEMUIR COACHES

Slaemuir Coaches Ltd, 2 Dellingburn Street, Greenock, PA15 4RN

K237SFJ	Mercedes-Benz 709D	Reeve Burgess Beaver	B25F	1991	Avondale Coaches, Greenock, 2002
K239SFJ	Mercedes-Benz 709D	Reeve Burgess Beaver	B25F	1991	Avondale Coaches, Greenock, 2002
K85DTM	Mercedes-Benz 811D	Wright NimBus	B33F	1992	Comet, Greenock, 2002
K241SFJ	Mercedes-Benz 709D	Reeve Burgess Beaver	B25F	1992	Citybus, Plymouth, 2002
K580YOJ	Mercedes-Benz 811D	Wright NimBus	B33F	1992	Comet, Greenock, 2003
L641DNA	Mercedes-Benz 709D	Plaxton Beaver	B27F	1993	Arriva Midlands, 2002
L94LND	Mercedes-Benz 709D	Plaxton Beaver	B27F	1993	Walsh, Middleton, 1999
L253YOD	Mercedes-Benz 709D	Plaxton Beaver	B25F	1994	Citybus, Plymouth, 2005
L254YOD	Mercedes-Benz 709D	Plaxton Beaver	B25F	1994	Citybus, Plymouth, 2005
L637DNA	Mercedes-Benz 709D	Marshall C19	B27F	1994	AA Buses, Ayr, 1996
M20BLU	Mercedes-Benz 811D	Marshall C16	B33F	1994	Bluebird, Rochdale, 2000
M123YCM	Mercedes-Benz 709D	Alexander Sprint	B27F	1995	Arriva North West, 2002
M124YCM	Mercedes-Benz 709D	Alexander Sprint	B27F	1995	Arriva North West, 2002
M7JPT	Mercedes-Benz 709D	Marshall C19	B27F	1995	Hughes, Greenock, 2000
N943MGG	Mercedes-Benz 709D	Marshall C19	B29F	1995	Argyle Bus, Port Glasgow, 1997
N990FNK	Mercedes-Benz 709D	Marshall C19	B27F	1996	Reg's, Hertford, 2002
N991FNK	Mercedes-Benz 709D	Marshall C19	B27F	1996	Reg's, Hertford, 2002
N798PDS	Mercedes-Benz 709D	Marshall C19	B29F	1996	Avondale Coaches, Greenock, 2002
N799PDS	Mercedes-Benz 709D	Marshall C19	B29F	1996	Avondale Coaches, Greenock, 2002
N616DWY	Mercedes-Benz 709D	Plaxton Beaver	B27F	1995	Silverwing, Brislington, 1999
N34GSX	Mercedes-Benz 709D	Alexander Sprint	B29F	1996	
P151LSC	Mercedes-Benz 709D	Alexander Sprint	B29F	1996	Dart Buses, Paisley, 1999
P152LSC	Mercedes-Benz 709D	Alexander Sprint	B29F	1996	Dart Buses, Paisley, 1999
P477TGA	Mercedes-Benz 811D	Mellor	B31F	1996	Newark Coaches, Greenock, 2000

One of the less-common body builders to the industry is Mellor who produces bodywork from a facility in Rochdale. The company's styling is seen on Mercedes-Benz 811D P477TGA which was operating the Clynder Road service in Greenock. *Bob Downham*

Recent changes to the fleet have seen several low-floor buses enter service with Slaemuir Coaches. Two arrivals from Ireland include T404EGD, a Volvo B10BLE with Wright Renown bodywork. It is seen in Glasgow shortly after entering service in 2006. *Murdoch Currie*

T403EGD	Volvo B10BLE	Wright Renown	N40F	1999	Bus Eireann, 2006
T404EGD	Volvo B10BLE	Wright Renown	N40F	1999	Bus Eireann, 2006
V10CBC	Mercedes-Benz Vario 0814	Plaxton Beaver 2	B31F	1999	Coakley Bus, Motherwell, 2002
V500CBC	Mercedes-Benz Vario 0814	Plaxton Beaver 2	B31F	1999	Coakley Bus, Motherwell, 2002
W301GCW	Volvo B10M-62	Plaxton Paramount 3200	C49FT	2000	Blackburn Buses, 2003
W814UAG	Dennis Dart SLF 8.8m	Plaxton Pointer MPD	N29F	2000	Alpha, Anlaby, 2003
W815UAG	Dennis Dart SLF 8.8m	Plaxton Pointer MPD	N29F	2000	Alpha, Anlaby, 2003
W816UAG	Dennis Dart SLF 10.7m	Plaxton Pointer 2	N39F	2000	Alpha, Anlaby, 2003
W991XDM	Dennis Dart SLF 8.8m	Plaxton Pointer MPD	N29F	2000	Bleasdale, Liverpool, 2002
W814UAG	Dennis Dart SLF 8.8m	Plaxton Pointer MPD	N29F	2000	Bleasdale, Liverpool, 2002
Y489PTU	Dennis Dart SLF 8.8m	Plaxton Pointer MPD	N29F	2000	Bleasdale, Liverpool, 2002
Y187KCS	Volvo B10M-62	Jonckheere Mistral 50	C51F	2001	Highland Heritage, 2005
Y523UOS	Volvo B10M-62	Jonckheere Mistral 50	C51F	2001	Highland Heritage, 2005
Y797GDV	Volvo B10M-62	Caetano Enigma	C53F	2001	Bus Eireann, 2005
Y805GDV	Volvo B10M-62	Caetano Enigma	C53F	2001	Bus Eireann, 2005
CV02KFX	Mercedes-Benz Vario 0814	Cymric	B31F	2002	First Stop, Renfrew, 2005
AA02BUS	TransBus Dart 8.8m	TransBus Mini Pointer	N25F	2002	
AA52BUS	TransBus Dart 8.8m	TransBus Mini Pointer	N25F	2002	
SF53KUK	TransBus Dart 10.1m	TransBus Pointer	N37F	2003	
SF53KUN	TransBus Dart 10.1m	TransBus Pointer	N37F	2003	
SF05FNU	Mercedes-Benz Vario 0814	Plaxton Cheetah	C33F	2005	
YF02SKX	Optare Solo M920	Optare	N33F	2002	DAC, St Ann's Chapel, 2004
YF02SKZ	Optare Solo M920	Optare	N33F	2002	DAC, St Ann's Chapel, 2004

Previous registrations:

K85DTM	K8BUS			
L94LND	L94LND, L5BUS		Y805GDV	01D69361
T403EGD	?		Y187KCS	LSK500
T404EGD	?		Y523UOS	LSK505

SMITH & SONS

Messrs Smith, The Coach Depot, West Balgersho, Woodside, Coupar Angus, PH13 9LW

Reg	Chassis	Body	Type	Year	History
KRU847W	Bristol VRT/SL3/6LXB	Eastern Coach Works	B43/31F	1980	Rennie, Dunfermline, 2001
CAZ1577	Volvo B10M-62	Van Hool Alizée HE	C53F	1994	Park's of Hamilton, 1996
L631AYS	Volvo B10M-62	Van Hool Alizée HE	C53F	1994	Park's of Hamilton, 1996
N505PYS	Volvo B10M-62	Van Hool Alizée HE	C53F	1996	Park's of Hamilton, 1999
P681DCK	Ford Transit	Ford	M14	1997	Smith-Kenning, 1999
P871AFV	Ford Transit	Ford	M14	1997	Smith-Kenning, 1999
R567UOT	Dennis Dart SLF	UVG UrbanStar	N40F	1997	Daybird, Killamarsh, 2002
T523GSR	Volvo B10M-62	Van Hool Alizée	C53F	1999	
SIL8697	Ford Transit	Ford	M14	2000	
MU51FMV	Mercedes-Benz Sprinter 413cdi	Onyx	M16	2001	
ST02GDA	Mercedes-Benz Vario 0814	Plaxton Cheetah	C33F	2002	
ST02GDE	Mercedes-Benz Vario 0814	Plaxton Cheetah	C33F	2002	
YD02RBX	DAF SB120	Wrightbus Cadet 2	N39F	2002	
YD02RBY	DAF SB120	Wrightbus Cadet 2	N39F	2002	
YD02RBZ	DAF SB120	Wrightbus Cadet 2	N39F	2002	
SP53GZB	Mercedes-Benz Vario 0815	Sitcar Beluga	C33F	2004	
SP53GZC	Mercedes-Benz Vario 0815	Sitcar Beluga	C33F	2004	
SP04EUY	Mercedes-Benz Vario 0815	Sitcar Beluga	C33F	2004	
SP04EUZ	VDL Bova Futura FHD12.340	VDL Bova	C53FT	2004	
SP04EVB	VDL Bova Futura FHD12.340	VDL Bova	C53FT	2004	
SP05CXX	VDL Bova Futura FHD12.340	VDL Bova	C49FT	2005	
SP05CXY	Mercedes-Benz Vario 0815	Sitcar Beluga	C33F	2005	

Prevous registrations:

CAZ1577	LSK835, L633AYS		N505PYS	LSK844
L631AYS	LSK827			

Smith & Sons operates the Broxden Park & Ride service in Perth using three DAF SB120s with Wrightbus Cadet 2 bodywork. Seen on the service is YD02RBZ. *Bob Downham*

SOUTHERN

Southern Coaches (NM) Ltd, Barshagra Garage, Lochlibo Road, Barrhead, G78 1LF

W500SOU	Volvo B10M-62	Plaxton Première 320	C53F	2000
Y40SOU	Volvo B9M	Van Hool T9 Alizée	C38FT	2001
SA02SOU	Mercedes-Benz Vario 0815	Sitcar Beluga	C22FT	2002
SB02SOU	Volvo B12M	Van Hool T9 Alizée	C57F	2002
SC02SOU	Volvo B12M	Van Hool T9 Alizée	C51FT	2002
SD03SOU	Volvo B12M	Plaxton Parargon	C57F	2003
SE03SOU	Volvo B12M	Plaxton Paragon	C51FT	2003
SF04SOU	DAF SB4000	Van Hool T9 Alizée	C51FT	2004
SG04SOU	Volvo B12M	Van Hool T9 Alizée	C51FT	2004
XU05SOU	Toyota Coaster BB50R	Caetano Optimo V	C22F	2005
SJ05SOU	Volvo B12M	Plaxton Paragon	C51FT	2005
SK05SOU	Volvo B12B	Van Hool T9 Alicron	C51FT	2005
SL06SOU	Volvo B12M	Plaxton Paragon	C51FT	2006
SM06SOU	Volvo B12B	Plaxton Paragon	C57F	2006
SO06SOU	Volvo B12B	Van Hool T9 Alicron	C51FT	2006

The Southern Coaches fleet is now entirely comprised of vehices with SOU index marks. Illustrating the cream livery is Volvo Y800SOU, a recently withdrawn example of the Van Hool T9 Alizée body which is the standard product for this fleet. It is seen in Blackpool. *Bob Downham*

STOKES

William Stokes & Sons Ltd, 22 Carstairs Road, Carstairs, Lanark, ML11 8QD

HSB703Y	Leyland Tiger TRCTL11/2R	Plaxton Paramount 3200 Exp	C49F	1983	
A386XOS	Leyland Tiger TRCTL11/2R	Duple Laser Express	C53F	1983	
D298HMT	Van Hool T815	Van Hool Alizée	C53FT	1987	Clarkes of London, 1988
F479FGE	Leyland Tiger TRBTL11/2RP	Plaxton Derwent	B54F	1988	
F480FGE	Leyland Tiger TRBTL11/2RP	Plaxton Derwent	B54F	1988	
F343GUS	Leyland Tiger TRBTL11/2RP	Plaxton Derwent	B54F	1988	
F344GUS	Leyland Tiger TRBTL11/2RP	Plaxton Derwent	B54F	1988	
WSU857	Volvo B10M-60	Van Hool Alizée	C53F	1989	Skyeways, Kyle of Lochalsh, 1994
WSU859	Volvo B10M-60	Ikarus Blue Danube 350	C49FT	1989	
WSU860	Dennis Javelin 8.5m	Plaxton Paramount 3200 III	C32FT	1989	Green, Kirkintilloch, 1990
WSU858	Volvo B10M-60	Van Hool Alizée	C53FT	1990	Crawford, Neilston, 1994
WSU871	Van Hool T815	Van Hool Alicron	C49FT	1991	
L292USU	Dennis Dart 9m	Plaxton Pointer	B35F	1993	
L293USU	Dennis Dart 9m	Plaxton Pointer	B35F	1993	
N753LSU	Volvo B6-9.9	Alexander Dash	B40F	1995	
N971MGG	Volvo B6-9.9	Alexander Dash	B40F	1995	
WSU557	Dennis Javelin 12m GX	Berkhof Axial 50	C51FT	1998	Pullman, Crofty, 2001
T80LRT	Dennis Javelin 12m GX	Berkhof Axial 50	C51FT	1998	Lothian Buses, 2002
T409BGB	Mercedes-Benz Vario 0814	Marshall Master	B31F	1999	
V677FPO	Dennis Dart SLF	Caetano Compass	N38F	1999	Stonehouse Coaches, 2002
WSU209	Mercedes-Benz Vario 0814	Plaxton Cheetah	C33F	2001	
WSU864	Volvo B10M-62	Berkhof Axial 50	C51FT	2002	Maynes of Buckie, 2004

Previous registrations:

A386XOS	A846TDS, WSU858		WSU858	H262XDS
D298HMT	D298HMT, WSU864		WSU859	G586KKU
HSB703Y	MSU299Y, WSU857		WSU860	G850VAY
WSU209	from new		WSU864	KM02GSM
WSU557	R3PCL		WSU871	H290TDT
WSU857	G93PGB			

Lanark is the location for this view of Stokes' F480FGE, a Leyland Tiger with Plaxton Derwent bodywork and one of four currently operated. *Bob Downham*

STONEHOUSE COACHES

N Collison, 48 New Street, Stonehouse, Lanark, ML9 3LT

C793UGS	Volvo Citybus B10M-50	Alexander RV	B47/33F	1986	Stagecoach, 2005
C801UGS	Volvo Citybus B10M-50	Alexander RV	B47/33F	1986	Stagecoach, 2005
G808LAG	Scania N113DRB	East Lancashire	B51/27F	1989	Coachmasters, Rochdale, 1999
H809WKH	Scania N113DRB	East Lancashire	B47/37F	1990	Coachmasters, Rochdale, 2000
H201LOM	Scania N113DRB	Alexander RV	B45/31F	1990	Alex Head, Lutton, 2005
L441DBU	Mercedes-Benz 811D	Mellor	BC33F	1993	Oldham MB, 2003
M195TMG	Mercedes-Benz 709D	Plaxton Beaver	B24FL	1994	Mitchell, Plean, 2004
X799AVN	LDV Convoy	Crest	M16	2000	Wilson, Strathaven, 2005
SJ04LLA	Mercedes-Benz Vario 0814	TransBus Beaver 2	BC33F	2004	Mitchell, Plean, 2004
VX54CKK	Mercedes-Benz Vario 0814	Plaxton Beaver 2	BC33F	2004	

Depots: Aye Road, Larkhall; New Street, Stonehouse and Loch Park Industrial Estate, Stonehouse

While the larger 12 and 13 metre coaches are popular for the capacity, a demand for the 8.5 metre Dennis Javelin has been high with over a hundred built by 1996. The body on this Stokes vehicle, WSU860, is a Plaxton Paramount 3200 mark III. *Phillip Stephenson*

STUARTS of CARLUKE

Stuarts Coaches Ltd, Castlehill, Airdrie Road, Carluke, ML8 5EP

Reg	Chassis	Body	Seating	Year	History
MOD572P	Bristol VRT/SL3/6LXB	Eastern Coach Works	B43/31F	1976	Stokes, Carstairs, 2005
BPF134Y	Leyland Olympian ONTL11/1R	Roe	B43/29F	1983	Sovereign, Stevenage, 2002
DWW932Y	Leyland Olympian ONLXB/1R	Eastern Coach Works	B43/32F	1983	Sovereign, Stevenage, 2002
A713YFS	Leyland Olympian ONLXB/2R	Eastern Coach Works	B51/32D	1983	Lothian Buses, 2000
A714YFS	Leyland Olympian ONLXB/2R	Eastern Coach Works	B51/32D	1983	Lothian Buses, 2000
A317XWG	Leyland Olympian ONLXB/1R	Eastern Coach Works	B43/32F	1984	Stagecoach East Midland, 2001
A741JAY	Volvo B10M-61	Duple 320	C57F	1984	Docherty, Stevenston, 2003
B769GSC	Leyland Olympian ONLXB/2R	Eastern Coach Works	B51/32D	1985	Lothian Buses, 2002
C364BUV	MCW Metrobus DR101/17	MCW	B43/28D	1985	Coakley Bus, Motherwell, 2002
CKZ8187	Volvo B10M-61	Van Hool Alizée	C53F	1986	Shaws of Maxey, 2001
OBZ2241	Volvo B10M-61	Van Hool Alizée	C53F	1986	Giles, Newtonards, 2001
C770SFS	Leyland Olympian ONLXB/2R	Eastern Coach Works	B51/32D	1986	Lothian Buses, 2002
C771SFS	Leyland Olympian ONLXB/2R	Eastern Coach Works	B51/32D	1986	Lothian Buses, 2002
C774SFS	Leyland Olympian ONLXB/2R	Eastern Coach Works	B51/32D	1986	Lothian Buses, 2002
D154THG	Leyland Tiger TRBTL11/2RP	East Lancs	B55F	1987	East End, Clydach, 2003
E324BVO	Volvo Citybus B10M-50	East Lancs	B47/38D	1987	City of Nottingham, 2005
F723LRG	Leyland Lynx LX1126LXCTZR1R	Leyland Lynx	B39F	1989	Chester, Walkden, 2004
G38VME	Leyland Lynx LX2R11C15Z4S	Leyland Lynx	B49F	1989	Local Link, Stansted, 2004
G904UPP	Mercedes-Benz 709D	Reeve Burgess Beaver	B25F	1989	Sovereign, Stevenage, 2000
H11JYM	Mercedes-Benz 709D	Reeve Burgess Beaver	B25F	1990	Moffat & Williamson, Gauldry, 2005
RIL9350	Mercedes-Benz 811D	Reeve Burgess Beaver	BC25F	1990	Simpson, Rosehearty, 2001
VAZ2534	Volvo B10M-60	Jonckheere Jubilee P50	C49FT	1991	Turners Chumleigh, 2005
CKZ8184	Dennis Dart 10.2m	Plaxton Pointer	BC35F	1992	LB Barking, 2003
J388GKH	Dennis Dart 8.8m	Plaxton Pointer	B28F	1992	Irvine, Law, 2004
J937WHJ	Mercedes-Benz 709D	Plaxton Beaver	B23F	1992	Warnock, Gourock, 2003
JCZ2065	Volvo B10M-60	Jonckheere Deauville P599	C53F	1992	Regal, Edinburgh, 2005
B15STA	Volvo B10M-62	Van Hool Alizée	C48FT	1993	Statton, Dewsbury, 2005
L657HKS	Volvo B10M-62	Van Hool Alizée	C53F	1994	Irvine, Law, 2005
M152LPL	Mercedes-Benz 709D	Plaxton Beaver	B25F	1995	Phoenix, Blackpool, 1999
M975WES	Mercedes-Benz 709D	Plaxton Beaver	B25F	1995	Moffat & Williamson, Gauldry, 2005
USV803	Dennis Javelin 12m	Wadham Stringer Vanguard III	BC70F	1995	Go-Goodwin, Eccles, 2003
N862FWG	Ford Transit	Ford	M14	1996	Stewart, Portleithen, 2004
N208CKP	Mercedes-Benz 709D	Plaxton Beaver	B27F	1996	Stonehouse Coaches, 2005
2450PP	DAF SB3000	Van Hool Alizée HE	C49FT	1996	North Kent Express, 2001

Another operator to use the mid-life vehicles displaced from the capital is Stuarts. Among the Olympians operated, three were latterly dual-doored buses with Lothian. B769GSC is seen at the Carluke depot.
Mark Doggett

With over six thousand Darts now in service, and the most popular body for the product being the Pointer, it is hard to travel far in the country without seeing the type. The colours of Stuarts of Carluke are carried on Mini Pointer SL52CPX as it departs Glasgow for Kirkintilloch. *Phillip Stehenson*

CSV651	Volvo B10M-62	Van Hool Alizée HE	C51FT	1997	
KSV980	Volvo B10M-62	Van Hool Alizée HE	C51FT	1997	
HUI8156	Volvo B10M-62	Caetano Algarve	C48FT	1997	Diamond, Morriston, 2002
YKJ798	Volvo B10M-62	Jonckheere Mistral 50	C51FT	1998	
T674TSG	Dennis Dart SLF 10.8m	Alexander ALX200	N38F	1999	Mitchell, Plean, 2004
W895AGA	Dennis Dart SLF 8.8m	Plaxton Pointer MPD	N29F	2000	
YKJ798	Volvo B10M-62	Caetano Algarve	C49F	2000	Collison, Stonehouse, 2003
LSV380	Volvo B10M-62	Van Hool Alizée	C49FT	2000	Bassetts, Tittensor, 2003
X705UKS	Dennis Dart SLF	Plaxton Pointer MPD	N29F	2001	
SK02VMO	Dennis Dart SLF	Plaxton Pointer MPD	N29F	2002	
SN02NMP	Bova Futura FHD12.340	Bova	C49FT	2002	Woods, Tillicoultry, 2004
SF02EWG	Ford Transit	Ford	M16	2002	
SL52CPX	TransBus Dart 8.8m	TransBus Mini Pointer	N29F	2002	
YN03NDF	Optare Solo M920	Optare	N33F	2003	Bailey Group, Blackburn, 2003
SP53JZA	TransBus Dart 8.8m	TransBus Mini Pointer	N29F	2003	
SJ04DZY	TransBus Dart 8.8m	TransBus Mini Pointer	N29F	2004	
SJ04DZZ	TransBus Dart 8.8m	TransBus Mini Pointer	N29F	2004	
YN04AGO	Scania K114IB4	Irizar InterCentury 12.32	C49FT	2004	
MX54KXU	Optare Solo M850	Optare	N24F	2004	Silverdale, New Stevenston, 2005
MX54KXV	Optare Solo M850	Optare	N24F	2004	Silverdale, New Stevenston, 2005
MX55BYG	Optare Solo M850SL	Optare	N28F	2005	
MX55WCT	Optare Solo M920	Optare	N28F	2005	

Previous registrations:

2450PP	P722RWU	JCZ2065	K617SBV
B15STA	K805HUM, 8665WA, K513KWT, RIL7555	LSV380	W899VRE
CKZ8184	J130GMP	M152LPL	M152LPL, CKZ8187
CKZ8187	D557MVR	OBZ2241	C335DND, ESU121, C431GVM
CSV651	P825XGD	RIL9350	G444JAW
G904UPP	G904UPP, CKZ8184	SN02NMP	JW02BUS
H11JYM	H907SHL	USV803	M516TVM, WSV552, CX61AA
HUI8156	P338CEP	YKJ798	W304SBC

TRAVEL DUNDEE

Travel Dundee - Wisharts

Tayside Public Transport Company Ltd, 44-48 East Dock Street, Dundee, DD1 3JS

Part of the National Express group.

TC1	2133PL	Volvo B10M-62	Plaxton Première 350	C53FT	1995	Skills, Nottingham, 1999
TC3	CTS917	Volvo B10M-62	Plaxton Première 350	C49FT	1994	
TC10	PYJ136	Volvo B10M-62	Plaxton Première 350	C49FT	1996	
TC11	A8TPT	Mercedes-Benz Vario O814	Plaxton Cheetah	C29F	1999	
TC17	JSU506	Volvo B10M-60	Plaxton Paramount 3500 III	C49FT	1990	Speedlink, 1997
TC22	NSV621	Volvo B10M-62	Plaxton Première 350	C48FT	1999	
TC23	NSV622	Volvo B10M-62	Plaxton Première 350	C48FT	1999	
TC25	USU661	Volvo Olympian	Northern Counties Palatine 2	BC39/29F	1998	National Express, 2003
TC26	USU662	Volvo Olympian	Northern Counties Palatine 2	BC39/29F	1998	National Express, 2003

1 - 18		Volvo B7TL		Wrightbus Eclipse Gemini		N45/29F	2005

1	DD	SP54CHF	6	DD	SP54CHL	11	DD	SP54CGO	15	DD	SP54CGY
2	DD	SP54CHG	7	DD	SP54CHN	12	DD	SP54CGU	16	DD	SP54CGZ
3	DD	SP54CHH	8	DD	SP54CHO	13	DD	SP54CGV	17	DD	SP54CHC
4	DD	SP54CHJ	9	DD	SP54CGG	14	DD	SP54CGX	18	DD	SP54CHD
5	DD	SP54CHK	10	DD	SP54CGK						

Travel Dundee is owned by National Express and uses the colours of Travel West Midlands with whom many vehicles are transferred. The coaching arm is Travel Greyhound using a purple scheme seen here on Plaxton Paramount 3500 JSU506. *Mark Doggett*

Eighteen Wrightbus Eclipes Gemini double-deck buses joined the Travel Dundee allocation in 2004. These are built on Volvo B7TL chassis built in Poland. Illustrating the batch is 2, SP54CHG. *Billy Nicol*

59	P521EJW	Volvo B6BLE	Wright Crusader	N37F	1996	Travel West Midlands, 2004
60	P522EJW	Volvo B6BLE	Wright Crusader	N37F	1996	Travel West Midlands, 2004
61	P523EJW	Volvo B6BLE	Wright Crusader	N37F	1996	Travel West Midlands, 2004
62	P527EJW	Volvo B6BLE	Wright Crusader	N37F	1996	Travel West Midlands, 2004
63	P531EJW	Volvo B6BLE	Wright Crusader	N37F	1996	Travel West Midlands, 2004
64	P398FVP	Scania L113CRL	Wright Axcess-ultralow	N43F	1996	Travel West Midlands, 2001
65	P399FVP	Scania L113CRL	Wright Axcess-ultralow	N43F	1996	Travel West Midlands, 2001
66	R466YDT	Scania L94UB	Wright Axcess-ultralow	N43F	1998	Travel West Midlands, 1999
67	Y722CJW	Volvo B7L	Wright Eclipse	N37F	1996	Travel West Midlands, 2004

84 - 87		Dennis Dart SLF 10.1m	Wright Crusader	N36F	1997	Travel West Midlands, 2003
84	DD R84GNW	**85** DD R85GNW	**86** DD R86GNW	**87** DD R87GNW		

88	S742RJX	Dennis Dart SLF 11.3m	Plaxton Pointer SPD	N38F	1998	Travel West Midlands, 1999
89	S743RJX	Dennis Dart SLF 11.3m	Plaxton Pointer SPD	N38F	1998	Travel West Midlands, 1999

114	L3LOW	Scania N113CRL	East Lancashire	N42F	1993	
115	R466XDA	Volvo B10L	Wright Liberator	N43F	1997	Travel West Midlands, 2003
121	P121GSR	Dennis Dart SLF	Plaxton Pointer	N37F	1996	

First of three Volvo B6BLEs with Wright Crusader bodies is 162, R162TSR, seen here with route branding for service 9X from Barnhill. *Bob Downham*

122 - 151   Volvo B10L   Wright Liberator   N43F   1997

122	P122KSL	130	P130KSL	138	P138KSL	145	P145RSN
123	P123KSL	131	P131KSL	139	P139KSL	146	P146RSN
124	P124KSL	132	P132KSL	140	P140KSL	147	P147RSN
125	P125KSL	133	P133KSL	141	P141KSL	148	P148RSN
126	P126KSL	134	P134KSL	142	P142RSN	149	P149RSN
127	P127KSL	135	P135KSL	143	P143RSN	150	P150RSN
128	P128KSL	136	P136KSL	144	P144RSN	151	P151RSN
129	P129KSL	137	P137KSL				

152 - 161   Volvo B10BLE   Wright Renown   N45F   1998

152	R152RSN	155	R155RSN	158	R158RSN	160	R160RSN
153	R153RSN	156	R156RSN	159	R159RSN	161	R161RSN
154	R154RSN	157	R157RSN				

162	R162TSR	Volvo B6LE	Wright Crusader	N38F	1998
163	R163TSR	Volvo B6LE	Wright Crusader	N38F	1998
164	R164TSR	Volvo B6LE	Wright Crusader	N38F	1998

165 - 179   Volvo B10BLE   Wright Renown   N45F   1999

165	V165ESL	169	V169ESL	173	V173ESL	177	V177ESL
166	V166ESL	170	V170ESL	174	V174ESL	178	V178ESL
167	V167ESL	171	V171ESL	175	V175ESL	179	V179ESL
168	V168ESL	172	V172ESL	176	V176ESL		

200	T304UOX	Optare Solo M850	Optare	N27F	1999	Travel West Midlands, 2005
201	S282AOX	Optare Solo M850	Optare	N27F	1998	Travel West Midlands, 2005

202-208		Optare Excel L960	Optare	N34F	1997	Travel London, 2005

202	R410HWU	**204**	R418HWU	**206**	R403HWU	**208**	R415HWU
203	R412HWU	**205**	R413HWU	**207**	R419HWU		

W240	JSU542	Volvo B10M-62	Plaxton Première 350	C53FT	1995	Skills, Nottingham, 1999
W253	OTS271	Volvo B10M-62	Plaxton Première 350	C49FT	1994	
W257	EUE489	Scania K93CRB	Plaxton Première 320	C47FT	1993	Speedlink, 1998
268	P226EJW	Mercedes-Benz 811D	Marshall C16	B27F	1997	Travel West Midlands, 2005
W300	5414PH	Mercedes-Benz 412D	Aitken	M15	1998	
W304	P206GSR	Optare Metrorider MR17	Optare	B29F	1996	
W305	LVG263	Mercedes-Benz Vario O814	Plaxton Cheetah	C29F	1999	
W306	P973KTS	Mercedes-Benz 814D	Plaxton Beaver	C32F	1997	
W307	P972KTS	Mercedes-Benz 814D	Plaxton Beaver	C32F	1997	
W308	T577ASN	Optare Solo M920	Optare	N31F	1999	
W309	T307UOX	Optare Solo M850	Optare	N31F	1999	Travel West Midlands, 1999
W310	P238EJW	Mercedes-Benz 811D	Marshall C16	B27F	1996	Travel West Midlands, 1999
521	P521EJW	Volvo B6LE	Wright Crusader	N37F	1997	Travel West Midlands, 1999
531	P531EJW	Volvo B6LE	Wright Crusader	N37F	1997	Travel West Midlands, 1999
4023	N23FWU	DAF DE02LTSB220	Ikarus CitiBus	B43F	1995	Travel West Midlands, 2005

Special event vehicle:

184	ETS964	Daimler CVG6	Metro-Cammell	B37/28R	1955	

Previous registrations:

2133PL	M36TRR			NSV621	V74DSN
5414PH	R884TSR			NSV622	V73DSN
A8TPT	T434GSP			OTS271	M200TPT
CTS917	M100TPT			PSR781	H290WSE
E737KSP	E737KSP, LIW9279			PYJ136	P10TAY
EVE489	L55SAS			USU661	R91GTM
JSU506	G804BPG			USU662	R92GTM
JSU542	M37TRR				

Depots: East Dock Street, Dundee and Friockheim (G&N Wishart).
Web: www.traveldundee.co.uk

Seven of the Optare Excel buses operated by Travel London, another National Express operation, moved north in 2005. Now carrying provincial colours is 206, R403HWU. *Mark Doggett*

WATERMILL COACHES

A J Clark & B Smith, 88 College Bounds, Fraserburgh, AB43 9QS

CWG694V	Leyland Atlantean AN68A/1R	Alexander AL	B45/33F	1979	Moffat & Williamson, 2005
YBK338V	Leyland Atlantean AN68A/1R	Alexander AL	B45/34F	1979	Moffat & Williamson, 2002
YBK341V	Leyland Atlantean AN68A/1R	Alexander AL	B45/34F	1979	Moffat & Williamson, 2004
HSV725	Volvo B10M-60	Plaxton Paramount 3200 III	C57F	1989	John Keir, Glass, 1997
MIL3960	Volvo B10M-60	Plaxton Paramount 3500 III	C57F	1990	Nefyn Coaches 2002
SIL5523	Volvo B10M-60	Van Hool Alizée	C49FT	1990	Reid, Rhynie, 1999
MIL3982	Volvo B10M-60	Van Hool Alizée	C49FT	1990	Reid, Rhynie, 1999
M8SKY	Volvo B10M-62	Van Hool Alizée HE	C53F	1994	Skyeways, Kyle of Lochalsh, 1999
N5BUS	Mercedes-Benz 811D	Marshall City	B33F	1996	Stonehouse Coaches, 1999
VRY357	Volvo B10M-62	Caetano Algarve 2	C49FT	1996	Reid, Rhynie, 2001
N195RGD	Dennis Javelin 12m	Wadhams Stringer Vanguard	BC70F	1996	MoD, 2005
N245RGD	Dennis Javelin 12m	Wadhams Stringer Vanguard	BC70F	1996	MoD, 2005
N350VSO	Mercedes-Benz 711D	Devon Conversions	B23F	1996	Ferguson, East Whitburn, 2002
P787BJU	Mercedes-Benz 709D	Leicester Carriage	C29F	1996	
JIL8207	Mercedes-Benz Vario 0814	Plaxton Cheetah	C33F	1996	Pearl, Skene, 2002
R651RSE	Volvo B10M-62	Plaxton Première 320	C57F	1997	John Keir, Glass, 2004
R111WCS	Mercedes-Benz 711D	Mellor	BC29F	1998	
T111WCS	Mercedes-Benz Vario 0814	Plaxton Beaver 2	BC31F	1999	

Seen in Edinburgh is Neoplan Skyliner EIJ4016 operating in Watermill Coaches. This coach has been replaced leaving a wholly single-deck coach fleet. *Billy Nicol*

For the Mercedes-Benz Vario the Plaxton bus version is the Beaver 2, while the coach version is the Cheetah. Pictured in Fraserburgh is Watermill Coaches' SF54CHO, a Beaver 2 bus that features high-back seating.
Murdoch Currie

W777WCS	Volvo B10M-62	Plaxton Première 350	C51F	2000	
W999WCS	Ford Transit VE6	Ford	M16	2000	
W885NNT	Ford Transit VE6	Ford	M16	2000	van, 2002
W496JHE	Ford Transit VE6	Ford	M16	2000	van, 2002
Y228RSO	Volvo B10M-62	Van Hool T9 Alizée	C49FT	2001	Whytes, Newmachar, 2005
SN51LVB	Mercedes-Benz Vario 0814	Plaxton Beaver 2	BC33F	2001	
SK02OAA	Mercedes-Benz Vario 0814	Plaxton Beaver 2	BC33F	2002	
ML02PFN	Mercedes-Benz Sprinter 614	Onyx	BC24F	2002	
SW02VFX	Dennis Javelin 12m	Wadham Stringer Vanguard II	BC70F	2002	MoD, 2004
SW02VGY	Dennis Javelin 12m	Wadham Stringer Vanguard II	BC70F	2002	MoD, 2004
YP52KRG	Volvo B7R	Plaxton Prima 70	BC70F	2002	
YN53EJC	Mercedes-Benz Vario 0814	TransBus Cheetah	C29F	2003	
SH04YZB	Ford Transit	Ford	M16	2004	Lowe, Cuminestown, 2005
SF54CHO	Mercedes-Benz Vario 0814	Plaxton Beaver 2	BC33F	2004	
YN55LMO	Mercedes-Benz Vario 0814	Plaxton Cheetah	C33F	2005	
MX55HXP	Mercedes-Benz Vario 0814	Onyx	BC24F	2005	

Previous registrations:

G247XLO	A2YOU	SIL5523	G802OSS, HSK174, HSK815
HSV725	F46TMU	VRY357	N85LSE, HSK815
JIL8207	P612UGE	W999WCS	SIL5523
MIL3960	G60RGG		
MIL3982	G803OSS, HSK175, HSK816		

WAVERLEY TRAVEL

R Jack, 11 Turnhouse Business Park, Turnhouse Road, Edinburgh, EH12 0AL

MVS380	MAN SR280	MAN	C49FT	1985	Richardson, Washington, 2002
RIB7002	Dennis Dart 9m	Carlyle Dartline	B36F	1990	Metroline, Harrow, 2001
V478FSF	Mercedes-Benz Vario 0814	Plaxton Beaver 2	B27F	1999	
X185BNH	Dennis Dart SLF 8.8m	Plaxton Pointer MPD	N29F	2000	Top Line, York, 2003
KX03HZK	Dennis Dart SLF 8.8m	Plaxton Pointer MPD	N29F	2003	
BU05EGD	BMC Probus 850 RE	BMC	C35F	2005	
SN54FCE	ADL Dart	ADL Mini Pointer	N29F	2004	
SN54FCF	ADL Dart	ADL Mini Pointer	N29F	2004	
KX54HKZ	ADL Dart	ADL Mini Pointer	N29F	2005	

Previous registrations:

MVS380	700CPO	RIB7002	CMN12A, H403HDY

Pictured leaving Edinburgh for Ratho, KP02PUX is one of four Plaxton Pointer MPD Darts in the fleet. Waverley Travel operates from a depot close to Edinburgh Airport. *Bob Downham*

WEST COAST MOTORS

Craig of Campbeltown Ltd, Benmhor, Campbeltown, PA28 6DN
Oban & District Buses Ltd, 2 Glengallen, Oban, PA34 4HH
Glasgow Citybus Ltd, 739 South Street, Glasgow, G14 0BX

ON	CUL197V	Leyland Titan TNLXB2RR	Park Royal	O44/26D	1979	Stagecoach, 2004
AG	GCS35V	Leyland Leopard PSU3E/4R	Alexander AY	B53F	1980	Clydeside, 1997
ON	GCS42V	Leyland Leopard PSU3E/4R	Alexander AY	B53F	1980	Clydeside, 1997
ON	GCS50V	Leyland Leopard PSU3E/4R	Alexander AY	B53F	1980	Clydeside, 1997
ON	WFS145W	Leyland Leopard PSU3F/4R	Alexander AYS	B53F	1980	Midland Bluebird, 1992
ON	WFS151W	Leyland Leopard PSU3F/4R	Alexander AYS	B60F	1980	Midland Bluebird, 1992
ON	LMS380W	Leyland Leopard PSU3F/4R	Alexander AYS	B60F	1980	Midland Bluebird, 1992
ON	CSF157W	Leyland Leopard PSU3F/4R	Alexander AYS	B53F	1981	Midland Bluebird, 1992
ON	CAS519W	Leyland Leopard PSU3G/4R	Alexander AY	BC49F	1981	Midland Bluebird, 1992
ON	CAS520W	Leyland Leopard PSU3G/4R	Alexander AY	BC49F	1981	Midland Bluebird, 1992
RY	GYE273W	Leyland Titan TNLXB2RR	Leyland	B44/24D	1981	Stagecoach, 2004
	MSL276X	Leyland Leopard PSU3G/4R	Plaxton Supreme V Express	C53F	1982	Tayside Travel, 1996
	A169UGB	Leyland Tiger TRCLXC/2RH	Plaxton Paramount 3200 Exp	C49F	1984	Midland Bluebird, 1992
DN	A824SUL	Leyland Titan TNLXB2RR	Leyland	B44/24D	1983	Stagecoach, 2004
DN	B79WUV	Leyland Titan TNLXB2RR	Leyland	O44/29F	1984	Stagecoach, 2005
AG	SSU727	Volvo B10M-56	Plaxton Paramount 3200 II	C53F	1985	Tellings-Golden Miller, 1989
DN	B108CCS	Volvo Citybus B10M-50	Alexander RV	B47/37F	1985	Stagecoach, 2004
DN	C791USG	Volvo Citybus B10M-50	Alexander RV	B47/33F	1986	Stagecoach, 2004
DN	C794USG	Volvo Citybus B10M-50	Alexander RV	BC47/33F	1986	Stagecoach, 2004
CN	FSU319	Volvo B10M-61	Plaxton Paramount 3200 III	C57F	1988	Bakers, Biddulph, 1996
CN	NDZ3026	Leyland Tiger TRCTL11/3RZ	Plaxton Paramount 3200 Exp	BC70F	1988	Holmeswood Coaches, 2004
RY	E870BGG	Volvo B10M-56	Duple 300	B53F	1988	Hutchison, Overtown, 1996
RY	E871BGG	Volvo B10M-56	Duple 300	B53F	1988	Hutchison, Overtown, 1996
DN	F727ASB	Volvo B10M-61	Plaxton Paramount 3200 III	C53F	1989	
CN	J807HSB	MAN 11.190	Optare Vecta	B41F	1992	
RY	J301BRM	Dennis Dart 9.8m	Alexander Dash	B40F	1992	Stagecoach, 2004
RY	J302BRM	Dennis Dart 9.8m	Alexander Dash	B40F	1992	Stagecoach, 2004
AG	J303BRM	Dennis Dart 9.8m	Alexander Dash	B40F	1992	Stagecoach, 2004
DN	J304BRM	Dennis Dart 9.8m	Alexander Dash	B40F	1992	Stagecoach, 2004

Oban & District received a pair of Alexander Dash-bodied Dennis Darts in 1996. N202WSB is seen with Oban and District names although recent transfers have led to both now being based at Dunoon. *Billy Nicol*

West Coast Motors celebrated its 80th Anniversary in 2003 and to commemorate this event, Van Hool-bodied DAF SB4000, Y80WCM, entered service in this special version of the livery. It is seen departing Glasgow for Campbeltown on Scottish Citylink service 926. *Billy Nicol*

RY	J305BRM	Dennis Dart 9.8m	Alexander Dash	B40F	1992	Stagecoach, 2004
ON	J306BRM	Dennis Dart 9.8m	Alexander Dash	B40F	1992	Stagecoach, 2004
DN	J308BRM	Dennis Dart 9.8m	Alexander Dash	B40F	1992	Stagecoach, 2004
RY	J309BRM	Dennis Dart 9.8m	Alexander Dash	B40F	1992	Stagecoach, 2004
RY	J310BRM	Dennis Dart 9.8m	Alexander Dash	B40F	1992	Stagecoach, 2004
CN	K103XHG	Dennis Dart 9m	Alexander Dash	B40F	1993	Stagecoach, 2004
AG	NDZ3024	Dennis Dart 9m	Wright HandyBus	B35F	1993	Stagecoach, 2004
CN	NDZ3025	Dennis Dart 9m	Wright HandyBus	B35F	1993	Stagecoach, 2004
RY	K400WCM	DAF SB3000	Van Hool Alizée	C49FT	1993	
CN	L146VRH	Dennis Dart 9m	Plaxton Pointer	B40F	1993	Stagecoach, 2004
AG	L400WCM	DAF SB3000	Van Hool Alizée HE	C53F	1993	
AG	L700WCM	DAF SB3000	Van Hool Alizée HE	C53F	1994	
AG	L300WCM	Volvo B10M-60	Jonckheere Deauville P599	C53FT	1994	
CN	L200WCM	Optare Metrorider MR15	Optare	B25F	1994	
ON	L937WFW	DAF 400	Onyx	M14	1994	
ON	L263AAG	DAF 400	Onyx	M16	1994	
ON	L264AAG	DAF 400	Onyx	M16	1994	
ON	M200WCM	DAF SB3000	Van Hool Alizée HE	C53F	1995	
CN	M300WCM	DAF SB3000	Van Hool Alizée HE	C53F	1995	
ON	M400WCM	DAF SB3000	Van Hool Alizée HE	C51FT	1995	
CN	M500WCM	Optare Metrorider MR15	Optare	B30F	1995	
AG	M700WCM	DAF SB3000	Van Hool Alizée HE	C51FT	1995	Armchair, Brentford, 1995
ON	M800WCM	DAF SB3000	Van Hool Alizée HE	C51FT	1995	Armchair, Brentford, 1995
ON	N100WCM	Optare Metrorider MR15	Optare	B30F	1995	
ON	N200WCM	Optare Metrorider MR15	Optare	B25F	1995	
DN	N603VSS	Mercedes-Benz 709D	Alexander Sprint	B18F	1995	Stagecoach, 2004
RY	N623VSS	Mercedes-Benz 709D	Alexander Sprint	B25F	1995	Stagecoach, 2004
RY	N629VSS	Mercedes-Benz 709D	Alexander Sprint	B19F	1995	Stagecoach, 2004
AG	N300WCM	Volvo B9M	Van Hool Alizée HE	C45F	1996	
ON	N400WCM	Mercedes-Benz 814D	Plaxton Beaver	BC33F	1996	
DN	N101WSB	Dennis Dart 9.8 m	Alexander Dash	B40F	1996	
DN	N202WSB	Dennis Dart 9.8 m	Alexander Dash	B40F	1996	
ON	P600WCM	Ford Transit VE6	Deansgate	M16	1996	Sail & Tap, Salford, 2000
ON	P720RWU	DAF SB3000	Van Hool Alizée HE	C49FT	1996	North Kent Express, 2005
SC	P100WCM	DAF SB3000	Van Hool Alizée HE	C49FT	1997	
AG	P200WCM	DAF SB3000	Van Hool Alizée HE	C49FT	1997	
ON	P204RUM	DAF SB220	Ikarus Citibus	B49F	1997	BCP, Gatwick, 2004
ON	R303VSB	Mercedes-Benz 711D	Onyx	BC24F	1997	
CN	K500WCM	DAF SB3000	Van Hool Alizée HE	C49FT	1998	Wood, Barnsley, 2003
SC	R100WCM	DAF SB3000	Van Hool Alizée HE	C49FT	1998	
SC	R200WCM	DAF SB3000	Van Hool Alizée HE	C49FT	1998	

The Scottish Bus Handbook

In recent years products from DAF, and its successor VDL Bus, have been chosen for this fleet. One of two Wrightbus Cadets new in 2001 for Oban & District is Y802WBT. *Billy Nicol*

SC	R300WCM	DAF SB3000	Van Hool Alizée HE	C49FT	1998	
	R177GNW	DAF SB3000	Van Hool Alizée HE	C35F	1998	North Kent Express, 2005
	R180GNW	DAF SB3000	Van Hool Alizée HE	C35F	1998	North Kent Express, 2005
DN	R24GNW	DAF SB220	Ikarus Citibus	B51F	1998	Hallmark, Luton, 2005
ON	R74GNW	DAF SB220	Ikarus Citibus	B51F	1998	Bowman, Craignure, 2004
AG	R400WCM	Mercedes-Benz 814D	Plaxton Beaver	C33F	1998	
ON	S555WCM	LDV Convoy	LDV	M16	1999	
SC	S400WCM	DAF SB3000	Van Hool T9 Alizée	C51FT	1999	
CN	T190AUA	Dennis Dart SLF 8.5m	Plaxton MPD	N29F	1999	
CN	T191AUA	Dennis Dart SLF 8.5m	Plaxton MPD	N29F	1999	
ON	W689XSB	Dennis Dart SLF 9.m	Plaxton Pointer 2	N39F	2000	
ON	W100WCM	DAF SB3000	Van Hool T9 Alizée	C51FT	2000	
SC	M100WCM	DAF SB3000	Van Hool T9 Alizée	C48FT	2001	
SC	M600WCM	DAF SB3000	Van Hool T9 Alizée	C48FT	2001	
ON	Y801WBT	DAF SB120	Wright Cadet	N39F	2001	
ON	Y802WBT	DAF SB120	Wright Cadet	N39F	2001	
SC	SA02CJO	Mercedes-Benz Vito 110cdi	Traveller	M8	2002	
SC	SC02HHE	Mercedes-Benz Vito 110cdi	Traveller	M8	2002	
SC	R900WCM	DAF SB4000	Van Hool T9 Alizée	C53F	2002	
SC	S900WCM	DAF SB4000	Van Hool T9 Alizée	C53F	2002	
SC	T900WCM	DAF SB4000	Van Hool T9 Alizée	C49FT	2002	
CN	Y80WCM	DAF SB4000	Van Hool T9 Alizée	C53F	2002	
SC	K200WCM	DAF SB4000	Van Hool T9 Alizée	C49FT	2003	
SC	K300WCM	DAF SB4000	Van Hool T9 Alizée	C49FT	2003	
ON	YJ03PNY	DAF SB120	Wrightbus Cadet 2	N39F	2003	
ON	YJ03PNZ	DAF SB120	Wrightbus Cadet 2	N39F	2003	
CN	T600WCM	Mercedes-Benz Vario 0814	Onyx	BC24F	2003	
	SF54HWA	Mercedes-Benz Vario 0814	Onyx	BC24F	2004	
CN	YJ54ZYH	Optare Solo M850	Optare	N27F	2005	
AG	YJ54ZYK	Optare Solo M850	Optare	N27F	2005	
AG	YJ54ZYL	Optare Solo M850	Optare	N27F	2005	
RY	YJ54ZYM	Optare Solo M850	Optare	N27F	2005	
DN	YJ05PVF	VDL Bus SB120	Wrightbus Cadet 2	N39F	2005	
DN	YJ05PVK	VDL Bus SB120	Wrightbus Cadet 2	N39F	2005	
DN	YJ05PVL	VDL Bus SB120	Wrightbus Cadet 2	N39F	2005	

The Scottish Bus Handbook

West Coast Motors operates several duties on Scottish Citylink services. Seen in Buchanan Street bus station in Glasgow is T900WCM, one of the latest Van Hool T9 Alizée coaches on a DAF SB4000 chassis. The SB 4000 is intended as coach chassis varying in length between 10.5 and 13 metres, the range encompasses two engine ranges, four gearboxes, two retarders. *Billy Nicol*

DN	YJ05PYT	VDL Bus SB120	Wrightbus Cadet 2	N39F	2005	
DN	YJ05PWU	VDL Bus SB120	Wrightbus Cadet 2	N39F	2005	
SC	YJ05PYO	VDL Bus SB4000	Van Hool T9 Alizée	C49FT	2005	
SC	YJ05PYP	VDL Bus SB4000	Van Hool T9 Alizée	C49FT	2005	

Glasgow Citybus:

GW	G215HCP	DAF SB220	Optare Delta	B49F	1990	
GW	G217HCP	DAF SB220	Optare Delta	B49F	1990	
GW	H114MOB	Dennis Dart 8.5 m	Carlyle Dartline	B25F	1990	London United, 1999
GW	H158NON	Dennis Dart 8.5 m	Carlyle Dartline	B28F	1991	London United, 1999
GW	H166NON	Dennis Dart 8.5 m	Carlyle Dartline	B28F	1991	London United, 1999
GW	J806KHD	DAF SB220	Ikarus Citibus	BC42F	1992	Capital, Twickenham, 2000
GW	J809KHD	DAF SB220	Ikarus Citibus	BC42F	1992	Capital, Twickenham, 2000
GW	J619KCU	Dennis Dart 9.8 m	Wright HandyBus	B40F	1992	Go-North East, 2001
GW	J619KCU	Dennis Dart 9.8 m	Wright HandyBus	B40F	1992	Go-North East, 2001
GW	L654MYG	Mercedes-Benz 709D	Plaxton Beaver	B27F	1993	Blue Bus, Bolton, 2004
GW	L152FRJ	Mercedes-Benz 709D	Alexander Sprint	B25F	1993	Arriva Cymru, 2002
GW	N169WNF	Mercedes-Benz 709D	Alexander Sprint	B23F	1995	Arriva Midlands, 2004
GW	N171WNF	Mercedes-Benz 709D	Alexander Sprint	B23F	1995	Arriva Midlands, 2004
GW	R551UOT	Dennis Dart SLF 10.1m	UVG UrbanStar	B42F	1997	Teandeck, Hanley, 2005
GW	W173CDN	Mercedes-Benz Vario O814	Alexander ALX100	B27F	2000	
GW	YJ03PGF	DAF SB120	Wrightbus Cadet 2	N39F	2003	
GW	YJ04HUU	VDL Bus SB200	Wrightbus Commander	N44F	2004	

Previous registrations:

FSU319	KGS305X, 7017PF, MSL276X		M700WCM	M837RCP
K200WCM	L937WFW		M800WCM	M838RCP
K500WCM	K547OGA		P600WCM	P605SBG
M100WCM	Y485HUA		S555WCM	S373PGB
M600WCM	Y486HUA		SSU727	A169UGB

Depots: Chalmers Street, Ardrishaig; Saddell Street, Campbeltown; Blochairn Road, Glasgow; Argyll Road, Dunoon; Soroba Lane, Oban; High Road, Port Blantyre; Riverbank Ind Park, Alloa.

WHITELAWS

G Whitelaw & Partners, Loch Ind Est, Stonehouse, Lanark, ML9 3LR

Reg	Chassis	Body	Seating	Year	History
OLS539P	Leyland Leopard PSU3C/3R	Alexander AYS	B53F	1975	Midland Scottish, 1991
XMS254R	Leyland Leopard PSU3C/3R	Alexander AY	B53F	1977	Midland Scottish, 1991
MRJ280W	Leyland Leopard PSU5D/4R	Plaxton Supreme IV	C50F	1981	Ribble, 1991
FAS373X	Leyland Leopard PSU3F/4R	Alexander AYS	B62F	1982	Rapsons, 2001
FAS374X	Leyland Leopard PSU3F/4R	Alexander AYS	B62F	1982	Rapsons, 2001
FAS375X	Leyland Leopard PSU3F/4R	Alexander AYS	B62F	1982	Highland Country, 1999
D375RHS	Volvo B10M-61	Duple Dominant	B55F	1987	Allander, Milngavie, 1996
D377RHS	Volvo B10M-61	Duple Dominant	B55F	1987	Allander, Milngavie, 1996
S947NGB	Iveco EuroRider 391.12..29	Marshall Maxibus	B51F	1998	
T290ROF	Volvo B6BLE	Wrightbus Crusader 2	N37F	1999	Volvo demonstrator, 1999
V452NGA	Volvo B6BLE	Wrightbus Crusader 2	N37F	2000	
W671WGG	Volvo B6BLE	Wrightbus Crusader 2	N37F	2000	
W674WGG	Volvo B10MT	Van Hool T9 Alizée	C49FT	2000	
W675WGG	Volvo B10MT	Van Hool T9 Alizée	C49FT	2000	
W613KFE	Mercedes-Benz O1223L	Optare Ferqui Solera	C39F	2000	Optare demonstrator, 2001
191WHW	Mercedes-Benz O1223L	Optare Ferqui Solera	C30FT	2001	
SJ51LYP	Volvo B6BLE	Wrightbus Crusader 2	N38F	2001	

Whitelaws operates a mix of older buses, mostly Leyland Leopards, on school services and modern low-floor buses on commercial services. Pictured in Motherwell while operating route 253 from Hamilton to Wishaw is SA02CDE, one of several Volvo B7RLEs with Wrightbus bodywork currently on front-line service.
Bob Downham

A pair of Volvo B10M-61s with Duple Dominant bus bodywork continues to provide service from the base in Stonehouse. Pictured in nearby Hamilton is D377RHS seen on the Netherburn service. *Phillip Stephenson*

9396WW	Volvo B12M	Sunsundegui Sideral 330	C49FT	2002
SA02CCY	Volvo B12M	Sunsundegui Sideral 330	C49FT	2002
SA02CCZ	Volvo B12M	Sunsundegui Sideral 330	C49FT	2002
SA52AZV	Mercedes-Benz Vario 0814	TransBus Beaver 2	B31F	2002
7173WW	Volvo B12M	Sunsundegui Sideral 330	C49FT	2003
SF03TLX	Volvo B12M	Sunsundegui Sideral 330	C49FT	2003
SF03TLY	Volvo B12M	Sunsundegui Sideral 330	C49FT	2003
1716WW	Volvo B12M	Sunsundegui Sideral 330	C49FT	2003
GW4343	Volvo B12M	Sunsundegui Sideral 330	C49FT	2004
SJ04DVG	Volvo B7RLE	Wrightbus Eclipse Urban	N43F	2004
SJ04DVH	Volvo B7RLE	Wrightbus Eclipse Urban	N43F	2004
SJ04DVK	Volvo B7RLE	Wrightbus Eclipse Urban	N43F	2004
SJ04DVL	Volvo B7RLE	Wrightbus Eclipse Urban	N43F	2004
SJ04DVM	Volvo B7RLE	Wrightbus Eclipse Urban	N43F	2004
SL54JUO	Volvo B7RLE	Wrightbus Eclipse Urban	N43F	2003
SJ55HHA	Volvo B7RLE	Wrightbus Eclipse Urban	N43F	2005
SJ55HHB	Volvo B7RLE	Wrightbus Eclipse Urban	N43F	2005
SJ55HHC	Volvo B7RLE	Wrightbus Eclipse Urban	N43F	2005
SJ55HHD	Volvo B7RLE	Wrightbus Eclipse Urban	N43F	2005
SJ55HHE	Volvo B7RLE	Wrightbus Eclipse Urban	N43F	2005
7994WW	Volvo B12B	Volvo 9700	C48FT	2006

Previous registration:

191WHW   Y783THS

Web: www.whitelaws.co.uk

WHYTES

Whytes Coach Tours, Scotts Road, Newmachar, Aberdeen, AB21 7PP

S591ACT	Mercedes-Benz Sprinter 410D	Autobus Classique	M16	1999
V878DSS	Ford Transit	Ford	M14	1999
X622CWN	Mercedes-Benz Sprinter 614	Cymric	BC24F	2001
SL52BTY	Mercedes-Benz Sprinter 413cdi	KVC	M16	2002
SV52VHY	Mercedes-Benz Vario 0815	Sitcar Beluga	C33F	2002
SF03AUC	Bova Futura FHD12.340	Bova	C49FT	2003
SF03AUE	Bova Futura FHD12.340	Bova	C49FT	2003
SF03AUH	Bova Futura FHD12.340	Bova	C49FT	2003
SV53ELJ	Mercedes-Benz Vario 0815	Sitcar Beluga	C33F	2003
SV04CVA	Bova Futura FHD12.340	Bova	C49FT	2004
SN04CVB	Volvo B7R	Plaxton Profile	C57F	2004
SN04GUF	Volkswagen LT46	KVC	M16	2004
SD04POV	Ford Transit	Ford	M8	2004
SN04MJS	Ford Transit	Ford	M14	2004
SV54EPJ	Mercedes-Benz Vario 0815	Sitcar Beluga	C33F	2004
SV06CEJ	VDL Bova Futura FHD12.370	VDL Bova	C49FT	2006
SV06CEK	VDL Bova Futura FHD12.370	VDL Bova	C49FT	2006
SV06CEN	VDL Bova Futura FHD12.370	VDL Bova	C49FT	2006
SV06CEO	VDL Bova Futura FHD12.370	VDL Bova	C49FT	2006
SV06	VDL Bova Futura FHD12.370	VDL Bova	C49FT	2006
SV06	VDL Bova Futura FHD12.370	VDL Bova	C49FT	2006
SV06	VDL Bova Futura FHD12.370	VDL Bova	C49FT	2006

Web: www.whytescoachtours.co.uk

Whytes latest arrivals are VDL Bova Futura coaches. The Futura is available in two height versions with lengths between 10 and 15 metres and various engine packages, the basic information being shown in the code. One of the trio delivered in 2003 is SF03AUC, seen taking a rest in Moffat. *Bob Downham*

WILSON'S of RHU

G H Wilson, Manse Brae, Rhu, Helensburgh, G84 8RE

K76OCR	Mercedes-Benz 811D	Alexander Sprint	B31F	1992	British Gas, Southampton, 2001
641RHU	Volvo B10M-62	Van Hool T9 Alizée	C51FT	2001	Southern, Barrhead, 2005
Y257KNB	Optare Solo M920	Optare	N33F	2001	
YG02FWJ	Optare Solo M920	Optare	N33F	2002	
SK52ODE	Mercedes-Benz Vario 0814	Plaxton Cheetah	C33F	2003	
SJ03FPW	Volvo B7R	Plaxton Profile	C57F	2003	
MX04DSZ	Mercedes-Benz Sprinter 413cdi	Mercedes-Benz	M16	2004	
YG54BSU	Optare Solo M920	Optare	N33F	2005	
SF05ONH	Mercedes-Benz Vario 0815	Sitcar Beluga	C33F	2005	
SF55UGB	Mercedes-Benz Vario 0814	Plaxton Cheetah	C33F	2005	
YJ06FZL	Optare Solo M920	Optare	N33F	2006	

Previous registration:
641RHU   Y800SOU

The Wilson's of Rhu fleet is represented by a picture of Plaxton Cheetah SN03FHD which is seen in Glasgow on private hire work. Late in 2005 a replacement new model arrived allowing this vehicle to be sold. *Billy Nicol*

VEHICLE INDEX

Reg	Operator	Reg	Operator	Reg	Operator	Reg	Operator
1RWM	Park's of Hamilton	9237AT	Allander Travel	A939SUL	McKindless	B460KRM	Rapsons
2HAN	Park's of Hamilton	9396WW	Whitelaws	A980SYF	McKindless	B496MFS	Mackie's
2HW	Park's of Hamilton	9446AT	Allander Travel	A990SYF	McKindless	B500MPY	MacEwan's
2RW	Park's of Hamilton	A1VOL	Keenan	AA02BUS	Slaemuir Coaches	B509YAT	Rapsons
2RWM	Park's of Hamilton	A5MWN	Nicoll	AA05DOT	Dodds of Troon	B742GSC	Rapsons
3HWS	Park's of Hamilton	A8AAA	Essbee	AA52BUS	Slaemuir Coaches	B743GSC	Rapsons
3RWM	Park's of Hamilton	A8TPT	Travel Dundee	AE06HBP	Munro's of Jedburgh	B744GSC	Rapsons
7MCB	Maynes Coaches	A12MWN	Nicoll	AEF91A	Keenan	B745GSC	Rapsons
12HM	Park's of Hamilton	A15MWN	Nicoll	AEF223Y	Jays Coaches	B759GSC	Prentice Westwood
15RWM	Park's of Hamilton	A16RNY	Rennie's	AEF228Y	McDade's Travel	B760GSC	Prentice Westwood
36RP	Prentice Westwood	A17MWN	Nicoll	AEF229Y	M-Line	B762GSC	Marbill
52GYY	McKindless	A17RNY	Rennie's	AHN391T	MacEwan's	B763GSC	Marbill
81CBK	Prentice Westwood	A19MWN	Nicoll	ANA173Y	Billy Davies	B769GSC	Stuarts of Carluke
121ASV	Moffat & Williamson	A19RNY	Rennie's	ANA184Y	Billy Davies	B774AOC	McColl Coaches
122ASV	Moffat & Williamson	A20MWN	Nicoll	AR03AAA	AAA Coaches	B777AOC	McColl Coaches
123TRL	Irvine's	A39XHE	Kineil Coaches	AR04AAA	AAA Coaches	B803AOP	Rapsons
138ASV	Prentice Westwood	A44XHE	Kineil Coaches	ASC665B	Lothian Buses	B810AOP	McColl Coaches
162EKH	Rapsons	A104OUG	Rennie's	AT2472	Allander Travel	B811YTC	McDade's Travel
191WHW	Whitelaws	A106MAC	Rapsons	AVK155V	Keenan	B820AOP	McColl Coaches
200UWX	Rapsons	A114WVP	McColl Coaches	AVK165V	Keenan	B821RSH	Billy Davies
240BBU	Prentice Westwood	A121XNH	Bowman	B1AFC	Jays Coaches	B825AOP	McColl Coaches
246AJF	Keenan	A145DPE	Lothian Buses	B3VOL	Keenan	B826AOP	McColl Coaches
318DHR	Rapsons	A157PKR	Rapsons	B4VOL	Keenan	B848AOP	McColl Coaches
367NHA	Prentice Westwood	A158FPG	Lothian Buses	B5VOL	Keenan	B852AOP	McColl Coaches
383OVF	Prentice Westwood	A159FPG	Lothian Buses	B10DPC	Prentice	B852OSB	McColl Coaches
408UFC	Essbee	A169UGB	West Coast Motors	B10MDP	Prentice	B853AOP	McColl Coaches
439BUS	Rennie's	A227LFX	Ayrways	B10VOL	Keenan	B857XYR	Rapsons
444VNX	Rapsons	A236GHN	Allander Travel	B12DPC	Prentice	B858AOP	McColl Coaches
448GWL	Rapsons	A246SVW	Golden Eagle	B21TVU	M-Line	B858XYR	Rapsons
485CLT	Lothian Buses	A317XWG	Stuarts of Carluke	B22TVU	M-Line	B860XYR	Rapsons
490SVX	Mackie's	A346ASF	E & M Horsburgh	B30TVU	M-Line	B864DOM	McColl Coaches
520PXR	Rapsons	A375BDL	MacEwan's	B79WUV	West Coast Motors	B867DOM	McColl Coaches
535LXB	Rapsons	A386XOS	Stokes	B108CCS	West Coast Motors	B875DOM	McKindless
540FFX	Rapsons	A416SPS	Rapsons	B109WUL	McKindless	B884DOM	McColl Coaches
550XBV	Rapsons	A446BGM	Rapsons	B121WUL	McKindless	B885DOM	MacEwan's
571BWT	MacEwan's	A449HJF	Rapsons	B121WUV	Rennie's	B908TVR	M-Line
641RHU	Wilson's of Rhu	A615KRT	Rapsons	B129WUL	McKindless	BAO867T	Dodds of Troon
650GXJ	Rapsons	A648THV	Rennie's	B131WUL	McKindless	BB05DOT	Dodds of Troon
671YWC	Kineil Coaches	A686UOE	McColl Coaches	B132WUL	Rennie's	BHZ9542	Rennie's
673EXA	Rapsons	A694UOE	McColl Coaches	B133WUL	McKindless	BHZ9543	Rennie's
700CWL	Rapsons	A700UOE	McKindless	B141KSF	E & M Horsburgh	BHZ9545	Rennie's
719CEL	Rapsons	A703UOE	McColl Coaches	B142KSF	E & M Horsburgh	BHZ9546	Rennie's
720RXJ	Rapsons	A705YFS	Prentice Westwood	B143KSF	E & M Horsburgh	BHZ9548	Rennie's
755ABL	Prentice Westwood	A706YFS	Prentice Westwood	B144KSF	E & M Horsburgh	BHZ9549	Rennie's
803DYE	Lothian Buses	A709YFS	Prentice Westwood	B145KSF	E & M Horsburgh	BJI6863	Marbill
828EWB	Prentice Westwood	A713YFS	Stuarts of Carluke	B146KSF	E & M Horsburgh	BKE832T	Rapsons
850RFX	Rapsons	A714YFS	Stuarts of Carluke	B147KSF	E & M Horsburgh	BL03NRE	Doig's
858DYE	Lothian Buses	A715YFS	Marbill	B154WUL	McKindless	BP02FMX	Irvine's
875YYA	Shuttle Buses	A716YFS	Marbill	B159WUL	McKindless	BPF134Y	Stuarts of Carluke
900HKU	Rapsons	A717ASJ	Kineil Coaches	B15STA	Stuarts of Carluke	BSJ931T	Keenan
900RWX	Rapsons	A718YFS	Marbill	B164WUL	McKindless	BSK790	Moffat & Williamson
930GJF	Rapsons	A722YFS	Marbill	B16AFC	Jays Coaches	BSK791	Moffat & Williamson
935BRU	H Crawford	A723YFS	Marbill	B193DVL	Rapsons	BU05EGD	Waverley
953HBU	Kineil Coaches	A724YFS	Marbill	B209WUL	Rennie's	BU51AYL	McDade's Travel
973BUS	H Crawford	A725YFS	E & M Horsburgh	B220WEU	Nicoll	BU51AYM	McDade's Travel
1716WW	Whitelaws	A726YFS	E & M Horsburgh	B281WUL	McKindless	BUI5220	McKendry
2133PC	Travel Dundee	A729YFS	McKindless	B291WUL	McKindless	BX04NCD	Rennie's
2154K	Marbill	A730YFS	McKindless	B293WUL	McKindless	BX06NZU	Rennie's
2367AT	Allander Travel	A731YFS	McKindless	B294KPF	Galson	BX06NZV	Rennie's
2396FH	McDade's Travel	A732YFS	Marbill	B296WUL	McKindless	C12RNY	Rennie's
2450PP	Stuarts of Carluke	A733YFS	Marbill	B297WUL	McKindless	C13RNY	Rennie's
3788AT	Allander Travel	A734YFS	E & M Horsburgh	B298WUL	McKindless	C55HOM	Rapsons
4143AT	Allander Travel	A735YFS	Marbill	B299WUL	McKindless	C56HOM	Rapsons
4670AT	Allander Travel	A736YFS	E & M Horsburgh	B301KVO	Irvine's	C57HOM	Rapsons
5414PH	Travel Dundee	A741JAY	Stuarts of Carluke	B302KVO	Irvine's	C58HOM	Rapsons
6308YG	Jays Coaches	A752WVP	MacEwan's	B303KVO	Irvine's	C59HOM	Rapsons
7173WW	Whitelaws	A766WVP	McColl Coaches	B303WUL	McKindless	C63PSG	E & M Horsburgh
7921AT	Allander Travel	A768WVP	McColl Coaches	B304KVO	Irvine's	C64PSG	E & M Horsburgh
7994WW	Whitelaws	A777NLG	McKindless	B305KVO	Irvine's	C268XSC	Rapsons
8212RU	Dunn's	A824SUL	West Coast Motors	B307KVO	Irvine's	C318BUV	Golden Eagle
8578AT	Allander Travel	A938SYE	Rennie's	B450GCB	Rapsons	C321PRM	Rapsons

Reg	Operator	Reg	Operator	Reg	Operator	Reg	Operator
C322PRM	Rapsons	D502NWG	City Sprinter	E919KYR	Rennie's	F747TRE	MacEwan's
C364BUV	Stuarts of Carluke	D518VSX	Rowe & Tudhope	E920KYR	Rennie's	F758FDV	City Sprinter
C402BUV	Golden Eagle	D522DSX	Clyde Coast	E987VUK	McColl Coaches	F774JYS	Mackie's
C406BUV	McKindless	D541RCK	City Sprinter	E993YNS	E & M Horsburgh	F852YJX	Jays Coaches
C663EHU	Rapsons	D660XPS	Rapsons	E996FRA	Nicoll	FAO426V	Rapsons
C770SFS	Stuarts of Carluke	D702EES	Pride of the Clyde	EBM439T	Ayrways	FAS373X	Whitelaws
C771FBH	Rapsons	D713CSC	Rowe & Tudhope	ECS65V	Jays Coaches	FAS374X	Whitelaws
C771OCN	Moffat & Williamson	D935NDA	McColl Coaches	ECS882V	Rapsons	FAS375X	Whitelaws
C771SFS	Stuarts of Carluke	D947NDA	McColl Coaches	ECS883V	Pride of the Clyde	FBV912Y	Nicoll
C774SFS	Stuarts of Carluke	D954NDA	McColl Coaches	EEH905Y	Rapsons	FE51RFJ	M-Line
C775SFS	Marbill	DLS520Y	Mackie's	EGB60T	Fairline	FJ04ESU	Rennie's
C776SFS	E & M Horsburgh	DLZ4298	Prentice Westwood	EJR104W	Ayrways	FJ04ETD	Lochs & Glens
C777SFS	Lothian Buses	DM04GSM	Maynes Coaches	EJR122W	McKindless	FJ04ETE	Lochs & Glens
C778OCN	Moffat & Williamson	DM05GSM	Maynes Coaches	EKA156Y	M-Line	FJ04ETF	Lochs & Glens
C780SFS	E & M Horsburgh	DM06GSM	Maynes Coaches	EPK1V	Fairline	FJ04ETK	Lochs & Glens
C781SFS	E & M Horsburgh	DOC36V	Rapsons	ESF801C	Lothian Buses	FJ04ETL	Lochs & Glens
C782SFS	E & M Horsburgh	DSP928V	Rapsons	ESK675	Jays Coaches	FJ04ETY	Mackie's
C783SFS	Jays Coaches	DSP934V	Rapsons	ESK930	Rapsons	FJ05ANX	Doig's
C784SFS	Jays Coaches	DSU355	Prentice Westwood	ESU512	Eve Coaches	FJ05AOM	Lochs & Glens
C786SFS	E & M Horsburgh	DSU707	Rapsons	ETS964	Travel Dundee	FJ05AON	Lochs & Glens
C787GGB	Scottish Travel	DSU755	Kineil Coaches	EU03EUD	Irvine's	FJ05AOO	Lochs & Glens
C788SFS	Prentice Westwood	DWW932Y	Stuarts of Carluke	EUE489	Travel Dundee	FJ05AOP	Lochs & Glens
C789SFS	Prentice Westwood	E72MVV	D B Travel	EUI656	Rapsons	FJ05AOR	Lochs & Glens
C790SFS	Prentice Westwood	E73MVV	D B Travel	F49CWY	D B Travel	FJ05HXX	Irvine's
C791SFS	Rapsons	E89VWA	M-Line	F61RFS	Puma	FJ06BSO	Lochs & Glens
C791USG	West Coast Motors	E173FRA	Nicoll	F69LNU	Dunn's	FJ06BSU	Lochs & Glens
C793UGS	Stonehouse Cs	E176TWW	Rapsons	F70DDA	Rapsons	FJ06BSV	Lochs & Glens
C794SFS	Rapsons	E205YGC	Dunn's	F113TML	Irvine's	FJ06BSX	Lochs & Glens
C794USG	West Coast Motors	E300MSG	Lothian Buses	F122PHM	Irvine's	FJ06BSY	Lochs & Glens
C801UGS	Stonehouse Cs	E301MSG	Lothian Buses	F134PHM	Irvine's	FLZ6854	Prentice Westwood
CAS519W	West Coast Motors	E302MSG	Lothian Buses	F135PHM	Irvine's	FLZ7953	Prentice Westwood
CAS520W	West Coast Motors	E303MSG	Lothian Buses	F171JKH	Golden Eagle	FN04JZK	Clyde Coast
CAZ1577	Smith & Sons	E304MSG	Lothian Buses	F189PRE	Dunn's	FN04JZM	Clyde Coast
CBZ4622	Prentice Westwood	E305MSG	Lothian Buses	F207DGT	Dunn's	FN04JZR	Rapsons
CBZ9062	McColl Coaches	E306MSG	Lothian Buses	F214DCC	D B Travel	FN04JZT	Rapsons
CCZ5837	Rennie's	E307EVW	M-Line	F218DCC	D B Travel	FN52HRU	Lochs & Glens
CHL772	Irvine's	E307MSG	Lothian Buses	F219DCC	D B Travel	FSU319	West Coast Motors
CJZ9222	Rowe & Tudhope	E308KES	Bryans of Denny	F252DLS	Galson	FSU331	Rapsons
CKZ8184	Stuarts of Carluke	E308MSG	Lothian Buses	F281GNB	Dunn's	FSU371	Moffat & Williamson
CKZ8187	Stuarts of Carluke	E309MSG	Lothian Buses	F311DET	Avondale Coaches	FSU372	Moffat & Williamson
CLZ1838	MacEwan's	E310MSG	Lothian Buses	F319EJO	Dickson's	FSU373	Moffat & Williamson
CM03GSM	Maynes Coaches	E311MSG	Lothian Buses	F335RWK	Marbill	FSU374	Moffat & Williamson
CM05GSM	Maynes Coaches	E312MSG	Lothian Buses	F336RWK	Marbill	FSU375	Moffat & Williamson
CNZ2978	Billy Davies	E313MSG	Lothian Buses	F337RWK	Marbill	FSU394	Moffat & Williamson
CSF157W	West Coast Motors	E314MSG	Lothian Buses	F338RWK	Marbill	FSU718	Rapsons
CSL612V	Marbill	E315MSG	Lothian Buses	F343GUS	Stokes	FSU797	Rapsons
CSV651	Stuarts of Carluke	E316MSG	Lothian Buses	F344GUS	Stokes	FTN702W	McColl Coaches
CTS917	Travel Dundee	E317MSG	Lothian Buses	F354WSC	Lothian Buses	FUM473Y	M-Line
CUL197V	West Coast Motors	E318MSG	Lothian Buses	F356WSC	Lothian Buses	FXU355	Pride of the Clyde
CUV203C	Lothian Buses	E319MSG	Lothian Buses	F357WSC	Lothian Buses	G38VME	Stuarts of Carluke
CUV210C	Lothian Buses	E320MSG	Lothian Buses	F358WSC	Lothian Buses	G44VME	McKindless
CUV241C	Lothian Buses	E321MSG	Lothian Buses	F360WSC	Lothian Buses	G83EOG	Rapsons
CUV248C	Lothian Buses	E322MSG	Lothian Buses	F361WSC	Lothian Buses	G103EOG	Rapsons
CV02KFX	Slaemuir Coaches	E324BVO	Stuarts of Carluke	F362WSC	Lothian Buses	G111EOG	Rapsons
CWG694V	Watermill	E327BVO	Irvine's	F363WSC	Lothian Buses	G118KUB	McColl Coaches
CWR505Y	McDade's Travel	E329BVO	Irvine's	F364WSC	Lothian Buses	G132EOG	Rapsons
CWR510Y	Rapsons	E333MSG	Lothian Buses	F365WSC	Lothian Buses	G146LRM	Lippen
CXP742	Rapsons	E334MSG	Lothian Buses	F366WSC	Lothian Buses	G149YAS	Rapsons
D5DOT	Dodds of Troon	E335MSG	Lothian Buses	F367WSC	Lothian Buses	G150EOG	Rapsons
D11DOT	Dodds of Troon	E342RSC	Prentice Westwood	F368WSC	Lothian Buses	G160YRE	City Sprinter
D20DOT	Dodds of Troon	E359NEG	McDade's Travel	F369WSC	Lothian Buses	G161YRE	City Sprinter
D31RYB	Rapsons	E452SON	Prentice Westwood	F370WSC	Lothian Buses	G162YRE	City Sprinter
D36ONY	Ayrways	E453SON	Prentice Westwood	F371WSC	Lothian Buses	G169FJC	Avondale Coaches
D126ACX	Bowman	E455SON	Prentice Westwood	F410KDD	City Sprinter	G173EOG	Rapsons
D131UGB	Rowe & Tudhope	E511YSU	Avondale Coaches	F424EJC	Dickson's	G175FJC	Avondale Coaches
D154THG	Stuarts of Carluke	E564YBU	Dunn's	F427DUG	Ayrways	G176EOG	Rapsons
D181TSB	Rapsons	E564YBU	Dunn's	F427EJC	D B Travel	G201RKK	City Sprinter
D216NCS	Rowe & Tudhope	E607KSP	Allander Travel	F428GAT	D B Travel	G202RKK	City Sprinter
D217NCS	Rowe & Tudhope	E766MSC	Henderson Travel	F469WFX	Rapsons	G203RKK	City Sprinter
D218NCS	Rowe & Tudhope	E870BGG	West Coast Motors	F479FGE	Stokes	G215HCP	West Coast Motors
D220NCS	Rowe & Tudhope	E871BGG	West Coast Motors	F480FGE	Stokes	G217HCP	West Coast Motors
D221NCS	Rowe & Tudhope	E911KYR	Rennie's	F481WFX	Ayrways	G233FJC	Dunn's
D298HMT	Stokes	E915NAC	Marbill	F624XMS	D B Travel	G238FJC	Dickson's
D375RHS	Whitelaws	E916NAC	Marbill	F723LRG	Stuarts of Carluke	G253VPK	Rapsons
D377RHS	Whitelaws	E917NAC	Marbill	F727ASB	West Coast Motors	G262TSL	McColl Coaches
D451CNR	Rapsons	E918NAC	Marbill	F736FDV	City Sprinter	G284EOG	Rapsons

The Scottish Bus Handbook

Reg	Operator	Reg	Operator	Reg	Operator	Reg	Operator
G285TSL	McColl Coaches	GCS42V	West Coast Motors	HCC100	H Crawford	J306BRM	West Coast Motors
G288TSL	Dickson's	GCS48V	Keenan	HCC296	H Crawford	J308BRM	West Coast Motors
G289EOG	Rapsons	GCS50V	West Coast Motors	HCC440	H Crawford	J309BRM	West Coast Motors
G293TSL	Avondale Coaches	GCS57V	E & M Horsburgh	HCC551	H Crawford	J310BRM	West Coast Motors
G336CSG	Lothian Buses	GDZ3363	Rennie's	HCC882	H Crawford	J316XVX	Coakley
G337CSG	Lothian Buses	GFM882	MacEwan's	HCC974	H Crawford	J319BVO	McKindless
G338CSG	Lothian Buses	GGE173T	Millport Motors	HCO514	Hutchison's	J324BVO	McKindless
G339CSG	Lothian Buses	GHG348W	Ayrways	HDZ5407	Rapsons	J325BVO	McKindless
G340CSG	Lothian Buses	GIL1685	Allander Travel	HDZ5417	Rapsons	J383GKH	Shuttle Buses
G341CSG	Lothian Buses	GIL2754	Clyde Coast	HDZ5427	Rapsons	J384GKH	Dickson's
G342CSG	Lothian Buses	GIL5407	Clyde Coast	HGD214T	Keenan	J387GKH	Irvine's
G343CSG	Lothian Buses	GJI627	Marbill	HHA122L	Essbee	J388GKH	Irvine's
G344CSG	Lothian Buses	GJI926	Marbill	HIL7467	Rapsons	J388GKH	Stuarts of Carluke
G345CSG	Lothian Buses	GM04GSM	Maynes Coaches	HIL7589	Gibson of Moffat	J389GKH	Irvine's
G512VYE	McKindless	GM06GSM	Maynes Coaches	HIL7590	Gibson of Moffat	J392AWB	First Stop
G636WJS	Rapsons	GN55XTD	Garelochhead	HIL8441	McKendry	J392GKH	Irvine's
G681AAD	City Sprinter	GNZ9360	Clyde Coast	HIL8645	Ayrways	J397GKH	Dickson's
G710HOP	Rapsons	GOG208W	Golden Eagle	HKM884V	Rapsons	J414PRW	Rapsons
G756SRB	McColl Coaches	GSC667X	Lothian Buses	HM03GSM	Maynes Coaches	J420JBV	Jays Coaches
G757SRB	Shuttle Buses	GSD779	Dodds of Troon	HM05GSM	Maynes Coaches	J422JBV	Jays Coaches
G780CFA	Rapsons	GSK675	Jays Coaches	HRO2Y	Rapsons	J494NBD	Munro's of Jedburgh
G800GSX	Lothian Buses	GSO84V	Fairline	HSB703Y	Stokes	J495DJS	Bus Na Comhairle
G801GSX	Lothian Buses	GSO89V	MacEwan's	HSK641	Park's of Hamilton	J498VMS	Mackie's
G802GSX	Lothian Buses	GSU342	Shuttle Buses	HSK642	Park's of Hamilton	J500BCS	Munro's of Jedburgh
G803GSX	Lothian Buses	GSU370	Eve Coaches	HSK643	Park's of Hamilton	J500CCH	Ayrways
G804GSX	Lothian Buses	GSU375	Rapsons	HSK644	Park's of Hamilton	J605KCU	McKindless
G805GSX	Lothian Buses	GSU551	Shuttle Buses	HSK645	Park's of Hamilton	J608KCU	McKindless
G806GSX	Lothian Buses	GTO303V	Pride of the Clyde	HSK646	Park's of Hamilton	J609XHL	McKindless
G806JRH	Rowe & Tudhope	GW4343	Whitelaws	HSK647	Park's of Hamilton	J610KCU	Rapsons
G807GSX	Lothian Buses	GXI153	Irvine's	HSK648	Park's of Hamilton	J611XHL	McKindless
G807LAG	Ayrways	GYE273W	West Coast Motors	HSK649	Park's of Hamilton	J612XHL	Coakley
G808GSX	Lothian Buses	GYE469W	McKindless	HSK650	Park's of Hamilton	J612XHL	Mackie's
G808LAG	Stonehouse Cs	GYE530W	McKindless	HSK651	Park's of Hamilton	J613XHL	McKindless
G809GSX	Lothian Buses	GYE544W	McKindless	HSK652	Park's of Hamilton	J614KCU	McKindless
G810GSX	Lothian Buses	H11JYM	Stuarts of Carluke	HSK653	Park's of Hamilton	J615XHL	Scottish Travel
G811GSX	Lothian Buses	H102THE	McKindless	HSK654	Park's of Hamilton	J619KCU	West Coast Motors
G812GSX	Lothian Buses	H103THE	McKindless	HSK655	Park's of Hamilton	J619KCU	West Coast Motors
G813GSX	Lothian Buses	H105THE	McKindless	HSK656	Park's of Hamilton	J623KCU	Rapsons
G814GSX	Lothian Buses	H106THE	McKindless	HSK657	Park's of Hamilton	J626KCU	McKindless
G815GSX	Lothian Buses	H107THE	McKindless	HSK658	Park's of Hamilton	J629KCU	McKindless
G816GSX	Lothian Buses	H108THE	McKindless	HSK659	Park's of Hamilton	J634KCU	McKindless
G817GSX	Lothian Buses	H109THE	McKindless	HSK660	Park's of Hamilton	J782KHD	Bowman
G818GSX	Lothian Buses	H110THE	McKindless	HSK857	Irvine's	J806KHD	West Coast Motors
G819GSX	Lothian Buses	H114MOB	West Coast Motors	HSL660	Scottish Travel	J807HSB	West Coast Motors
G820GSX	Lothian Buses	H114THE	McKindless	HSR37X	Pride of the Clyde	J809KHD	West Coast Motors
G821GSX	Lothian Buses	H141MOB	Caledonian Buses	HSR43X	Pride of the Clyde	J812HMC	Irvine's
G822GSX	Lothian Buses	H149SKU	Marbill	HSR49X	Pride of the Clyde	J814HMC	Irvine's
G823GSX	Lothian Buses	H150SKU	Marbill	HSR50X	Pride of the Clyde	J818HMC	Irvine's
G824GSX	Lothian Buses	H151SKU	Marbill	HSV725	Watermill	J836TSC	Lothian Buses
G825GSX	Lothian Buses	H152SKU	Marbill	HUI4553	Caledonian Buses	J837TSC	Lothian Buses
G826GSX	Lothian Buses	H153SKU	Marbill	HUI8156	Stuarts of Carluke	J838TSC	Lothian Buses
G827GSX	Lothian Buses	H154SKU	Marbill	IDZ636	Rapsons	J839TSC	Lothian Buses
G828GSX	Lothian Buses	H155SKU	Marbill	IDZ828	Rapsons	J840TSC	Lothian Buses
G829GSX	Lothian Buses	H156SKU	Marbill	IIL3504	Rennie's	J841TSC	Lothian Buses
G830GSX	Lothian Buses	H157SKU	Marbill	IIL4595	Prentice	J842TSC	Lothian Buses
G831GSX	Lothian Buses	H158NON	West Coast Motors	IUI9892	Shuttle Buses	J843TSC	Lothian Buses
G831RDS	Shuttle Buses	H158SKU	Marbill	J10WBT	Avondale Coaches	J844TSC	Lothian Buses
G832GSX	Lothian Buses	H159SKU	Marbill	J17BUS	Hutchison's	J845TSC	Lothian Buses
G833GSX	Lothian Buses	H166NON	West Coast Motors	J34MKB	McKendry	J846TSC	Lothian Buses
G834GSX	Lothian Buses	H166WWT	Rapsons	J48SNY	Moffat & Williamson	J847TSC	Lothian Buses
G835GSX	Lothian Buses	H177JVT	Coakley	J55BUS	Dunn's	J848TSC	Lothian Buses
G864RNC	Mackie's	H201LOM	Stonehouse Cs	J75FPS	Rapsons	J849TSC	Lothian Buses
G872SKE	McDade's Travel	H201TWE	First Stop	J118HGF	McKindless	J850TSC	Lothian Buses
G901UPP	First Stop	H213TWE	First Stop	J122HGF	McKindless	J851TSC	Lothian Buses
G904UPP	Stuarts of Carluke	H223LOM	Ayrways	J156GAT	McKindless	J852TSC	Lothian Buses
G909UPP	First Stop	H224LOM	Ayrways	J158GAT	McKindless	J853TSC	Lothian Buses
G926WGS	Key Coaches	H242TSS	Nicoll	J211KTT	Key Coaches	J854TSC	Lothian Buses
G931MYG	Munro's of Jedburgh	H410DPS	Rapsons	J224HGY	McKindless	J855TSC	Lothian Buses
G935MYG	McKindless	H611TKU	McKindless	J235NNC	Rapsons	J856TSC	Lothian Buses
G948TDV	City Sprinter	H809WKH	Stonehouse Cs	J292NNB	E & M Horsburgh	J857TSC	Lothian Buses
G951TDV	City Sprinter	H837AHS	Bowman	J293NNB	E & M Horsburgh	J858TSC	Lothian Buses
GBZ7212	Dunn's	H916XYT	Coakley	J301BRM	West Coast Motors	J859TSC	Lothian Buses
GBZ8812	Lippen	H921XYT	Coakley	J302BRM	West Coast Motors	J860TSC	Lothian Buses
GBZ9059	Lippen	H922XYT	Coakley	J303BRM	West Coast Motors	J861TSC	Lothian Buses
GCS35V	West Coast Motors	HCC49	H Crawford	J304BRM	West Coast Motors	J862TSC	Lothian Buses
GCS38V	Keenan	HCC60	H Crawford	J305BRM	West Coast Motors	J863TSC	Lothian Buses

Reg	Operator	Reg	Operator	Reg	Operator	Reg	Operator
J864TSC	Lothian Buses	K98SAG	McKindless	K544RJX	McKendry	KSK930	Hutchison's
J865TSC	Lothian Buses	K102SAG	McKindless	K546RJX	Munro's of Jedburgh	KSK933	Hutchison's
J866TSC	Lothian Buses	K103OMW	Puma	K578PHU	Allander Travel	KSK934	Hutchison's
J867TSC	Lothian Buses	K103SAG	McKindless	K579MGT	Lippen	KSK950	Park's of Hamilton
J868TSC	Lothian Buses	K103XHG	West Coast Motors	K579PHU	Allander Travel	KSK951	Park's of Hamilton
J869TSC	Lothian Buses	K104OGB	McColl Coaches	K580MGT	Lippen	KSK952	Park's of Hamilton
J870TSC	Lothian Buses	K104SAG	McKindless	K580YOJ	Slaemuir Coaches	KSK953	Park's of Hamilton
J871TSC	Lothian Buses	K105SAG	McKindless	K581MGT	Avondale Coaches	KSK954	Park's of Hamilton
J937WHJ	Stuarts of Carluke	K106SAG	McKindless	K583MGT	Avondale Coaches	KSK976	Park's of Hamilton
J938WHJ	Key Coaches	K113XHG	Davidson Buses	K593MGT	Avondale Coaches	KSK977	Park's of Hamilton
J945MFT	McKindless	K117CSG	Lothian Buses	K620DMS	Mackie's	KSK978	Park's of Hamilton
J946MFT	McKindless	K118CSG	Lothian Buses	K621PGO	McKindless	KSK979	Park's of Hamilton
J947MFT	MacEwan's	K119CSG	Lothian Buses	K622PGO	McKindless	KSK980	Park's of Hamilton
J955SBU	Munro's of Jedburgh	K120CSG	Lothian Buses	K667NGB	Marbill	KSK981	Park's of Hamilton
J967JNL	Caledonian Buses	K121CSG	Lothian Buses	K719DAO	John Morrow	KSK982	Park's of Hamilton
J968JNL	Caledonian Buses	K122CSG	Lothian Buses	K725UTT	Gullivers Travel	KSK983	Park's of Hamilton
J972OGV	Munro's of Jedburgh	K123CSG	Lothian Buses	K732DAO	John Morrow	KSK984	Park's of Hamilton
JA5515	Docherty's Midland	K132XRE	City Sprinter	K766DAO	MacEwan's	KSK985	Park's of Hamilton
JAZ4632	Rapsons	K151LGO	Avondale Coaches	K770AFS	Shuttle Buses	KSK986	Park's of Hamilton
JAZ9850	Rapsons	K153LGO	Avondale Coaches	K773DAO	John Morrow	KSU317	McKindless
JAZ9851	Rapsons	K163FYG	Caledonian Buses	K788DAO	MacEwan's	KSU674	Rapsons
JAZ9852	Rapsons	K173CAV	Gullivers Travel	K816WFJ	Gullivers Travel	KSV980	Stuarts of Carluke
JAZ9853	Rapsons	K186YDW	Caledonian Buses	K818NKH	Bryans of Denny	KSX105X	E & M Horsburgh
JAZ9854	Rapsons	K200WCM	West Coast Motors	K851RBB	MacEwan's	KU02YUL	MacEwan's
JAZ9855	Rapsons	K210SAG	McKindless	K852RBB	MacEwan's	KU02YUN	MacEwan's
JAZ9856	Rapsons	K221VTB	Avondale Coaches	K866ODY	Dickson's	KU52YJX	Jays Coaches
JAZ9857	Rapsons	K222VTB	Avondale Coaches	K872CSF	Lothian Buses	KU52YJY	Jays Coaches
JAZ9858	Rapsons	K223VTB	Avondale Coaches	K873CSF	Lothian Buses	KU52YJZ	Jays Coaches
JAZ9859	Rapsons	K224VTB	Avondale Coaches	K874CSF	Lothian Buses	KVF246V	Rapsons
JBZ4910	McDade's Travel	K225VTB	Avondale Coaches	K875CSF	Lothian Buses	KX03HZK	Waverley
JCZ2065	Stuarts of Carluke	K226BJA	Dunn's	K876CSF	Lothian Buses	KX54HKZ	Waverley
JDS77J	Docherty's Midland	K229SFJ	First Stop	K877CSF	Lothian Buses	KYV652X	McKindless
JDZ2401	McKindless	K235AHG	Munro's of Jedburgh	K878CSF	Lothian Buses	KYV661X	McKindless
JDZ2403	McKindless	K236SFJ	First Stop	K879CSF	Lothian Buses	KYV682X	McKindless
JDZ2404	McKindless	K237SFJ	Slaemuir Coaches	K880CSF	Lothian Buses	KYV702X	McKindless
JDZ2405	Caledonian Buses	K238SFJ	First Stop	K881CSF	Lothian Buses	KYV714X	McKindless
JDZ2409	Caledonian Buses	K239SFJ	Slaemuir Coaches	K882CSF	Lothian Buses	KYV721X	McKindless
JDZ2410	McKindless	K241SFJ	Slaemuir Coaches	K883CSF	Lothian Buses	KYV732X	McKindless
JDZ2411	McKindless	K242SFJ	City Sprinter	K884CSF	Lothian Buses	KYV752X	McKindless
JDZ2412	McKindless	K243SFJ	Davidson Buses	K885CSF	Lothian Buses	KYV756X	Rennie's
JDZ2413	Caledonian Buses	K244SUS	Avondale Coaches	K886CSF	Lothian Buses	KYV765X	McKindless
JDZ2414	Caledonian Buses	K245SFJ	Davidson Buses	K887CSF	Lothian Buses	KYV772X	McKindless
JIL3713	Galson	K247MOS	Rapsons	K889BRW	McKindless	KYV773X	McKindless
JIL5144	McKindless	K247SFJ	Davidson Buses	K889CSF	Lothian Buses	KYV798X	McKindless
JIL5145	McKindless	K300SOU	Galson	K890CSF	Lothian Buses	L1PPN	Lippen
JIL5809	Rapsons	K300WCM	West Coast Motors	K891CSF	Lothian Buses	L2PPN	Lippen
JIL8207	Watermill	K310YKG	Rapsons	K892CSF	Lothian Buses	L3LOW	Travel Dundee
JIL8208	Prentice Westwood	K314YKG	Rapsons	K893BEG	Dunn's	L3PPN	Lippen
JIL8553	Golden Eagle	K316YKG	Rapsons	K893CSF	Lothian Buses	L4LCC	Kineil Coaches
JIL8559	Golden Eagle	K322BTM	Dunn's	K894CSF	Lothian Buses	L4PPN	Lippen
JIL8560	Golden Eagle	K325YKG	Rapsons	K930HSO	E & M Horsburgh	L5PPN	Lippen
JIL8561	Golden Eagle	K327FAL	McKindless	K96RGA	Key Coaches	L7PPN	Lippen
JIL8562	Golden Eagle	K328FAL	McKindless	K983CBO	McKindless	L8BUS	Billy Davies
JIL8813	Irvine's	K32WND	Key Coaches	K991CBO	McKindless	L8PPN	Lippen
JJD432D	Scottish Travel	K330FAL	McKindless	K994CBO	McKindless	L9PPN	Lippen
JNM742Y	H Crawford	K336FAL	McKindless	KAZ2065	Rapsons	L11PPN	Lippen
JSJ746	Lothian Buses	K337FAL	McKindless	KDZ5801	Coakley	L23WGA	Moffat & Williamson
JSJ747	Lothian Buses	K338FAL	McKindless	KFO809	Rapsons	L35OKV	Rapsons
JSJ748	Lothian Buses	K339FAL	McKindless	KHT121P	Rapsons	L52LSG	Coakley
JSJ749	Lothian Buses	K342FAL	McKindless	KIW4388	Kineil Coaches	L53LSG	Coakley
JSU384	Kineil Coaches	K359SCN	Caledonian Buses	KKG109W	Essbee	L54LSG	Coakley
JSU506	Travel Dundee	K392SLB	First Stop	KKN752	Maynes Coaches	L82RHL	Moffat & Williamson
JSU542	Travel Dundee	K393SLB	First Stop	KKZ5534	Rapsons	L91NSF	Henderson Travel
JSU550	Prentice	K400WCM	West Coast Motors	KLZ2315	Rapsons	L94LND	Slaemuir Coaches
JSV331	Dunn's	K416MGN	Caledonian Buses	KLZ2316	Rapsons	L98PTW	Eve Coaches
JSV440	Prentice Westwood	K433OKH	Coakley	KLZ2317	Rapsons	L98WSW	H Crawford
JSV486	Galson	K433OKH	Mackie's	KLZ2318	Rapsons	L101SDY	McKindless
JSX595T	Lothian Buses	K470SKO	Coakley	KLZ858	Rapsons	L103GBO	Caledonian Buses
K5SKY	Kineil Coaches	K476FYN	Scottish Travel	KM03GSM	Maynes Coaches	L106GBO	Caledonian Buses
K10EVE	Eve Coaches	K477SSM	MacEwan's	KM04GSM	Maynes Coaches	L106YGD	Moffat & Williamson
K17CJT	Galson	K478SSM	MacEwan's	KM05GSM	Maynes Coaches	L139XDS	Avondale Coaches
K21CDW	McKindless	K500WCM	West Coast Motors	KM06GSM	Maynes Coaches	L140XDS	Avondale Coaches
K31WND	Key Coaches	K504NST	Rapsons	KPJ281W	E & M Horsburgh	L141BFV	McKindless
K76OCR	Wilson's of Rhu	K515RJX	Munro's of Jedburgh	KPS701T	Rapsons	L146VRH	West Coast Motors
K85DTM	Slaemuir Coaches	K523RJX	Munro's of Jedburgh	KRE278P	Rapsons	L151WAG	McKindless
K97SAG	McKindless	K538PHU	Allander Travel	KRU847W	Smith & Sons	L152FRJ	West Coast Motors

Reg	Operator	Reg	Operator	Reg	Operator	Reg	Operator
L152WAG	McKindless	L733MWW	McGill's	LSK500	Park's of Hamilton	M193HTT	Gullivers Travel
L154WAG	McKindless	L735PUA	First Stop	LSK501	Park's of Hamilton	M195TMG	Stonehouse Cs
L155UEM	Nicoll	L736PUA	McGill's	LSK502	Park's of Hamilton	M200WCM	West Coast Motors
L155WAG	McKindless	L737PUA	Coakley	LSK503	Park's of Hamilton	M201EGF	Coakley
L156UEM	Nicoll	L738PUA	D B Travel	LSK504	Park's of Hamilton	M201VSX	Lothian Buses
L156WAG	McKindless	L742NHE	Garelochhead	LSK505	Park's of Hamilton	M202EGF	Coakley
L157WAG	McKindless	L748LWA	Dickson's	LSK506	Park's of Hamilton	M202VSX	Lothian Buses
L158WAG	McKindless	L749JSX	E & M Horsburgh	LSK507	Park's of Hamilton	M203VSX	Lothian Buses
L160XRH	McKindless	L776AUS	Lippen	LSK508	Park's of Hamilton	M204VSX	Lothian Buses
L162XRH	McKindless	L807TFY	Caledonian Buses	LSK510	Park's of Hamilton	M205VSX	Lothian Buses
L164XRH	McKindless	L851WDS	Avondale Coaches	LSK511	Park's of Hamilton	M206EGF	Coakley
L165YAT	McKindless	L866LFS	Coakley	LSK512	Park's of Hamilton	M206VSX	Lothian Buses
L166YAT	McKindless	L868LFS	Coakley	LSK513	Park's of Hamilton	M207EGF	Coakley
L167YAT	McKindless	L870LFS	Coakley	LSK514	Park's of Hamilton	M207VSX	Lothian Buses
L168YAT	McKindless	L906ANS	Coakley	LSK555	Park's of Hamilton	M208EGF	City Sprinter
L169YAT	McKindless	L910JRN	Millport Motors	LSK611	Park's of Hamilton	M208VSX	Lothian Buses
L200WCM	West Coast Motors	L930UGA	Kineil Coaches	LSK612	Park's of Hamilton	M209EGF	City Sprinter
L202ONU	D B Travel	L937WFW	West Coast Motors	LSK613	Park's of Hamilton	M209VSX	Lothian Buses
L203ONU	D B Travel	L947HTM	First Stop	LSK614	Park's of Hamilton	M210VSX	Lothian Buses
L245CCK	Dickson's	L948HTM	First Stop	LSK615	Park's of Hamilton	M211EGF	Avondale Coaches
L248YOD	First Stop	L950MSC	Lothian Buses	LSK812	Park's of Hamilton	M211VSX	Lothian Buses
L253YOD	Slaemuir Coaches	L951MSC	Lothian Buses	LSK814	Park's of Hamilton	M211YAS	Rapsons
L254YOD	Slaemuir Coaches	L952MSC	Lothian Buses	LSK830	Park's of Hamilton	M212VSX	Lothian Buses
L255YOD	Davidson Buses	L953MSC	Lothian Buses	LSK831	Park's of Hamilton	M213VSX	Lothian Buses
L260YOD	First Stop	L954MSC	Lothian Buses	LSK832	Park's of Hamilton	M214VSX	Lothian Buses
L263AAG	West Coast Motors	L955MSC	Lothian Buses	LSK835	Park's of Hamilton	M215EGF	Coakley
L264AAG	West Coast Motors	L956MSC	Lothian Buses	LSK839	Park's of Hamilton	M215VSX	Lothian Buses
L292USU	Stokes	L957MSC	Lothian Buses	LSK844	Park's of Hamilton	M216EGF	Coakley
L293USU	Stokes	L958MSC	Lothian Buses	LSK845	Park's of Hamilton	M216VSX	Lothian Buses
L299BGA	First Stop	L959MSC	Lothian Buses	LSK870	Park's of Hamilton	M217VSX	Lothian Buses
L300RHU	Avondale Coaches	L960MSC	Lothian Buses	LSK871	Park's of Hamilton	M218VSX	Lothian Buses
L300WCM	West Coast Motors	L961MSC	Lothian Buses	LSK872	Park's of Hamilton	M219VSX	Lothian Buses
L314KSS	Kineil Coaches	L962MSC	Lothian Buses	LSK873	Park's of Hamilton	M220VSX	Lothian Buses
L345ERU	Galson	L963MSC	Lothian Buses	LSK874	Park's of Hamilton	M221VSX	Lothian Buses
L374BGA	Avondale Coaches	L964MSC	Lothian Buses	LSK875	Park's of Hamilton	M223VSX	Lothian Buses
L375BGA	Avondale Coaches	L965MSC	Lothian Buses	LSK876	Park's of Hamilton	M224VSX	Lothian Buses
L376BGA	Avondale Coaches	L966MSC	Lothian Buses	LSK877	Park's of Hamilton	M225VSX	Lothian Buses
L377TFT	Caledonian Buses	L967MSC	Lothian Buses	LSK878	Park's of Hamilton	M226VSX	Lothian Buses
L383TFT	Caledonian Buses	L968MSC	Lothian Buses	LSK879	Park's of Hamilton	M227VSX	Lothian Buses
L385TFT	Caledonian Buses	L969MSC	Lothian Buses	LST873	Lothian Buses	M228VSX	Lothian Buses
L386TFT	Caledonian Buses	L970MSC	Lothian Buses	LSU689	Prentice Westwood	M229VSX	Lothian Buses
L387TFT	Caledonian Buses	L971MSC	Lothian Buses	LSV380	Stuarts of Carluke	M230VSX	Lothian Buses
L388BGA	McColl Coaches	L972MSC	Lothian Buses	LTU284	Rapsons	M231VSX	Lothian Buses
L389AVK	Caledonian Buses	L973MSC	Lothian Buses	LTU284	Rapsons	M232VSX	Lothian Buses
L395BGA	Avondale Coaches	L974MSC	Lothian Buses	LVG263	Travel Dundee	M233VSX	Lothian Buses
L400WCM	West Coast Motors	L975MSC	Lothian Buses	M6SEL	Bus Na Comhairle	M234VSX	Lothian Buses
L413BGA	Coakley	L976MSC	Lothian Buses	M7JPT	Slaemuir Coaches	M238UTM	Caledonian Buses
L416BGA	Avondale Coaches	L977MSC	Lothian Buses	M7SEL	Bus Na Comhairle	M243JHB	Rapsons
L441DBU	Stonehouse Cs	L978MSC	Lothian Buses	M8SKY	Watermill	M291OUR	MacEwan's
L464BGA	Avondale Coaches	L979MSC	Lothian Buses	M17YNE	Maynes Coaches	M300WCM	West Coast Motors
L465BGA	Avondale Coaches	L980MSC	Lothian Buses	M20BLU	Slaemuir Coaches	M303YWE	Moffat & Williamson
L472YVK	Caledonian Buses	L981MSC	Lothian Buses	M37FGG	E & M Horsburgh	M304YWE	Moffat & Williamson
L481BGA	Avondale Coaches	L982MSC	Lothian Buses	M70TCC	Dodds of Troon	M308BAV	Prentice Westwood
L482BGA	Avondale Coaches	L983MSC	Lothian Buses	M100WCM	West Coast Motors	M318RSO	Puma
L483BGA	Henderson Travel	LCZ1890	McKendry	M101WKA	Scottish Travel	M327TSF	Scottish Travel
L493BGA	Avondale Coaches	LDC84P	McDade's Travel	M102WKA	Nicoll	M354SDC	Riverside
L500GSM	Rapsons	LFJ848W	MacEwan's	M103BLE	City Sprinter	M358LFX	McKendry
L502YGD	Kineil Coaches	LFJ849W	MacEwan's	M104WKA	Nicoll	M365AMA	Bus Na Comhairle
L512LNR	Pride of the Clyde	LFJ850W	MacEwan's	M110KBO	Caledonian Buses	M366AMA	Bus Na Comhairle
L631AYS	Smith & Sons	LHS747V	Jays Coaches	M115KBD	Coakley	M366KVR	Henderson Travel
L637DNA	Slaemuir Coaches	LIJ595	Rapsons	M116KBO	Caledonian Buses	M367KVR	Henderson Travel
L638DNA	Dunn's	LIL8970	MacEwan's	M121KBD	Coakley	M373MUV	Anderson Coaches
L641DNA	Slaemuir Coaches	LIL9814	Keenan	M121YCM	Scottish Travel	M378EFD	Scottish Travel
L642DNA	Dunn's	LMS380W	West Coast Motors	M123KBO	Caledonian Buses	M394KVR	Scottish Travel
L649DNA	Key Coaches	LS04OSL	Mackie's	M123YCM	Slaemuir Coaches	M400WCM	West Coast Motors
L654MYG	West Coast Motors	LSK444	Park's of Hamilton	M124KBO	Caledonian Buses	M480FGG	E & M Horsburgh
L657HKS	Stuarts of Carluke	LSK473	Park's of Hamilton	M124YCM	Slaemuir Coaches	M481CSD	Bowman
L670PWT	Moffat & Williamson	LSK478	Rennie's	M125KBO	Caledonian Buses	M481FGG	E & M Horsburgh
L684UYS	Hutchison's	LSK479	Rennie's	M126YCM	Scottish Travel	M487WAS	Rapsons
L700WCM	West Coast Motors	LSK481	Park's of Hamilton	M127KBO	Caledonian Buses	M490FGG	E & M Horsburgh
L703AGA	Dickson's	LSK483	Park's of Hamilton	M128YCM	Scottish Travel	M491FGG	E & M Horsburgh
L704AGA	Rowe & Tudhope	LSK495	Park's of Hamilton	M129KBO	Caledonian Buses	M498XSP	Moffat & Williamson
L705AGA	Coakley	LSK496	Park's of Hamilton	M132KBD	Coakley	M500WCM	West Coast Motors
L715WCC	Dunn's	LSK497	Park's of Hamilton	M152LPL	Stuarts of Carluke	M506ALP	City Sprinter
L716WCC	Dunn's	LSK498	Park's of Hamilton	M158WWM	Nicoll	M507ALP	McKindless
L733MWV	D B Travel	LSK499	Park's of Hamilton	M191HTT	Gullivers Travel	M534NCG	Harris Coaches

Reg	Operator	Reg	Operator	Reg	Operator	Reg	Operator
M578BSM	MacEwan's	MRJ40W	Billy Davies	N169WNF	West Coast Motors	N752LUS	McGill's
M599GMR	Galson	MRJ55W	Billy Davies	N171WNF	West Coast Motors	N753LSU	Stokes
M600WCM	West Coast Motors	MSL276X	West Coast Motors	N182CMJ	Gullivers Travel	N753OYR	Anderson Coaches
M601RFS	Jays Coaches	MTU118Y	M-Line	N183CMJ	Gullivers Travel	N779OGA	Riverside
M602BCA	Bus Na Comhairle	MU51FMV	Smith & Sons	N195RGD	Watermill	N790EES	Moffat & Williamson
M609WFS	Henderson Travel	MUD490	McColl Coaches	N200BUS	Garelochhead	N796PDS	D B Travel
M623WAS	Rapsons	MV04GXF	Henderson Travel	N200WCM	West Coast Motors	N798FSD	Dickson's
M627RCP	Bowman	MVS380	Waverley	N202WSB	West Coast Motors	N798PDS	Slaemuir Coaches
M628HDV	Gullivers Travel	MX03OBG	Munro's of Jedburgh	N207GCS	Dickson's	N799FSD	Puma
M631KVU	Ayrways	MX03YCM	Henderson Travel	N208CKP	Stuarts of Carluke	N799PDS	Slaemuir Coaches
M631RCP	Munro's of Jedburgh	MX03YCV	Henderson Travel	N208GCS	Puma	N801FSD	Puma
M634FJF	Garelochhead	MX03YCW	Henderson Travel	N209FSM	MacEwan's	N804GRV	Millport Motors
M636HDV	Gullivers Travel	MX03YDB	Henderson Travel	N210FSM	MacEwan's	N810PDS	Riverside
M637HDV	Gullivers Travel	MX04DSZ	Wilson's of Rhu	N221MUS	Riverside	N830DKU	Dodds of Troon
M640HDV	Gullivers Travel	MX05ENC	Garelochhead	N224THO	Galson	N839LGA	McDade's Travel
M658ROS	Galson	MX06ACZ	Moffat & Williamson	N228MUS	McGill's	N840LGA	McDade's Travel
M664UCT	E & M Horsburgh	MX06ADO	Moffat & Williamson	N245RGD	Watermill	N841LGA	McDade's Travel
M665JFP	Caledonian Buses	MX51VCT	Eve Coaches	N249PGD	City Sprinter	N843LGA	McDade's Travel
M679CSU	Hutchison's	MX54KXU	Stuarts of Carluke	N250MNS	E & M Horsburgh	N862FWG	Stuarts of Carluke
M700WCM	West Coast Motors	MX54KXV	Stuarts of Carluke	N250PGD	City Sprinter	N943MGG	Slaemuir Coaches
M742UUA	Coakley	MX54KXZ	Henderson Travel	N254PGD	McGill's	N950MGG	Dickson's
M743UUA	Coakley	MX54KYG	Moffat & Williamson	N256PGD	McGill's	N965LHS	McDade's Travel
M744UUA	Coakley	MX54PJU	McDade's Travel	N258PGD	McGill's	N966LHS	McDade's Travel
M745UUA	Coakley	MX54VWJ	Hebridean Coaches	N275FNS	Dickson's	N971MGG	Stokes
M753WWR	First Stop	MX55BYG	Stuarts of Carluke	N300WCM	West Coast Motors	N982FWT	Bowman
M760ASL	Moffat & Williamson	MX55BYH	Garelochhead	N317DAG	MacEwan's	N990FNK	Slaemuir Coaches
M771TFS	Puma	MX55HXP	Watermill	N345OBC	Scottish Travel	N991FNK	Slaemuir Coaches
M783ASL	Moffat & Williamson	MX55MCW	E & M Horsburgh	N345OBC	Scottish Travel	N993KUS	Marbill
M788ASL	Moffat & Williamson	MX55WCT	Stuarts of Carluke	N350VSO	Watermill	N996CCC	Puma
M791EUS	Coakley	MX55WDS	Munro's of Jedburgh	N400WCM	West Coast Motors	N997CCC	Puma
M796ASL	Moffat & Williamson	MX55WDT	Munro's of Jedburgh	N401GSX	Lothian Buses	NCH868	Prentice Westwood
M800WCM	West Coast Motors	N1CLL	Nicoll	N402GSX	Lothian Buses	NDZ3024	West Coast Motors
M802ASL	Moffat & Williamson	N1EVE	Eve Coaches	N403GSX	Lothian Buses	NDZ3025	West Coast Motors
M804ASM	MacEwan's	N2CLL	Nicoll	N404GSX	Lothian Buses	NDZ3026	West Coast Motors
M808ASL	Moffat & Williamson	N2SBL	Shuttle Buses	N405GSX	Lothian Buses	NDZ3146	Puma
M814ASL	Moffat & Williamson	N3CLL	Nicoll	N406GSX	Lothian Buses	NDZ7925	Scottish Travel
M823ASL	Moffat & Williamson	N3SBL	Shuttle Buses	N406SPC	Hebridean Coaches	NDZ7927	Coakley
M827HNS	Pride of the Clyde	N4SKY	Rapsons	N407GSX	Lothian Buses	NDZ7928	Coakley
M868FSU	Hutchison's	N5BUS	Watermill	N407SPC	Hebridean Coaches	NDZ7930	Coakley
M880DDS	Coakley	N5SBL	Shuttle Buses	N409SPC	Hebridean Coaches	NDZ7937	Pride of the Clyde
M893WLG	Harris Coaches	N6SBL	Shuttle Buses	N468SPA	Scottish Travel	NEO832R	McColl Coaches
M901NKS	Munro's of Jedburgh	N7DOT	Dodds of Troon	N469PYS	Pride of the Clyde	NFL881	Rapsons
M975WES	Stuarts of Carluke	N7SBL	Shuttle Buses	N469SPA	McDade's Travel	NFS172Y	Jays Coaches
M983HNS	Pride of the Clyde	N10CLL	Nicoll	N470SPA	Scottish Travel	NFS179Y	Jays Coaches
M984HNS	Pride of the Clyde	N11JDP	Rapsons	N479VPA	Hebridean Coaches	NGH456	Prentice Westwood
MBZ6454	Rapsons	N18SCP	Prentice	N491FDT	Riverside	NIB2796	Essbee
MDX540	M-Line	N22DTS	McKindless	N501KCD	McGill's	NIB6535	Essbee
MFR125P	MacEwan's	N23FWU	Travel Dundee	N502KCD	McGill's	NIL2266	Prentice Westwood
MFR126P	MacEwan's	N23KYS	Anderson Coaches	N503KCD	McGill's	NIL2734	Rapsons
MFR41P	MacEwan's	N33CLL	Nicoll	N504KCD	McGill's	NIL2735	Rapsons
MFS444P	Prentice	N34GSX	Slaemuir Coaches	N505PYS	Smith & Sons	NIL3416	M-Line
MIL3960	Watermill	N77JDS	Docherty's Midland	N506KCD	McGill's	NIL7707	Essbee
MIL3982	Watermill	N78LGD	McDade's Travel	N508KCD	McGill's	NML600E	McKindless
MIL5573	Rapsons	N79LGD	McDade's Travel	N511KCD	McGill's	NMY634E	Lothian Buses
MIL6548	McKendry	N81LGD	McDade's Travel	N513KCD	McGill's	NMY646E	Lothian Buses
MIL6676	Essbee	N86FHL	Moffat & Williamson	N516KCD	McGill's	NNF922	H Crawford
MIL6679	Jays Coaches	N87FHL	Moffat & Williamson	N517KCD	McGill's	NR04AAA	AAA Coaches
MIL7620	Essbee	N100WCM	West Coast Motors	N517PYS	Pride of the Clyde	NSK919	H Crawford
MIL7622	Essbee	N101WRC	Rapsons	N518KCD	McGill's	NSK920	H Crawford
MIL9752	Rapsons	N101WSB	West Coast Motors	N519KCD	McGill's	NSK921	H Crawford
MIL9753	Rapsons	N102EMB	Dickson's	N554SJF	McKendry	NST61Y	Rapsons
MIL9754	Rapsons	N102WRC	Rapsons	N602FWA	E & M Horsburgh	NSU552	Irvine's
MIL9755	Rapsons	N103WRC	Rapsons	N603VSS	West Coast Motors	NSV621	Travel Dundee
MIL9756	Rapsons	N104WRC	E & M Horsburgh	N608OGE	Hutchison's	NSV622	Travel Dundee
MK03OCB	Munro's of Jedburgh	N105WRC	E & M Horsburgh	N616DWY	Slaemuir Coaches	NTC640M	Essbee
MK52OKX	Munro's of Jedburgh	N106WRC	Rapsons	N620DMS	Mackie's	NTT573W	MacEwan's
MK52UGJ	Munro's of Jedburgh	N107WRC	E & M Horsburgh	N623VSS	West Coast Motors	NUW596Y	Rennie's
MK52UHG	Munro's of Jedburgh	N108WRC	Rapsons	N629VSS	West Coast Motors	NUW600Y	Rennie's
ML02PFN	Watermill	N109WRC	Rapsons	N638LGG	McDade's Travel	NX03MVL	Rennie's
MM03GSM	Maynes Coaches	N113NYS	Allander Travel	N639LGG	McDade's Travel	NXX451	Rennie's
MM04GSM	Maynes Coaches	N114DWE	MacEwan's	N640LGG	McDade's Travel	OAF990	Rapsons
MM05GSM	Maynes Coaches	N117FSM	MacEwan's	N642LGG	McDade's Travel	OAS624	Lothian Buses
MM06GSM	Maynes Coaches	N120NYS	E & M Horsburgh	N702FLN	Moffat & Williamson	OAZ9372	Gibson of Moffat
MM54GSM	Maynes Coaches	N128XEG	Caledonian Buses	N706FSM	MacEwan's	OBX51	Fairline
MOD572P	Stuarts of Carluke	N139PTG	Caledonian Buses	N744LUS	Dickson's	OBZ2241	Stuarts of Carluke
MRJ280W	Whitelaws	N142PTG	Coakley	N746YVR	Dickson's	OBZ6976	Munro's of Jedburgh

The Scottish Bus Handbook

Reg	Operator	Reg	Operator	Reg	Operator	Reg	Operator
OFS671Y	Marbill	P135KSL	Travel Dundee	P285PSX	Lothian Buses	P671MSC	E & M Horsburgh
OFS672Y	Marbill	P136KSL	Travel Dundee	P291MLD	Coakley	P675RWU	Dickson's
OFS674Y	Clyde Coast	P137KSL	Travel Dundee	P294MLD	City Sprinter	P675RWU	Scottish Travel
OFS675Y	Clyde Coast	P138KSL	Travel Dundee	P294MLD	Coakley	P677VJS	Rapsons
OFS676Y	M-Line	P139KSL	Travel Dundee	P295MLD	Coakley	P681DCK	Smith & Sons
OFS677Y	Marbill	P140KSL	Travel Dundee	P301MLD	Coakley	P683HND	Henderson Travel
OFS678Y	Clyde Coast	P141KSL	Travel Dundee	P301VWR	Gibson of Moffat	P691RWU	Scottish Travel
OFS685Y	Marbill	P142RSN	Travel Dundee	P316UHS	McKendry	P692RWU	Davidson Buses
OFS686Y	Marbill	P143RSN	Travel Dundee	P318MLD	Coakley	P694RWU	Gibson
OFS687Y	Marbill	P144RSN	Travel Dundee	P336JND	McKindless	P696BRS	Bowman
OFS688Y	Marbill	P145RSN	Travel Dundee	P337CEP	McKendry	P697RWU	Scottish Travel
OFS689Y	Clyde Coast	P146RSN	Travel Dundee	P340JND	McKindless	P698RWU	Davidson Buses
OFS690Y	Allander Travel	P147RSN	Travel Dundee	P343JAS	Rapsons	P707DPA	Hebridean Coaches
OFS691Y	Allander Travel	P148RSN	Travel Dundee	P349JND	McKindless	P718RYL	McKindless
OFS692Y	Marbill	P149RSN	Travel Dundee	P376NSX	Rowe & Tudhope	P720RWU	West Coast Motors
OFS694Y	Marbill	P150RSN	Travel Dundee	P385XGG	MacEwan's	P721RYL	McKindless
OFS695Y	Marbill	P151LSC	Slaemuir Coaches	P390OFS	Eve Coaches	P723RYL	McKindless
OFS696Y	Marbill	P151RSN	Travel Dundee	P398FEA	Scottish Travel	P730RYL	McKindless
OFS697Y	Marbill	P152LSC	Slaemuir Coaches	P398FVP	Travel Dundee	P736FMS	Coakley
OFS699Y	Marbill	P166LSC	Rapsons	P399FVP	Travel Dundee	P737FMS	Coakley
OFS700Y	Marbill	P200WCM	West Coast Motors	P408KSX	Lothian Buses	P738FMS	Coakley
OFV21X	McKendry	P203OLX	Coakley	P408RGG	Lippen	P743HND	Millport Motors
OHV697Y	Rennie's	P204OLX	Coakley	P409KSX	Lothian Buses	P787BJU	Watermill
OHV721Y	Rennie's	P204RUM	West Coast Motors	P410KSX	Lothian Buses	P798KSF	Eve Coaches
OHV744Y	Rennie's	P205OLX	Coakley	P411KSX	Lothian Buses	P817EST	Rapsons
OHV771Y	Rennie's	P206GSR	Travel Dundee	P412KSX	Lothian Buses	P871AFV	Smith & Sons
OHV804Y	Rennie's	P207OLX	Coakley	P413KSX	Lothian Buses	P905DST	Rapsons
OHV805Y	Rennie's	P208OLX	Coakley	P414KSX	Lothian Buses	P907DST	Rapsons
OHV812Y	Rennie's	P210OLX	Coakley	P414MFS	Henderson Travel	P939YSB	Riverside
OIL2939	Gibson of Moffat	P221EJW	McColl Coaches	P415KSX	Lothian Buses	P972KTS	Travel Dundee
OIL4570	Rapsons	P223EJW	McColl Coaches	P416KSX	Lothian Buses	P973KTS	Travel Dundee
OJD11R	Keenan	P224EJW	McColl Coaches	P417KSX	Lothian Buses	P995RHS	Hutchison's
OJI9456	Essbee	P224YGG	Pride of the Clyde	P418KSX	Lothian Buses	PA51LEY	Riverside
OJU106	Prentice Westwood	P225YGG	Pride of the Clyde	P419KSX	Lothian Buses	PAU195R	McDade's Travel
OKM317	Dodds of Troon	P226EJW	Travel Dundee	P420KSX	Lothian Buses	PAZ6344	Essbee
OLS539P	Whitelaws	P227YGG	Garelochhead	P421KSX	Lothian Buses	PCZ2674	Galson
ONR314	Prentice Westwood	P232EJW	McColl Coaches	P422JDT	McKindless	PDL252X	Kineil Coaches
OO05EVE	Eve Coaches	P238EJW	McColl Coaches	P422KSX	Lothian Buses	PDX782	Kineil Coaches
OO05GXZ	Eve Coaches	P240OSF	Henderson Travel	P423KSX	Lothian Buses	PDZ7762	Rapsons
OO05HCC	H Crawford	P241WWX	Shuttle Buses	P424KSX	Lothian Buses	PF04SVJ	AAA Coaches
OO06HCC	H Crawford	P253PSX	Lothian Buses	P425KSX	Lothian Buses	PFG362	Mackie's
OOB32X	Fairline	P254PSX	Lothian Buses	P426KSX	Lothian Buses	PGA833V	MacEwan's
OOX801R	Essbee	P255PSX	Lothian Buses	P427KSX	Lothian Buses	PH54PCH	Prentice
ORA450W	Jays Coaches	P255RUM	McColl Coaches	P428KSX	Lothian Buses	PIB9211	Rennie's
ORJ393W	Keenan	P256PSX	Lothian Buses	P429KSX	Lothian Buses	PIJ601	Rennie's
OSC54V	Jays Coaches	P256RUM	McColl Coaches	P430KSX	Lothian Buses	PIL2162	Prentice Westwood
OSJ636R	Lothian Buses	P257PSX	Lothian Buses	P431KSX	Lothian Buses	PIL2167	Jays Coaches
OSN852Y	McDade's Travel	P257RUM	McColl Coaches	P432KSX	Lothian Buses	PIL3750	Dunn's
OSN857Y	McDade's Travel	P258PSX	Lothian Buses	P433KSX	Lothian Buses	PIL3752	Dunn's
OSN870Y	Kineil Coaches	P259PSX	Lothian Buses	P454MFS	Henderson Travel	PIL6829	Rapsons
OSN875Y	Kineil Coaches	P259RUM	McColl Coaches	P455MFS	Henderson Travel	PIL7834	Prentice Westwood
OTS271	Travel Dundee	P260PSX	Lothian Buses	P470JEG	Caledonian Buses	PIL7835	McDade's Travel
OUR610	Prentice Westwood	P261PSX	Lothian Buses	P474JEG	Caledonian Buses	PIW6962	McColl Coaches
P11RVN	Irvine's	P262PSX	Lothian Buses	P476JEG	Caledonian Buses	PK02WVV	Garelochhead
P40BLU	Coakley	P263PSX	Lothian Buses	P477TGA	Slaemuir Coaches	PN05BJY	AAA Coaches
P50BLU	Coakley	P264PSX	Lothian Buses	P478JEG	Caledonian Buses	PNW59W	Jays Coaches
P61HUJ	Scottish Travel	P265PSX	Lothian Buses	P478TGA	Riverside	PO54VZT	AAA Coaches
P77JDS	Docherty's Midland	P266PSX	Lothian Buses	P484GNB	Coakley	POG524Y	McKindless
P100BUS	Billy Davies	P267PSX	Lothian Buses	P502VUS	Hutchison's	PSV114	Irvine's
P100WCM	West Coast Motors	P268PSX	Lothian Buses	P507VUS	Hutchison's	PSV223	Hutchison's
P111JDP	Rapsons	P269PSX	Lothian Buses	P508VUS	Hutchison's	PUF249M	Maynes Coaches
P121GSR	Travel Dundee	P270PSX	Lothian Buses	P521EJW	Travel Dundee	PVS20W	Rapsons
P122KSL	Travel Dundee	P271PSX	Lothian Buses	P521EJW	Travel Dundee	PWY49W	Rapsons
P123KSL	Travel Dundee	P272PSX	Lothian Buses	P522EJW	Travel Dundee	PYJ136	Travel Dundee
P124KSL	Travel Dundee	P273PSX	Lothian Buses	P523EJW	Travel Dundee	R24GNW	West Coast Motors
P125KSL	Travel Dundee	P274PSX	Lothian Buses	P526UGA	McGill's	R26USM	MacEwan's
P126KSL	Travel Dundee	P275PSX	Lothian Buses	P527EJW	Travel Dundee	R27VSM	Hutchison's
P127FRS	Nicoll	P276PSX	Lothian Buses	P531EJW	Travel Dundee	R28VSM	Hutchison's
P127KSL	Travel Dundee	P277PSX	Lothian Buses	P531EJW	Travel Dundee	R50TPB	Gibson of Moffat
P128KSL	Travel Dundee	P278PSX	Lothian Buses	P536PUB	MacEwan's	R60TPB	Gibson of Moffat
P129KSL	Travel Dundee	P279PSX	Lothian Buses	P600WCM	West Coast Motors	R74GNW	West Coast Motors
P130KSL	Travel Dundee	P279VUS	Jays Coaches	P611RGB	Rapsons	R83BRY	Jays Coaches
P131KSL	Travel Dundee	P281PSX	Lothian Buses	P612RGB	Rapsons	R83YVU	McKendry
P132KSL	Travel Dundee	P282PSX	Lothian Buses	P613RGB	E & M Horsburgh	R87GNW	Travel Dundee
P133KSL	Travel Dundee	P283PSX	Lothian Buses	P630FTV	MacEwan's	R91HUS	Hutchison's
P134KSL	Travel Dundee	P284PSX	Lothian Buses	P646MSE	Ayrways	R92HUS	Hutchison's

Reg	Operator	Reg	Operator	Reg	Operator	Reg	Operator
R93HUS	Hutchison's	R797OYS	McKindless	S905DUB	Henderson Travel	SF05KWE	Essbee
R94HUS	Hutchison's	R798OYS	McKindless	S947NGB	Whitelaws	SF05KWM	Marbill
R95HUS	Hutchison's	R809OYS	McKindless	S975CSG	John Morrow	SF05KWN	Marbill
R100WCM	West Coast Motors	R817OYS	McKindless	SA02BOU	Essbee	SF05KWO	Marbill
R102HUA	MacEwan's	R823RDS	Fairline	SA02CCY	Whitelaws	SF05KWR	Essbee
R111WCS	Watermill	R849CJS	Rapsons	SA02CCZ	Whitelaws	SF05NRY	Allander Travel
R113RLY	Coakley	R85GNW	Travel Dundee	SA02CJO	West Coast Motors	SF05ONH	Wilson's of Rhu
R114RLY	McKindless	R86GNW	Travel Dundee	SA02LHC	Garelochhead	SF51RCY	Doig's
R115RLY	Coakley	R86JAR	McKindless	SA02RMZ	Doig's	SF53KUK	Slaemuir Coaches
R116RLY	McKindless	R874RST	Rapsons	SA02RNE	Doig's	SF53KUN	Slaemuir Coaches
R118RLY	Coakley	R878FGE	John Morrow	SA02RYZ	Marbill	SF53NZU	Galson
R119RLY	Coakley	R886YOM	Pride of the Clyde	SA02RZB	Marbill	SF54CHK	Shuttle Buses
R120RLY	Coakley	R900WCM	West Coast Motors	SA02SOU	Southern Coaches	SF54CHO	Watermill
R121RLY	Coakley	R983FYS	Bryans of Denny	SA02UEX	Riverside	SF54HFT	Marbill
R152RSN	Travel Dundee	RAN645R	Rapsons	SA02UEY	Riverside	SF54HFU	Marbill
R153RSN	Travel Dundee	RIA5991	Prentice Westwood	SA02UHW	Marbill	SF54HWA	West Coast Motors
R154RSN	Travel Dundee	RIB6563	Billy Davies	SA02VKH	Gibson of Moffat	SF54HWG	Gibson
R155RSN	Travel Dundee	RIB7002	Waverley	SA03YDB	MacEwan's	SF54HWH	Gibson
R156RSN	Travel Dundee	RIB7742	Kineil Coaches	SA52AZV	Whitelaws	SF54KHV	Irvine's
R157RSN	Travel Dundee	RIB8035	Rapsons	SA52EXD	McGill's	SF54ORA	Gibson
R158RSN	Travel Dundee	RIL3749	Key Coaches	SA52GXO	Riverside	SF54ORC	Gibson
R159RSN	Travel Dundee	RIL4450	Key Coaches	SA52OCX	Fairline	SF54ORJ	Gibson
R160RSN	Travel Dundee	RIL7381	Key Coaches	SAS859T	Rapsons	SF54ORK	Gibson
R161RSN	Travel Dundee	RIL9350	Stuarts of Carluke	SB02SOU	Southern Coaches	SF54ORL	Gibson
R162TSR	Travel Dundee	RIL9404	Caledonian Buses	SC02DPC	Prentice	SF54ORM	Gibson
R163TSR	Travel Dundee	RIL9410	Caledonian Buses	SC02HHE	West Coast Motors	SF54ORN	Gibson
R164TSR	Travel Dundee	RIL9868	McKindless	SC02HLD	Garelochhead	SF54ORP	Gibson
R166GNW	Moffat & Williamson	RIL9964	Kineil Coaches	SC02SOU	Southern Coaches	SF55BKA	McDade's Travel
R177GNW	West Coast Motors	RM03GSM	Maynes Coaches	SC53VOM	AAA Coaches	SF55GXJ	Coakley
R178VLA	Coakley	RM05GSM	Maynes Coaches	SC53VPP	AAA Coaches	SF55GXL	Coakley
R178VLA	McKindless	RNY307Y	H Crawford	SD03SOU	Southern Coaches	SF55HBC	Coakley
R179VLA	Coakley	ROX641Y	MacEwan's	SD04POV	Whytes	SF55HBD	Coakley
R180GNW	West Coast Motors	ROX644Y	McColl Coaches	SE03SOU	Southern Coaches	SF55HGO	Essbee
R183VLA	Coakley	RR52AAA	AAA Coaches	SF02EWG	Stuarts of Carluke	SF55UGB	Wilson's of Rhu
R183VLA	McKindless	RRS320X	Clyde Coast	SF03ABU	Riverside	SG02ONA	Doig's
R185OCW	John Morrow	RSC192Y	Jays Coaches	SF03ABV	Marbill	SG03ZBH	Park's of Hamilton
R189LBC	Billy Davies	RX03HNN	Fairline	SF03ABX	Marbill	SG03ZBM	Park's of Hamilton
R200STL	AAA Coaches	RXW982	Rapsons	SF03AUC	Whytes	SG03ZCB	Park's of Hamilton
R200WCM	West Coast Motors	S2HMC	Moffat & Williamson	SF03AUE	Whytes	SG03ZCC	Park's of Hamilton
R300WCM	West Coast Motors	S4DPC	Prentice	SF03AUH	Whytes	SG03ZCH	Park's of Hamilton
R303VSB	West Coast Motors	S20HCC	H Crawford	SF03AWC	Marbill	SG03ZCR	Park's of Hamilton
R319NRU	Allander Travel	S26HCC	H Crawford	SF03OMP	Doig's	SG03ZEP	Park's of Hamilton
R321HDS	Kineil Coaches	S27DTS	Eve Coaches	SF03SCZ	Gibson	SG03ZER	Golden Eagle
R339RRA	Pride of the Clyde	S27HCC	H Crawford	SF03TLX	Whitelaws	SG03ZES	Park's of Hamilton
R400WCM	West Coast Motors	S28HCC	H Crawford	SF03TLY	Whitelaws	SG03ZEV	Park's of Hamilton
R403HWU	Travel Dundee	S29HCC	H Crawford	SF03YXP	Riverside	SG03ZEX	Park's of Hamilton
R410HWU	Travel Dundee	S30HCC	H Crawford	SF03YXR	Riverside	SG03ZEY	Park's of Hamilton
R412HWU	Travel Dundee	S48KSM	MacEwan's	SF04ETK	Keenan	SG03ZEZ	Park's of Hamilton
R412YWJ	Rapsons	S137JSO	Nicoll	SF04HXM	Rowe & Tudhope	SG03ZHS	Park's of Hamilton
R413HWU	Travel Dundee	S282AOX	Travel Dundee	SF04HXW	Hutchison's	SG03ZJA	Park's of Hamilton
R415HWU	Travel Dundee	S310KNW	Shuttle Buses	SF04HXX	Hutchison's	SG03ZJB	Park's of Hamilton
R418HWU	Travel Dundee	S332SET	Irvine's	SF04LHR	Riverside	SG03ZJC	Park's of Hamilton
R419HWU	Travel Dundee	S374PGB	Gibson	SF04LHU	Henderson Travel	SG03ZJD	Park's of Hamilton
R459VSD	E & M Horsburgh	S388JPS	Rapsons	SF04LKG	Docherty's Midland	SG03ZJF	Park's of Hamilton
R466XDA	Travel Dundee	S389JPS	Rapsons	SF04LKV	Essbee	SG03ZJH	Park's of Hamilton
R466YDT	Travel Dundee	S400EVE	Eve Coaches	SF04LKX	Essbee	SG04FKK	Bus Na Comhairle
R531PJH	Scottish Travel	S400WCM	West Coast Motors	SF04LKY	Doig's	SG04SOU	Southern Coaches
R551UOT	West Coast Motors	S445OGB	Fairline	SF04LLD	Marbill	SG52XMK	McGill's
R555GSM	Maynes Coaches	S456LGN	E & M Horsburgh	SF04RHJ	McColl Coaches	SG52XML	McGill's
R567UOT	Smith & Sons	S457LGN	E & M Horsburgh	SF04RHK	McColl Coaches	SG52XMO	McGill's
R584SKW	E & M Horsburgh	S458LGN	E & M Horsburgh	SF04RHU	McColl Coaches	SG52XMP	McGill's
R585HDS	John Morrow	S461LGN	Irvine's	SF04RHX	Dickson's	SG52XMR	McGill's
R598EAB	McKendry	S463LGN	E & M Horsburgh	SF04SOU	Southern Coaches	SH03XBE	M-Line
R611OFS	Kineil Coaches	S515GGD	Shuttle Buses	SF04SPZ	Hutchison's	SH04YZB	Watermill
R651RSE	Watermill	S555WCM	West Coast Motors	SF04SRU	Hutchison's	SH51KJY	Riverside
R681OYS	McKindless	S556OGB	Hutchison's	SF04YEK	Essbee	SHE306Y	Rapsons
R682OYS	McKindless	S581PGB	Gibson	SF04ZPE	Hutchison's	SIL1075	McDade's Travel
R691OYS	McKindless	S591ACT	Whytes	SF04ZPG	Hutchison's	SIL1075	McDade's Travel
R692OYS	McKindless	S617LRN	Rowe & Tudhope	SF04ZPV	Essbee	SIL1816	McKindless
R694OYS	McKindless	S690RWG	Rapsons	SF04ZXC	Gibson	SIL1895	Irvine's
R716TRV	John Morrow	S718MGB	Moffat & Williamson	SF05BEJ	Fairline	SIL5523	Watermill
R719JGD	Scottish Travel	S742RJX	Travel Dundee	SF05FMV	Gibson	SIL7058	Prentice Westwood
R733EGD	Key Coaches	S743RJX	Travel Dundee	SF05FNU	Slaemuir Coaches	SIL7566	McDade's Travel
R776MGB	Lippen	S751SCJ	Rapsons	SF05HNM	Essbee	SIL8697	Smith & Sons
R777GSM	Bus Na Comhairle	S900WCM	West Coast Motors	SF05KWA	Allander Travel	SJ03AOR	Marbill
R785GGU	E & M Horsburgh	S904DUB	Shuttle Buses	SF05KWB	Allander Travel	SJ03BZL	Marbill

The Scottish Bus Handbook

Reg	Operator	Reg	Operator	Reg	Operator	Reg	Operator
SJ03EHT	Rowe & Tudhope	SK52OJB	Lothian Buses	SN04ACV	Lothian Buses	SN05HCX	McGill's
SJ03FPW	Wilson's of Rhu	SK52OJC	Lothian Buses	SN04ACX	Lothian Buses	SN05HCY	McGill's
SJ04DVG	Whitelaws	SK52OJD	Lothian Buses	SN04ACY	Lothian Buses	SN05HCZ	McGill's
SJ04DVH	Whitelaws	SK52OJE	Lothian Buses	SN04ACZ	Lothian Buses	SN05HDA	McGill's
SJ04DVK	Whitelaws	SK52OJF	Lothian Buses	SN04ADU	Lothian Buses	SN05HDC	Davidson Buses
SJ04DVL	Whitelaws	SK52OJG	Lothian Buses	SN04ADV	Lothian Buses	SN05HDD	Davidson Buses
SJ04DVM	Whitelaws	SK52OJH	Lothian Buses	SN04ADX	Lothian Buses	SN05HDE	Davidson Buses
SJ04DZY	Stuarts of Carluke	SK52OJJ	Lothian Buses	SN04ADZ	Lothian Buses	SN05HDF	Davidson Buses
SJ04DZZ	Stuarts of Carluke	SK52OJL	Lothian Buses	SN04AEA	Lothian Buses	SN05LFT	Coakley
SJ04FLA	Shuttle Buses	SK52OJM	Lothian Buses	SN04AEB	Lothian Buses	SN05LFU	Coakley
SJ04LLA	Stonehouse Cs	SK52OJN	Lothian Buses	SN04AEC	Lothian Buses	SN05LFV	Coakley
SJ04MFV	MacEwan's	SK52OJO	Lothian Buses	SN04AEV	Lothian Buses	SN05LFW	Coakley
SJ05SOU	Southern Coaches	SK52OJP	Lothian Buses	SN04AEW	Lothian Buses	SN06ACO	Highland Heritage
SJ51BZA	Irvine's	SK52OJR	Lothian Buses	SN04AEX	Lothian Buses	SN06ACU	Highland Heritage
SJ51GCV	Gibson	SK52OJS	Lothian Buses	SN04AEY	Lothian Buses	SN06AEF	Prentice Westwood
SJ51LPA	Doig's	SK52OJT	Lothian Buses	SN04AEZ	Lothian Buses	SN51AAA	AAA Coaches
SJ51LYP	Whitelaws	SK52OJU	Lothian Buses	SN04AFA	Lothian Buses	SN51AXF	Lothian Buses
SJ51UDW	Irvine's	SK52OJW	Lothian Buses	SN04CVB	Whytes	SN51AXG	Lothian Buses
SJ53AXB	Davidson Buses	SK52OJX	Lothian Buses	SN04GFE	Kineil Coaches	SN51AXH	Lothian Buses
SJ53CUU	Prentice Westwood	SK52OJY	Lothian Buses	SN04GFK	Rennie's	SN51AXJ	Lothian Buses
SJ53CUV	Prentice Westwood	SK52OJZ	Lothian Buses	SN04GNJ	Prentice Westwood	SN51AXK	Lothian Buses
SJ54GDA	John Morrow	SK52OKA	Lothian Buses	SN04GUF	Whytes	SN51AXO	Lothian Buses
SJ54GDE	John Morrow	SK52OKB	Lothian Buses	SN04MJS	Whytes	SN51AXP	Lothian Buses
SJ55HHA	Whitelaws	SK52OKC	Lothian Buses	SN04NFZ	Lothian Buses	SN51AXR	Lothian Buses
SJ55HHB	Whitelaws	SK52OKD	Lothian Buses	SN04NGE	Lothian Buses	SN51AXS	Lothian Buses
SJ55HHC	Whitelaws	SK52OKE	Lothian Buses	SN04NGF	Lothian Buses	SN51AXT	Lothian Buses
SJ55HHD	Whitelaws	SK52OKF	Lothian Buses	SN04NGG	Lothian Buses	SN51AXU	Lothian Buses
SJ55HHE	Whitelaws	SK52UTT	MacEwan's	SN04NGJ	Lothian Buses	SN51AXV	Lothian Buses
SJI1631	Rapsons	SK52UTU	MacEwan's	SN04NGU	Lothian Buses	SN51AXW	Lothian Buses
SJI2765	Pride of the Clyde	SKF5T	Essbee	SN04NGX	Lothian Buses	SN51AXX	Lothian Buses
SJW515	Dodds of Troon	SL04OLS	Mackie's	SN04NGY	Lothian Buses	SN51AXY	Lothian Buses
SK02NYU	Galson	SL06SOU	Southern Coaches	SN04NGZ	Lothian Buses	SN51AXZ	Lothian Buses
SK02OAA	Watermill	SL52AFZ	Nicoll	SN04NHA	Lothian Buses	SN51AYA	Lothian Buses
SK02VCG	Nicoll	SL52AKN	Nicoll	SN04NHB	Lothian Buses	SN51AYB	Lothian Buses
SK02VCL	Nicoll	SL52BTY	Whytes	SN04NHC	Lothian Buses	SN51AYC	Lothian Buses
SK02VMO	Stuarts of Carluke	SL52CPE	Bryans of Denny	SN04NHD	Lothian Buses	SN51AYD	Lothian Buses
SK02VNX	Docherty's Midland	SL52CPX	Stuarts of Carluke	SN04NHE	Lothian Buses	SN51AYE	Lothian Buses
SK02ZYG	Hutchison's	SL54JUO	Whitelaws	SN04NHF	Lothian Buses	SN51AYF	Lothian Buses
SK02ZYH	Hutchison's	SL54OSL	Mackie's	SN04NHG	Lothian Buses	SN51AYG	Lothian Buses
SK02ZYJ	Hutchison's	SL8207	Mackie's	SN04NHH	Lothian Buses	SN51AYH	Lothian Buses
SK02ZYL	Hutchison's	SL8417	Mackie's	SN04NHJ	Lothian Buses	SN51AYJ	Lothian Buses
SK05SOU	Southern Coaches	SL9483	Mackie's	SN04NHK	Lothian Buses	SN51AYK	Lothian Buses
SK51AYC	Munro's of Jedburgh	SM04GSM	Maynes Coaches	SN04NHL	Lothian Buses	SN51AYL	Lothian Buses
SK51AYD	Munro's of Jedburgh	SM05GSM	Maynes Coaches	SN04NHM	Lothian Buses	SN51AYM	Lothian Buses
SK52HYP	Docherty's Midland	SM06GSM	Maynes Coaches	SN04NHP	Lothian Buses	SN51AYO	Lothian Buses
SK52OCO	Nicoll	SM06SOU	Southern Coaches	SN04NHT	Lothian Buses	SN51AYP	Lothian Buses
SK52ODE	Wilson's of Rhu	SMK697F	Scottish Travel	SN04NHU	Lothian Buses	SN51FZB	Lothian Buses
SK52OGT	Lothian Buses	SN02AAA	AAA Coaches	SN04NHV	Lothian Buses	SN51LVB	Watermill
SK52OGU	Lothian Buses	SN02NMP	Stuarts of Carluke	SN04NHX	Lothian Buses	SN51WYC	Nicoll
SK52OGV	Lothian Buses	SN03CLX	Hutchison's	SN04NHY	Lothian Buses	SN53AED	Lothian Buses
SK52OGW	Lothian Buses	SN03CLY	Hutchison's	SN04NHZ	Lothian Buses	SN53AEE	Lothian Buses
SK52OGX	Lothian Buses	SN03CLZ	Hutchison's	SN04NJE	Lothian Buses	SN53AEF	Lothian Buses
SK52OGY	Lothian Buses	SN03CME	Hutchison's	SN04NJF	Lothian Buses	SN53AEG	Lothian Buses
SK52OGZ	Lothian Buses	SN03LFV	Avondale Coaches	SN05DVW	Highland Heritage	SN53AEJ	Lothian Buses
SK52OHA	Lothian Buses	SN03LFW	Avondale Coaches	SN05DVX	Highland Heritage	SN53AEK	Lothian Buses
SK52OHB	Lothian Buses	SN03LFX	Avondale Coaches	SN05DVY	Highland Heritage	SN53AEL	Lothian Buses
SK52OHC	Lothian Buses	SN03NLJ	Fairline	SN05DVZ	Highland Heritage	SN53AEM	Lothian Buses
SK52OHD	Lothian Buses	SN03NLK	Fairline	SN05DWA	Highland Heritage	SN53AEP	Lothian Buses
SK52OHE	Lothian Buses	SN03NLL	Fairline	SN05DWC	Highland Heritage	SN53AET	Lothian Buses
SK52OHG	Lothian Buses	SN04AAE	Lothian Buses	SN05DWD	Highland Heritage	SN53AEU	Lothian Buses
SK52OHH	Lothian Buses	SN04AAF	Lothian Buses	SN05DWE	Highland Heritage	SN53AUW	Lothian Buses
SK52OHJ	Lothian Buses	SN04AAJ	Lothian Buses	SN05DWF	Highland Heritage	SN53AUX	Lothian Buses
SK52OHL	Lothian Buses	SN04AAK	Lothian Buses	SN05DWG	Highland Heritage	SN53AUY	Lothian Buses
SK52OHN	Lothian Buses	SN04AAU	Lothian Buses	SN05DWJ	Highland Heritage	SN53AVC	Lothian Buses
SK52OHO	Lothian Buses	SN04AAV	Lothian Buses	SN05DWK	Highland Heritage	SN53AVD	Lothian Buses
SK52OHP	Lothian Buses	SN04AAX	Lothian Buses	SN05DWL	Highland Heritage	SN53AVE	Lothian Buses
SK52OHR	Lothian Buses	SN04AAY	Lothian Buses	SN05EOV	Mackie's	SN53AVF	Lothian Buses
SK52OHS	Lothian Buses	SN04AAZ	Lothian Buses	SN05EOW	Mackie's	SN53AVG	Lothian Buses
SK52OHT	Lothian Buses	SN04ABF	Lothian Buses	SN05FBE	Prentice Westwood	SN53AVK	Lothian Buses
SK52OHU	Lothian Buses	SN04ABK	Lothian Buses	SN05FCF	Doig's	SN53AVL	Lothian Buses
SK52OHV	Lothian Buses	SN04ABU	Lothian Buses	SN05FCU	Rennie's	SN53AVM	Lothian Buses
SK52OHW	Lothian Buses	SN04ABV	Lothian Buses	SN05FCX	Rennie's	SN53AVO	Lothian Buses
SK52OHX	Lothian Buses	SN04ABX	Lothian Buses	SN05FHL	Docherty's Midland	SN53AVP	Lothian Buses
SK52OHY	Lothian Buses	SN04ABZ	Lothian Buses	SN05FHM	Docherty's Midland	SN53AVR	Lothian Buses
SK52OHZ	Lothian Buses	SN04ACJ	Lothian Buses	SN05FLR	Bryans of Denny	SN53AVT	Lothian Buses
SK52OJA	Lothian Buses	SN04ACU	Lothian Buses	SN05FPG	Clyde Coast	SN53AVU	Lothian Buses

Reg	Operator	Reg	Operator	Reg	Operator	Reg	Operator
SN53AVV	Lothian Buses	SP05CXX	Smith & Sons	T111WCS	Watermill	TSJ61S	Fairline
SN53AVW	Lothian Buses	SP05CXY	Smith & Sons	T131ARE	MacEwan's	TSJ71S	Keenan
SN53AVX	Lothian Buses	SP06DFZ	Docherty's Midland	T131AST	Rapsons	TSJ77S	MacEwan's
SN53AVZ	Lothian Buses	SP06DGE	Docherty's Midland	T132AST	Rapsons	TSO24X	Clyde Coast
SN53BHD	Rennie's	SP06DGF	Docherty's Midland	T133AST	Rapsons	TVP863S	Essbee
SN53DYA	Kineil Coaches	SP06EBJ	Moffat & Williamson	T134AST	Rapsons	TWH686T	Ayrways
SN53JNO	Lothian Buses	SP53GZB	Smith & Sons	T136ARE	MacEwan's	TXI4242	McColl Coaches
SN54FCE	Waverley	SP53GZC	Smith & Sons	T190AUA	West Coast Motors	TYS259W	Kineil Coaches
SN54FCF	Waverley	SP53HDD	Moffat & Williamson	T191AUA	West Coast Motors	UDT312Y	Rapsons
SN54FNL	Prentice	SP53JXJ	McGill's	T222GSM	Bryans of Denny	UHG741R	Essbee
SN54LRL	Highland Heritage	SP53JXK	McGill's	T290ROF	Whitelaws	UIJ412	Rapsons
SN54LRO	Highland Heritage	SP53JXL	McGill's	T304UOX	Travel Dundee	ULS618X	Billy Davies
SN55BJJ	Lothian Buses	SP53JXM	McGill's	T307UOX	Travel Dundee	UNA863S	Jays Coaches
SN55BJK	Lothian Buses	SP53JZA	Stuarts of Carluke	T337TVM	Shuttle Buses	UO6929	Prentice Westwood
SN55BJO	Lothian Buses	SP53KGE	McGill's	T341LGB	John Morrow	USU661	Travel Dundee
SN55BJU	Lothian Buses	SP53KGG	McGill's	T383GTH	Galson	USU662	Travel Dundee
SN55BJV	Lothian Buses	SP53KGJ	McGill's	T399OWA	MacEwan's	USV803	Stuarts of Carluke
SN55BJX	Lothian Buses	SP53KGK	McGill's	T401JSL	McGill's	USY858	Prentice Westwood
SN55BJY	Lothian Buses	SP54AHX	Moffat & Williamson	T403EGD	Slaemuir Coaches	V7CTL	Scottish Travel
SN55BJZ	Lothian Buses	SP54CGG	Travel Dundee	T404EGD	Slaemuir Coaches	V9DOT	Dodds of Troon
SN55BKA	Lothian Buses	SP54CGK	Travel Dundee	T409BGB	Stokes	V10CBC	Slaemuir Coaches
SN55BKD	Lothian Buses	SP54CGO	Travel Dundee	T415LGP	Caledonian Buses	V32JST	Rapsons
SN55BKE	Lothian Buses	SP54CGU	Travel Dundee	T416LGP	Caledonian Buses	V100CBC	Gibson
SN55BKF	Lothian Buses	SP54CGV	Travel Dundee	T417LGP	Caledonian Buses	V110ESF	McGill's
SN55BKG	Lothian Buses	SP54CGX	Travel Dundee	T432EBD	Munro's of Jedburgh	V151EFS	Lothian Buses
SN55BKJ	Lothian Buses	SP54CGY	Travel Dundee	T435EBD	Munro's of Jedburgh	V152EFS	Lothian Buses
SN55BKK	Lothian Buses	SP54CGZ	Travel Dundee	T501SSG	Lothian Buses	V153EFS	Lothian Buses
SN55BKL	Lothian Buses	SP54CHC	Travel Dundee	T502SSG	Lothian Buses	V154EFS	Lothian Buses
SN55BKU	Lothian Buses	SP54CHD	Travel Dundee	T503SSG	Lothian Buses	V155EFS	Lothian Buses
SN55BKV	Lothian Buses	SP54CHF	Travel Dundee	T504SSG	Lothian Buses	V156EFS	Lothian Buses
SN55BKX	Lothian Buses	SP54CHG	Travel Dundee	T505SSG	Lothian Buses	V157EFS	Lothian Buses
SN55BKY	Lothian Buses	SP54CHH	Travel Dundee	T506SSG	Lothian Buses	V158EFS	Lothian Buses
SN55BKZ	Lothian Buses	SP54CHJ	Travel Dundee	T507SSG	Lothian Buses	V159EFS	Lothian Buses
SN55BLF	Lothian Buses	SP54CHK	Travel Dundee	T508SSG	Lothian Buses	V160EFS	Lothian Buses
SN55BLJ	Lothian Buses	SP54CHL	Travel Dundee	T509SSG	Lothian Buses	V161EFS	Lothian Buses
SN55BLK	Lothian Buses	SP54CHN	Travel Dundee	T510SSG	Lothian Buses	V162EFS	Lothian Buses
SN55BLV	Lothian Buses	SP54CHO	Travel Dundee	T517EUB	McGill's	V163EFS	Lothian Buses
SN55BLX	Lothian Buses	SP54FML	Moffat & Williamson	T520EUB	McGill's	V164EFS	Lothian Buses
SN55BLZ	Lothian Buses	SP54FMM	Moffat & Williamson	T523GSR	Smith & Sons	V165EFS	Lothian Buses
SN55BMO	Lothian Buses	SP55EEF	Moffat & Williamson	T535EUB	Rapsons	V165ESL	Travel Dundee
SN55BMU	Lothian Buses	SSU727	West Coast Motors	T549HNH	Munro's of Jedburgh	V166EFS	Lothian Buses
SN55BMV	Lothian Buses	ST02GDA	Smith & Sons	T577ASN	Travel Dundee	V166ESL	Travel Dundee
SN55BMY	Lothian Buses	ST02GDE	Smith & Sons	T600WCM	West Coast Motors	V167EFS	Lothian Buses
SN55BMZ	Lothian Buses	ST52GZN	Moffat & Williamson	T608DGD	Bowman	V167ESL	Travel Dundee
SN55BNA	Lothian Buses	SV03JZK	Kineil Coaches	T645JWB	Moffat & Williamson	V168EFS	Lothian Buses
SN55BNB	Lothian Buses	SV04CVA	Whytes	T674TSG	Stuarts of Carluke	V168ESL	Travel Dundee
SN55BND	Lothian Buses	SV06CEJ	Whytes	T675ASN	Moffat & Williamson	V169EFS	Lothian Buses
SN55BNE	Lothian Buses	SV06CEK	Whytes	T676ASN	Moffat & Williamson	V169ESL	Travel Dundee
SN55BNF	Lothian Buses	SV06CEN	Whytes	T732JGB	Hutchison's	V170EFS	Lothian Buses
SN55BNJ	Lothian Buses	SV06CEO	Whytes	T735JGB	Hutchison's	V170ESL	Travel Dundee
SN55BNK	Lothian Buses	SV52AXV	Hebridean Coaches	T736JGB	Hutchison's	V171EFS	Lothian Buses
SN55BNL	Lothian Buses	SV52VHY	Whytes	T794TWX	Munro's of Jedburgh	V171ESL	Travel Dundee
SN55BNO	Lothian Buses	SV53ELJ	Whytes	T796BGD	Essbee	V172EFS	Lothian Buses
SN55BNU	Lothian Buses	SV54EPJ	Whytes	T900WCM	West Coast Motors	V172ESL	Travel Dundee
SN55BNV	Lothian Buses	SW02VFX	Watermill	T902JTD	Shuttle Buses	V173EFS	Lothian Buses
SN55BNX	Lothian Buses	SW02VGY	Watermill	T966JAO	First Stop	V173ESL	Travel Dundee
SN55BNY	Lothian Buses	SW52FCF	McKendry	T967JAO	First Stop	V174EFS	Lothian Buses
SN55BNZ	Lothian Buses	SY51EHT	Rapsons	T993PFH	Rapsons	V174ESL	Travel Dundee
SN55BOF	Lothian Buses	SY51EHU	Rapsons	TFX966	Rapsons	V175EFS	Lothian Buses
SN55BOH	Lothian Buses	SY51EHV	Rapsons	TGD759W	Rapsons	V175ESL	Travel Dundee
SN55BOJ	Lothian Buses	SY51EHX	Rapsons	TIL7490	Galson	V176ESL	Travel Dundee
SN55BOU	Lothian Buses	SY51EHZ	Rapsons	TIW7700	Kineil Coaches	V177ESL	Travel Dundee
SN55BOV	Lothian Buses	SY51EZU	Rapsons	TIW9829	Keenan	V178ESL	Travel Dundee
SN55BPE	Lothian Buses	SYJ961X	MacEwan's	TJI1328	Keenan	V179ESL	Travel Dundee
SN55BPF	Lothian Buses	T3DOT	Dodds of Troon	TJI1983	Jays Coaches	V326XDO	Kineil Coaches
SN55BPK	Lothian Buses	T3EVE	Eve Coaches	TJI3142	Galson	V400CBC	Gibson
SN55BPO	Lothian Buses	T9RVN	Irvine's	TJI3143	McKindless	V431EAL	AAA Coaches
SN55DUU	Irvine's	T9TAP	Kineil Coaches	TJI4024	Clyde Coast	V452NGA	Whitelaws
SN55FEF	AAA Coaches	T52JBA	McGill's	TJI5392	Dodds of Troon	V478FSF	Waverley
SO06SOU	Southern Coaches	T53JBA	McGill's	TJI5393	Dodds of Troon	V500CBC	Slaemuir Coaches
SO51AAA	AAA Coaches	T56RJL	Shuttle Buses	TJI5394	Dodds of Troon	V501FSF	Nicoll
SP02HMV	E & M Horsburgh	T75JBA	E & M Horsburgh	TJI6264	Clyde Coast	V502FSF	Nicoll
SP04EUY	Smith & Sons	T80LRT	Stokes	TJI7192	Rapsons	V511ESC	Lothian Buses
SP04EUZ	Smith & Sons	T87JBA	John Morrow	TJT196X	Prentice Westwood	V512ESC	Lothian Buses
SP04EVB	Smith & Sons	T92JBA	Henderson Travel	TMS407X	Rowe & Tudhope	V513ESC	Lothian Buses
SP05AKK	Shuttle Buses	T104GSE	Allander Travel	TPD108X	Rennie's	V514ESC	Lothian Buses

The Scottish Bus Handbook

Registration	Operator	Registration	Operator	Registration	Operator	Registration	Operator
V515ESC	Lothian Buses	W15HCT	Harris Coaches	W724WAK	Doig's	X442JHS	Essbee
V516ESC	Lothian Buses	W52WDS	Hutchison's	W743NAS	Rapsons	X443JHS	Garelochhead
V517ESC	Lothian Buses	W77JDS	Docherty's Midland	W745NAS	Rapsons	X461UKS	Rapsons
V518ESC	Lothian Buses	W100WCM	West Coast Motors	W747NAS	Rapsons	X462UKS	Rapsons
V519ESC	Lothian Buses	W137OSM	MacEwan's	W749GSE	Gibson of Moffat	X463UKS	Munro's of Jedburgh
V520ESC	Lothian Buses	W158WTA	MacEwan's	W777WCS	Watermill	X464UKS	Munro's of Jedburgh
V521ESC	Lothian Buses	W173CDN	West Coast Motors	W814UAG	Slaemuir Coaches	X465UKS	Munro's of Jedburgh
V522ESC	Lothian Buses	W189WNS	E & M Horsburgh	W814UAG	Slaemuir Coaches	X466UKS	Munro's of Jedburgh
V523ESC	Lothian Buses	W235AGA	Galson	W815UAG	Slaemuir Coaches	X466XAS	Rapsons
V524ESC	Lothian Buses	W272MKY	McKendry	W816UAG	Slaemuir Coaches	X467UKS	Rapsons
V525ESC	Lothian Buses	W291PFS	Lothian Buses	W877VGT	Moffat & Williamson	X578USC	Lothian Buses
V526ESC	Lothian Buses	W292PFS	Lothian Buses	W878VGT	Moffat & Williamson	X579USC	Lothian Buses
V527ESC	Lothian Buses	W293PFS	Lothian Buses	W885NNT	Watermill	X581USC	Lothian Buses
V528ESC	Lothian Buses	W294PFS	Lothian Buses	W895AGA	Stuarts of Carluke	X582USC	Lothian Buses
V529ESC	Lothian Buses	W295PFS	Lothian Buses	W991XDM	Slaemuir Coaches	X583USC	Lothian Buses
V530ESC	Lothian Buses	W296PFS	Lothian Buses	W999WCS	Watermill	X584USC	Lothian Buses
V531ESC	Lothian Buses	W301GCW	Slaemuir Coaches	WDA680T	McDade's Travel	X585USC	Lothian Buses
V532ESC	Lothian Buses	W322YSB	Irvine's	WDC218Y	Clyde Coast	X586USC	Lothian Buses
V533ESC	Lothian Buses	W348WCS	Rowe & Tudhope	WDF297	Lothian Buses	X587USC	Lothian Buses
V534ESC	Lothian Buses	W349WCS	Rowe & Tudhope	WDS323V	MacEwan's	X588USC	Lothian Buses
V535ESC	Lothian Buses	W365OSM	Gibson of Moffat	WDS343V	Keenan	X589USC	Lothian Buses
V536ESC	Lothian Buses	W386WGE	Gibson	WDZ4724	Gibson of Moffat	X591USC	Lothian Buses
V537ESC	Lothian Buses	W425CWX	Henderson Travel	WFO311	Rapsons	X592USC	Lothian Buses
V538ESC	Lothian Buses	W426CWX	Henderson Travel	WFS145W	West Coast Motors	X593USC	Lothian Buses
V539ESC	Lothian Buses	W462RSX	Nicoll	WFS147W	Dodds of Troon	X594USC	Lothian Buses
V540ESC	Lothian Buses	W463RSX	Nicoll	WFS151W	West Coast Motors	X595USC	Lothian Buses
V541ESC	Lothian Buses	W464RSX	Nicoll	WIB7085	Rapsons	X596USC	Lothian Buses
V542ESC	Lothian Buses	W496JHE	Watermill	WIB9256	Coakley	X597UKS	Lothian Buses
V543ESC	Lothian Buses	W49WDS	Hutchison's	WIL9201	McKindless	X598USC	Lothian Buses
V544ESC	Lothian Buses	W500SOU	Southern Coaches	WIL9202	McKindless	X622CWN	Whytes
V545ESC	Lothian Buses	W514PSF	McColl Coaches	WIL9203	McKindless	X675USX	Nicoll
V58KWO	Harris Coaches	W546RSG	Lothian Buses	WIL9204	McKindless	X704UKS	Shuttle Buses
V664FPO	Doig's	W547RSG	Lothian Buses	WIL9205	McKindless	X705UKS	Stuarts of Carluke
V677FPO	Stokes	W548RSG	Lothian Buses	WIL9206	McKindless	X799AVN	Stonehouse Cs
V700CBC	Gibson	W549RSG	Lothian Buses	WIL9207	McKindless	X974NRS	Kineil Coaches
V828GGA	Hebridean Coaches	W551RSG	Lothian Buses	WIL9208	McKindless	XAM826A	Dunn's
V829GGA	MacEwan's	W552RSG	Lothian Buses	WIL9216	Scottish Travel	XAT11X	Allander Travel
V878DSS	Whytes	W553RSG	Lothian Buses	WIL9217	Scottish Travel	XCD108	Rennie's
V943JST	Rapsons	W554RSG	Lothian Buses	WIL9218	McKindless	XCS961	Essbee
V944JST	Rapsons	W556RSG	Lothian Buses	WIL9220	McKindless	XIJ602	Rapsons
V958HEB	Hebridean Coaches	W557RSG	Lothian Buses	WIL9223	McKindless	XIL1483	Lothian Buses
VAH280X	Rapsons	W558RSG	Lothian Buses	WIL9224	McKindless	XIL6561	M-Line
VAZ2524	Stuarts of Carluke	W559RSG	Lothian Buses	WIL9225	McKindless	XJF448	Clyde Coast
VEF151Y	McDade's Travel	W561RSG	Lothian Buses	WIL9226	McKindless	XLM923	H Crawford
VIA488	Kineil Coaches	W562RSG	Lothian Buses	WIL9227	McKindless	XMS254R	Whitelaws
VIA963	Kineil Coaches	W563RSG	Lothian Buses	WIL9228	McKindless	XMS423Y	Dodds of Troon
VIB3264	Essbee	W564RSG	Lothian Buses	WLT371	Lothian Buses	XOV748T	Essbee
VIL4589	McKindless	W566RSG	Lothian Buses	WNB604	Prentice Westwood	XRY278	Marbill
VIL4714	Prentice	W567RSG	Lothian Buses	WSC571	Clyde Coast	XSV270	Mackie's
VJI3002	Rowe & Tudhope	W568RSG	Lothian Buses	WSD212V	Pride of the Clyde	XU05SOU	Southern Coaches
VJI9410	Rowe & Tudhope	W569RSG	Lothian Buses	WSD216V	Pride of the Clyde	XUF456	Hutchison's
VJI9411	Rowe & Tudhope	W571RSG	Lothian Buses	WSF989Y	Garelochhead	XXI3248	Irvine's
VJI9412	Rowe & Tudhope	W572RSG	Lothian Buses	WSU209	Stokes	Y8AMS	Jays Coaches
VLT143	Lothian Buses	W573RSG	Lothian Buses	WSU557	Stokes	Y10EVE	Eve Coaches
VLT163	Lothian Buses	W574RSG	Lothian Buses	WSU857	Stokes	Y40SOU	Southern Coaches
VLT235	Lothian Buses	W575RSG	Lothian Buses	WSU858	Stokes	Y58THS	Allander Travel
VLT237	Lothian Buses	W576RSG	Lothian Buses	WSU859	Stokes	Y77JDS	Docherty's Midland
VLT242	Lothian Buses	W577RSG	Lothian Buses	WSU860	Stokes	Y111EAD	MacEwan's
VLT281	Lothian Buses	W585PFS	Essbee	WSU864	Stokes	Y11EAD	MacEwan's
VO53OVA	Munro's of Jedburgh	W592PFS	Fairline	WSU871	Stokes	Y138TVV	MacEwan's
VO53OVB	Munro's of Jedburgh	W594PFS	E & M Horsburgh	WSU982	Prentice	Y173CGC	Irvine's
VRN830Y	M-Line	W595PFS	E & M Horsburgh	WUH704	Moffat & Williamson	Y176CFS	Lothian Buses
VRY357	Watermill	W596PFS	E & M Horsburgh	X2JPT	Moffat & Williamson	Y177CFS	Lothian Buses
VSV632	Prentice Westwood	W597PFS	E & M Horsburgh	X77JDS	Docherty's Midland	Y178CFS	Lothian Buses
VU02TSO	Avondale Coaches	W600SOU	McGill's	X109RGG	Riverside	Y179CFS	Lothian Buses
VU02TSV	Irvine's	W613KFE	Whitelaws	X185BNH	Waverley	Y181BGB	Hutchison's
VU02TSV	Irvine's	W631PSX	Lothian Buses	X233USC	Fairline	Y181CFS	Lothian Buses
VU02TTO	Avondale Coaches	W632PSX	Lothian Buses	X274SRM	Fairline	Y182BGB	Hutchison's
VU52UEA	Munro's of Jedburgh	W633PSX	Lothian Buses	X299DHF	Shuttle Buses	Y182CFS	Lothian Buses
VU52UEB	Munro's of Jedburgh	W634PSX	Lothian Buses	X303JGE	Hutchison's	Y183CFS	Lothian Buses
VU52UEC	Munro's of Jedburgh	W671WGG	Whitelaws	X304JGE	Hutchison's	Y184CFS	Lothian Buses
VX54CKK	Stonehouse Cs	W674WGG	Whitelaws	X311ABU	Shuttle Buses	Y185CFS	Lothian Buses
VX54CKL	Garelochhead	W675WGG	Whitelaws	X415CSC	E & M Horsburgh	Y186CFS	Lothian Buses
W1JAY	Jays Coaches	W689XSB	West Coast Motors	X416CSC	E & M Horsburgh	Y187CFS	Lothian Buses
W2JAY	Jays Coaches	W691NST	Rapsons	X417CSC	E & M Horsburgh	Y187KCS	Slaemuir Coaches
W7JDS	Docherty's Midland	W692NST	Rapsons	X441JHS	Essbee	Y188CFS	Lothian Buses

The Scottish Bus Handbook

Y189CFS	Lothian Buses	YG52DFX	Eve Coaches	YJ51XSH	E & M Horsburgh	YN04XZC	Docherty's Midland
Y191CFS	Lothian Buses	YG54BSU	Wilson's of Rhu	YJ51XSK	E & M Horsburgh	YN05HFY	Doig's
Y214BGB	Gibson	YIB4337	McKindless	YJ51XSL	E & M Horsburgh	YN05HFZ	Doig's
Y216BGB	Gibson	YIB4528	McKindless	YJ51XSM	E & M Horsburgh	YN06CYV	Fairline
Y228RSO	Watermill	YIB5488	McKindless	YJ51XSN	E & M Horsburgh	YN51HBF	Munro's of Jedburgh
Y257KNB	Wilson's of Rhu	YIB7073	McKindless	YJ51XSO	E & M Horsburgh	YN51HCJ	Munro's of Jedburgh
Y264KNB	Bryans of Denny	YIB9500	McKindless	YJ54UWN	Henderson Travel	YN51HCK	Munro's of Jedburgh
Y285YST	Rapsons	YIJ3053	Keenan	YJ54UWO	Henderson Travel	YN51XMH	Park's of Hamilton
Y396PSP	Moffat & Williamson	YIJ3053	Keenan	YJ54UXB	Henderson Travel	YN51XMJ	Park's of Hamilton
Y483TSU	Gibson	YIJ351	Prentice Westwood	YJ54UXC	Henderson Travel	YN51XMK	Park's of Hamilton
Y484TSU	Gibson	YIL1206	Golden Eagle	YJ54UXD	Henderson Travel	YN51XML	Park's of Hamilton
Y485TSU	Gibson	YIL1207	Golden Eagle	YJ54UXE	Henderson Travel	YN51XMU	Park's of Hamilton
Y489PTU	Slaemuir Coaches	YIL1208	Golden Eagle	YJ54ZYH	West Coast Motors	YN51XMV	Park's of Hamilton
Y500MRT	Irvine's	YIL6691	Golden Eagle	YJ54ZYK	West Coast Motors	YN51XMW	Park's of Hamilton
Y523UOS	Slaemuir Coaches	YIL8799	Prentice Westwood	YJ54ZYM	West Coast Motors	YN51XMX	Park's of Hamilton
Y556KSC	Prentice	YJ03PGF	West Coast Motors	YJ55BGY	Gibson	YN51XMZ	Park's of Hamilton
Y557KSC	Prentice	YJ03PNY	West Coast Motors	YJ55BGZ	Gibson	YN51XNC	Park's of Hamilton
Y573RSE	Allander Travel	YJ03PNZ	West Coast Motors	YJ55BHA	Gibson	YN51XND	Park's of Hamilton
Y633TYS	Allander Travel	YJ04HLC	Rapsons	YJ55BHD	Gibson	YN51XNE	Park's of Hamilton
Y668BKS	Munro's of Jedburgh	YJ04HUU	West Coast Motors	YJ55BHE	Gibson	YN53EJC	Watermill
Y722CJW	Travel Dundee	YJ04KWJ	McDade's Travel	YJ55BHK	Gibson	YN53WZJ	Munro's of Jedburgh
Y797GDV	Slaemuir Coaches	YJ05PVF	West Coast Motors	YJ55BJZ	Fairline	YN53YHJ	Irvine's
Y801WBT	West Coast Motors	YJ05PVK	West Coast Motors	YJ55YGD	Scottish Travel	YN54WCM	Moffat & Williamson
Y802WBT	West Coast Motors	YJ05PVL	West Coast Motors	YK04KWH	Rapsons	YN54WWZ	Kineil Coaches
Y804GDV	M-Line	YJ05PWU	West Coast Motors	YK05CDE	Moffat & Williamson	YN54XYK	Bus Na Comhairle
Y805GDV	Slaemuir Coaches	YJ05PYO	West Coast Motors	YK05CDF	Moffat & Williamson	YN55LMO	Watermill
Y80WCM	West Coast Motors	YJ05PYP	West Coast Motors	YK05FEK	Rapsons	YN55PVX	Doig's
Y989TSD	Marbill	YJ05PYT	West Coast Motors	YK51ADZ	Moffat & Williamson	YN55YHC	Henderson Travel
Y991TSD	Marbill	YJ05XNP	Avondale Coaches	YKJ798	Stuarts of Carluke	YP02AAY	MacEwan's
Y998TGG	Golden Eagle	YJ05XNR	Avondale Coaches	YKJ798	Stuarts of Carluke	YP02AAZ	MacEwan's
YAJ154Y	McDade's Travel	YJ05XNS	Avondale Coaches	YL02FKZ	Nicoll	YP02AAZ	Rapsons
YAZ6428	Rapsons	YJ05XNT	Avondale Coaches	YN02TOV	E & M Horsburgh	YP52KRG	Watermill
YBK159	Moffat & Williamson	YJ05XOA	Rapsons	YN03NDF	Stuarts of Carluke	YPJ207Y	John Morrow
YBK338V	Watermill	YJ05XOB	Rapsons	YN03NDY	E & M Horsburgh	YR02ZMO	Moffat & Williamson
YBK341V	Watermill	YJ05XOC	Rapsons	YN03NDZ	E & M Horsburgh	YR03UMR	Munro's of Jedburgh
YBL526	Mackie's	YJ05XOD	Rapsons	YN03UYJ	Rapsons	YR52VEX	Docherty's Midland
YBZ1462	McKindless	YJ05XOE	Rapsons	YN03WXH	Moffat & Williamson	YRR436	Prentice Westwood
YBZ4427	Rowe & Tudhope	YJ05XOF	Rapsons	YN03WYD	Docherty's Midland	YSL334	Lothian Buses
YBZ6469	McKindless	YJ05XOG	Rapsons	YN03ZXE	Henderson Travel	YSO40Y	Jays Coaches
YBZ7531	McKindless	YJ05XOH	Rapsons	YN04AGO	Stuarts of Carluke	YSU882	Rapsons
YBZ818	Rapsons	YJ05XOK	Rapsons	YN04HJD	Bus Na Comhairle	YSU990	Maynes Coaches
YD02RBX	Smith & Sons	YJ05XOL	Rapsons	YN04HJE	Bus Na Comhairle	YSV125	Prentice Westwood
YD02RBY	Smith & Sons	YJ05XOM	Rapsons	YN04HJF	Bus Na Comhairle	YSV607	Prentice Westwood
YD02RBZ	Smith & Sons	YJ05XOS	Henderson Travel	YN04HJK	Bus Na Comhairle	YSV608	Prentice Westwood
YDL318	McKindless	YJ05XOT	Henderson Travel	YN04LWZ	Henderson Travel	YU04XJT	Bus Na Comhairle
YF02SKX	Slaemuir Coaches	YJ05XOU	Henderson Travel	YN04LXE	Henderson Travel	YWE840	Dodds of Troon
YF02SKZ	Slaemuir Coaches	YJ06FZE	Fairline	YN04LXS	Henderson Travel	YX05DKK	AAA Coaches
YFS438	Mackie's	YJ06FZF	Fairline	YN04WTV	Moffat & Williamson	YXD507	Dodds of Troon
YG02FWJ	Wilson's of Rhu	YJ06FZL	Wilson's of Rhu			YXI7906	Dodds of Troon

ISBN 1 904875 01 7

© Published by British Bus Publishing Ltd , May 2005

British Bus Publishing Ltd, 16 St Margaret's Drive, Telford, TF1 3PH
Telephone: 01952 255669 - Facsimile: 01952 222397
e-mail: Office@britishbuspublishing.co.uk